ASSESSMENT STRATEGIES
IN TECHNICAL SERVICES

ALA Editions purchases fund advocacy, awareness, and accreditation programs for library professionals worldwide.

AN ALCTS MONOGRAPH

ASSESSMENT STRATEGIES IN TECHNICAL SERVICES

EDITED BY
Kimberley A. Edwards and Michelle Leonard

ALA
Editions
CHICAGO | 2019

Extensive effort has gone into ensuring the reliability of the information in this book; however, the publisher makes no warranty, express or implied, with respect to the material contained herein.

ISBNs
978-0-8389-1857-9 (paper)
978-0-8389-1884-5 (PDF)
978-0-8389-1882-1 (ePub)
978-0-8389-1883-8 (Kindle)

Library of Congress Cataloging-in-Publication Data

Names: Edwards, Kimberley A., editor. | Leonard, Michelle, 1968– editor.
Title: Assessment strategies in technical services / edited by Kimberley A. Edwards and Michelle Leonard.
Description: Chicago : ALA Editions, 2019. | Series: An ALCTS monograph | Includes bibliographical references and index.
Identifiers: LCCN 2018059760 | ISBN 9780838918579 (paper : alk. paper) | ISBN 9780838918821 (epub) | ISBN 9780838918845 (pdf) | ISBN 9780838918838 (kindle)
Subjects: LCSH: Technical services (Libraries)—United States—Evaluation. | Collection management (Libraries)—United States—Evaluation.
Classification: LCC Z688.6.U6 A86 2019 | DDC 025/.02—dc23
LC record available at https://lccn.loc.gov/2018059760

Cover design by Alejandra Diaz. Image © Adobe Stock.

Text composition by Dianne M. Rooney in the Adobe Caslon Pro and Archer typefaces.

♾ This paper meets the requirements of ANSI/NISO Z39.48–1992 (Permanence of Paper).

Printed in the United States of America

23 22 21 20 19   5 4 3 2 1

CONTENTS

PREFACE

This edited volume delves into the assessment strategies used by the various departments in libraries' technical services. These strategies encompass a variety of options, including approaches, plans, and policies that should be applicable in a department of any size. The sequence of this book's chapters encompasses the technical services life cycle and moves from the selection of materials through their acquisition, their entry into the catalog, and finally to their long-term preservation.

This book commences with an overview of the state of assessment in technical services, in which Botero and Carrico (chapter 1) discuss the growing need for work in that area. A holistic approach to collection management decisions is provided by Kelly and Smith (chapter 2), who provide a framework for creating and maintaining a collections assessment program. This then narrows down to the functionality of the acquisitions unit for placing orders, working with vendors, and tracking statistics in Shelton and Carrico's chapter (chapter 3), and examines the importance of the assessment of serials in Calvert and Jordan's chapter (chapter 4.) Once collections are ordered and maintained, the materials are cataloged. While this is quite an underrepresented field of assessment, Pettitt's expertise (chapter 5) deftly guides the reader through an easy methodological approach to cataloging and metadata assessment. In his chapter on preservation (chapter 6), Durant completes the discussion by outlining the ways in which assessment can enable library personnel to understand their physical collections and to direct their resources toward high-impact areas. Finally, in the concluding chapter (chapter 7), Servizzi promotes a vision for the future of technical services and the role that assessment will play in them.

Overall, these chapters will guide the reader into thinking about which strategy best relates to their own library culture. The book includes suggestions on which assessment approach is best utilized, the kinds of project management for which staff must be trained, and how to effectively communicate the various types of assessment to the target audience. This book offers guided expertise on developing a varied array of assessment strategies in technical services, as demonstrated by the authors' voices in each chapter.

ASSESSMENT OF TECHNICAL SERVICES

An Overview

Cecilia Botero and Steven Carrico

- def of technical services - responsible for acquiring, cataloging, organizing, and preserving all of the materials in library collections
- assessment needs to be tied to the larger assessment strategies of the library

T echnical services in libraries are responsible for acquiring, cataloging, organizing, and preserving all of the materials in library collections, whether print or electronic. Librarians and staff have been assessing their technical services for many decades. Historically, the staff working in technical services annually collected and compiled a wide range of statistics that were focused mainly on budget expenditures, and on the acquisition and cataloging of books and other tangible materials. Librarians used the gathered statistics for grant writing, accreditation reviews, or for surveys such as the Association of Research Libraries' annual statistics.[1] Technical service administrators and unit managers also applied library statistics during staff evaluations, and to monitor and revise the workflows within or between departments. Yet, in the past, these assessment activities in technical services were seldom tied to the larger assessment strategies of the library.

Two influential factors sparked the need to revise traditional assessment and statistical gathering in technical services: (1) the increased importance of efficiently and wisely allocating and expending the library's material resource budgets; and (2) the need to provide evidence-based information to university administrators and stakeholders regarding the library's evolving mission, user services, and operations. Since the units and staff handling both the materials resource budget and electronic resources (e-resources) are very often found in technical services, their assessment activities are becoming more crucial than ever. Assessing such things as the library's annual expenditures for licensed online resources, the usage of e-journal packages and databases, and users' preferences are all receiving increased attention by library administrators. In addition to employing the data from assessing budget expenditures and online usage to shape new collection development goals and activities, libraries are finding it necessary to develop assessment strategies in technical services that are measurable, not overly labor-intensive, and repeatable for consistent comparisons from year to year. This chapter will survey the past assessment and statistical gathering efforts employed by academic libraries, since many of these are still very useful and pertinent to libraries regardless of their size or type. The chapter also incorporates the highlights and lessons learned from an assessment project launched at a medium-sized academic library, at the University of Mississippi. This case study outlines the discussion, planning, and steps taken to develop a comprehensive, practical, pragmatic, and sustainable assessment program across the library and its technical services areas. Finally, the chapter will offer several topics for future assessment in technical services.

DEFINING TECHNICAL SERVICES

Libraries, whether academic, public, or special, differ in size, scope, and vision, and thus library technical services vary from institution to institution. Granted, in some libraries the designation of *technical services* may differ; for example, smaller libraries may have binding operations performed in the serials unit, or they may have the materials budget overseen by the library's main accounting department. Despite these variances in administrative structure, most technical services are defined by certain core operations and workflows regardless of how units and departments are organized and where the staff reside. In 1954, Tauber recognized acquisitions, cataloging and classification, binding, photographic reproduction, and circulation within the definition and operational parameters of library technical services.[2] As circulation and gate counts increased in the latter half of the twentieth century, many libraries relocated circulation units and departments from technical services to public services. The Association for Library Collections & Technical Services (ALCTS), a division of the American Library Association (ALA), does not include circulation in its list of sections.[3] With circulation removed from the list, the following areas are considered to be traditional technical services units: ☆

1. **Acquisitions:** includes management of the materials budget
2. **Cataloging:** includes original and enhanced cataloging
3. **Preservation:** includes repair and binding
4. **Serials and continuations:** includes print serial collections and series

With the rise of online resources beginning in the 1990s, the collection-building focus radically shifted in many libraries, particularly those serving academic and research institutions. Users increasingly accessed online resources, and particularly continuing resources such as electronic journals and databases. As libraries scrambled to add additional online resources to keep up with demand, significant changes occurred in collection-building and materials budget management. In the course of this shift from an emphasis on print to online resources, technical services adapted and evolved their areas of operations to include collection management.[4] In the current environment, with many libraries reducing the role of collection librarians in the daily selection of materials, and with licensing and budgets for online resources given such a high collection priority, acquisitions and collection management are on many levels working together. Absent from the ALCTS's sections is e-resources as a listed unit of operations, although the impact of the online environment can be seen in the organization's group activities, publications, and minutes of meetings across the sections.[5] It is not a stretch to state that online resources are overwhelmingly the largest current influence on library mission statements, user services, budgets, and staffing. For the purposes of this chapter, technical services will include the following areas of operations: *reframing technical services* ☆

1. **Acquisitions and collections:** now includes a percentage of collection management
2. **Cataloging and metadata:** now includes creating and organizing metadata
3. **Digital and preservation:** now includes operations for digitizing in-house print resources
4. **E-resources and serials:** now includes licensing and link resolving

ASSESSMENT IN TECHNICAL SERVICES— TRADITIONAL AND CONTEMPORARY

For decades, the data generated from assessment was often incorporated into annual staff appraisals, was used to revise position descriptions, and provided information to administrators for unit, department, or divisional reorganizations. While assessment and the metrics gathered were critical to technical services, the results were seldom incorporated into larger, library-wide assessment strategies. In an Association of Research Libraries (ARL) Spec Kit study conducted in 2007, all but one of the respondent academic libraries reported that they gathered statistics (Q. 1. N = 74; 99 percent), and the major impetus for conducting assessment activities was canvassing users (Q. 4. N = 63; 91 percent).[6] Assessment in technical services is no longer insular and conducted in a silo apart from the rest of the library. While academic libraries struggle to measure and demonstrate the value they provide to their university stakeholders, technical services must step up and be part of the process. To this end, an ALCTS e-forum was held for this very purpose with dozens of technical service librarians and administrators from ALA libraries sharing assessment strategies and issues from their institutions.[7]

However, several recent and significant trends have occurred to alter the collecting and service missions of libraries. Webster observes five generations of evolution to operations, service, and staffing in academic libraries, all produced by the online environment and its enormous impact on communication and research.[8] The emergence of the Web has influenced wholesale changes in library mission statements, user services, and collection-building. Yet, while most libraries continue to incorporate online resources into their collections as a high priority, maintaining and building on print and tangible material collections remains important. Users now want libraries to provide both traditional materials—such as print books—and access to online resources. For technical services units, the addition of online resources to the collections has simply meant an increase in responsibility; besides having to order, process, and maintain traditional print collections, technical services staff have added new workflows and have revised their staffing in order to accommodate the glut of online resources being acquired.

The changing landscape is having a sizable influence on the assessment strategies and activities that are taking place in libraries. Using the four main areas of operations in technical services previously defined—acquisitions and collection development, cataloging and metadata, digital and preservation,

focus on contemporary (handwritten)

and e-resources and serials—we have provided below a companion list of the metrics gathered and assessment activities undertaken in libraries in each of these areas. Each area is separated into two sections, "Traditional Metrics and Assessment" and "Contemporary Metrics and Assessment." The transition between what is "traditional" and what is "contemporary" occurred in the 1990s, which saw the emergence of the online environment. Yet the metric-gathering and assessment activities that took place in the previous era are still very relevant today, since most libraries maintain traditional print collections and services. The lists of metrics that are gathered are given in the sections starting below.

many special libraries not (handwritten marginal note)

Acquisitions and Collection Development

I disagree with verbiage (handwritten)

"Traditional Metrics and Assessment (handwritten quotation mark, then italic)

Firm order/approval plans: number of orders placed; number of orders received; number of print books purchased; books received on approval plan vs. firm order; circulation of books by firm vs. approval also by subject discipline; number of gift and exchange monographs and other materials received, reviewed, and sent to collections

Media: number of videos, CD-ROMs, CDs, microforms, and so on ordered and processed; this category now also includes individual e-books and stand-alone databases

Materials budget: percentage of budget spent on print monographs, print journals, media, and so on; percentage of budget spent on each subject discipline

Staffing/workflow: number of staff and staff hours (full-time equivalent = FTE) in each area of operations; FTEs spent on ordering, processing, paying invoices, and communicating/partnering with vendors

Acquisitions served collection management and librarians ordering materials; most libraries placed their emphasis on building print collections, so collecting, compiling, and reporting statistics on these materials to university and library organizations was a high priority. Collection managers were given wide authority for subject areas, and they built holdings through the purchase of print books and other materials, including gifts. Larger academic and science libraries having to support in-depth research emphasized the print journal collection, and so subsequently a large percentage of the materials budget was devoted to purchasing serial subscriptions. In this landscape, most assessment activities focused on vendor comparisons and determining the efficiency of services rendered, particularly vendors supplying monographs through firm or blanket ordering, approval plans, and shelf-ready services. Staff also conducted frequent budget analyses to improve the methods or formulas for library fund allocations.

Contemporary Metrics and Assessment

E-books, streaming video, and other online resources: in addition to collecting numerical metrics on resources that were paid for directly, there are resources received from other streams (i.e., HathiTrust, Open Access, etc.); reviewing online cost, use, and other metrics such as cost-per-use; online usage vs. print circulation statistics; comparison of usage by acquisition type (e.g., e-books acquired by use-driven acquisitions [UDA] vs. package purchase vs. firm order); usage and cost-per-use of e-books by subject discipline; and assisting collection managers or spearheading projects on usability and conducting qualitative studies on online use

Materials budget: percentage of the budget spent on ordering and processing e-books, e-journals (individual and via packages), and databases; percentage subdivided by purchase or subscription; percentage of the e-resources budget spent on each subject discipline

Staffing/workflow: number of staff and FTEs engaged in ordering and processing e-books; developing approval/UDA plans; and communicating/partnering with vendors and publishers, including setting up trials and engaging in consortial sharing

With acquisitions and collection management more intertwined, studies have become more interdepartmental, with librarians and staff analyzing intricate cost, usage, and cost-per-use data. More involved assessments of usability and qualitative user studies and surveys are ongoing in many libraries. As materials budgets have become tighter for libraries, the assessment of vendor-supplied resources such as use-driven acquisitions plans will become indispensable to librarians and administrators who must make tough choices on what online resources are selected or de-selected.

Cataloging and Metadata

Traditional Metrics and Assessment

Original monograph cataloging: number of print book volumes cataloged for different holding locations and by subject discipline

Enhanced monograph cataloging: number of print book volumes cataloged requiring record enhancement, again sorted and counted by holdings location and subject discipline

Serials cataloging: number of serial titles cataloged either originally or enhanced, subdivided by ongoing vs. static, serials cataloged by individual titles, analyzed, or pieces/volumes added to existing holdings

Media and specialized materials: number of VHS videos, CD-ROMs, CDs, microforms, and other media; rare books, maps, charts, music scores, and other items added to library collections

based on what? ?

Generally, most catalog departments or units were well-staffed, with workflows designed to catalog large amounts of incoming print and tangible materials. The staff conducted both original and enhanced cataloging and reported title and volume counts. Many of the assessment projects conducted were aimed at studying workflow, particularly the time and costs required to conduct various types and levels of cataloging. Compiling statistics was labor-intensive due to physical counting techniques, although this improved with automation; assessment studies were just as difficult, since most reports offered by the integrated library system (ILS) had limited report functionality.

Contemporary Metrics and Assessment

Original monograph cataloging: in addition to the number of print book volumes and e-resources cataloged for different holding locations and by subject discipline, there are running counts on vendor-supplied full records being purchased at ordering; original e-books cataloged

Enhanced monograph cataloging: in addition to the number of print and e-book volumes cataloged requiring record enhancement, the number of e-book records enhanced after loading

Serials cataloging: in addition to print serial titles cataloged either originally or enhanced, e-journals requiring either original or enhanced cataloging

Media and specialized materials: the number of DVDs and other emerging media, either stand-alone or attached to print materials, that are cataloged for collections

Despite the prevalence of online resources, assessment is rooted in traditional methodologies, since many cataloging departments still devote more time to creating or enhancing catalog records for print materials. Libraries are increasingly adopting vendor discovery tools that provide links to both purchased and native-born online resources which often require review by catalogers, but larger assessment projects are usually routed to vendors, central bibliographic utilities, or consortia. With the emphasis now placed on creating metadata rather than on traditional cataloging functions, assessments to review staff assignments, statistics, and workflows are helping administrators and managers transform, downsize, and reorganize departments and units. Title and volume counts continue to be collected in cataloging with varying degrees of difficulty depending on the ILS, which still offers limited report functionality. An emerging assessment area for study is automated record-loading and the quality control of both the bibliographic utility and vendor records being furnished.

Digital and Preservation

Traditional Metrics and Assessment

Print monographs and serials: the number of serial and monograph volumes bound; the number of monographs and brittle books repaired

Media and specialized materials: the number of volumes with media added to collections; the number of CDs, DVDs, and other materials requiring special processing

Scanning: limited scanning of in-house and native resources to microfilm

Shelf maintenance: the number of serials and monograph volumes withrawn, subdivided by holdings locations or call number/subject discipline ranges; early collaboration with regional and consortial libraries to consolidate holdings in centralized storage facilities

Preservation operations maintain and bind print collections, and assessment was usually performed on a project basis. As the collection concentration shifted from print to online resources, assessment projects became larger, more elaborate, and often involved collaboration with collection managers, assessment groups, and stack maintenance staff. Preservation units began photographing out-of-copyright print books and other library materials onto microfilm, and then later, with the emergence of the online environment, the staff began digitizing materials; creating microfilm and digitizing materials required frequent quality reviews and collection assessment.

Contemporary Metrics and Assessment

Monographs and serials: in addition to numerical counts of print serial and monograph volumes bound and repaired, there are metrics for books or bound serial volumes that have been withdrawn and supplied to partner library organizations (e.g., the Center for Research Libraries) or to nonprofit vendors (e.g., the Internet Archive)

Media and specialized materials: in addition to counts for materials requiring special processing, there are numerical figures for unique items including data, reports, publications, webcasts, and other resources generated by the university or library

Scanning: numerical figures for institutional online collections and items scanned and placed on library websites, as well as usage of the collections and items—includes the institutional repository

Shelf maintenance: in addition to the number of serials and monograph volumes withdrawn, there are also counts for items removed to or brought back from off-site and high-density storage facilities

— still a focus on what was previously known

As local digital initiatives have grown in size and importance, librarians and administrators in technical services are assessing the workflows and traditional staffing assignments that were previously dedicated to maintaining print collections. Libraries are increasing their collaboration with regional and consortial libraries in order to consolidate their holdings and collectively share print and digitized resources. To determine the appropriate items for shared holdings, assessing the library's print collections for quality, quantity, and duplication becomes critical. In general, print collection assessment is a collaborative undertaking, since technical services must work with units across the library on these large projects. The results from assessment provide

→ ch. focuses on print collections rather than other solutions

information for libraries that are making decisions on relocating print materials to off-site or high-density storage facilities. The birth of institutional repositories (IRs) creates a need for staff to assess the online usage and downloads of the resources offered by the library.

E-Resources and Serials

Traditional Metrics and Assessment

> *Periodicals:* periodical issues received, claimed, or missing; number of titles; track subscriptions and holdings updated; expenditures by subscription subdivided by budgets

> *Annuals:* number of volumes and titles; track subscriptions, serial holdings updated and claims; expenditures by subscription subdivided by budgets; number of gift and exchange titles and volumes in collections

> *Series:* number especially divided by call number/subject discipline ranges; series classed together or separately; expenditures by subscription subdivided by budgets

> *E-resources:* number of serial titles by subscription subdivided by budgets or subject areas; number of CD-ROMs, either stand-alone or inserted into print items, subdivided by budgets; e-books purchased individually or by package

Print serials were the cornerstone of academic library collections, but serials management was extremely labor-intensive for staff in technical services, so constant evaluations of daily workflows and assessing vendor services were crucial. Most libraries have inexact methods to monitor print serial use, making assessment difficult. When usage figures for a library's e-resources became available from vendors, the assessment of online journal use became possible. It was now necessary for staff to add statistical counts for e-resources along with print serials, while assessment activities evolved into a two-pronged review of print and online resources. As libraries began to switch their collections' focal point from print to online serials, technical service administrators and managers reassigned staff to manage the growing number of e-resources; but despite the increased emphasis placed on the selection and acquisition of online resources, assessment was in its infancy, and libraries relied heavily on vendor reports.

Contemporary Metrics and Assessment

Periodicals and e-journals: in addition to compiling and reporting statistics for all print journals and continuations, counts now include the number of online journals received directly by subscription, through journal packages from societies, vendors, and other sources; and counts also include titles and series received via databases. The distinction between identifying and counting annuals, series, and periodicals in the online environment is no longer relevant, although tracking and updating holdings and years of coverage remain important for access purposes.

Databases, e-books, streaming videos, and other resources: reports are now required for the usage of e-journals, databases, and other continuing resources, often from vendor-supplied data; cost and cost-per-use for individual packages, titles, and databases are standard metrics.

E-book usage and title count are often compiled by e-resource staff, often via the electronic resource management system (ERM), in-house ILS reports, or from vendor platforms.

focus on serials

With the escalating growth of users who are accessing e-resources, and with more publishers transforming from print to online publications, libraries are increasing the number of licenses for databases and large publisher or society packages of e-journals. It follows that assessment activities have become progressively more important in this area, especially as material budgets are continually reallocated to pay for the expensive licensing of these packages. Most libraries incorporate the statistical gathering for the new online resources into the pool of previously tracked print journal metrics, while new assessment efforts are needed for collecting and assessing COUNTER journal statistics, e-book usage, and other online metrics. Reviews of usage, costs by subject areas, and cost-per-use have all become important areas for assessment. In-house reports *is this true?* generated by electronic resource management systems or the ILS systems are not sophisticated enough to generate the information and assessment sought, so libraries continue to rely exceedingly on vendors' metrics and reports. Library assessment is growing more demanding, with entirely new social metrics to consider (e.g., altmetrics), and new requirements such as conducting overlap analyses of database and e-journal package content.

demanding? not enlightening?

FUTURE ASSESSMENT

Most academic, public, and special libraries are building collections that are increasingly online-centric. Libraries are adding online resources through various acquisition streams, mainly those purchased or licensed, but also items received by open-source means. While the bulk of resources offered to users are acquired individually, many libraries are seizing opportunities to broker better deals by engaging in group or consortial purchases and license agreements, or by participating in memberships with groups such as HathiTrust. In addition to providing thousands of e-journals, e-books, and other online resources such as citation indexes, many libraries are beginning to offer unpublished reports, papers, or even links to raw data and data sets, often through an institutional repository. *negative language*

Offering such a myriad of resources poses a stiff challenge for library assessment. Fortunately, online resources do provide the means for collecting usage statistics, whether these are library- or vendor-generated, and this is spurring libraries to launch a variety of more complex assessment studies. Despite the burgeoning online landscape, most libraries still build and maintain traditional print collections. In a new millennium, with libraries developing collections and offering user services for both print and online resources, libraries' assessment groups and staff will have to refocus and prioritize their assessment projects to encompass all formats and methods of acquisitions. Ideally, the assessment activities in technical services will be part of larger assessment strategies developed by the administration and committees. To assist libraries in these endeavors, the sections below are bulleted topics or areas to consider for future assessment strategies and projects.

Acquisitions and Collection Development

Will identify continual assessment for use-driven acquisition plans and combined print/e-book approval plans; such assessment will require a collaboration between libraries and vendors or publishers supplying the resources; more sophisticated reports need to be created and offered by vendors and publishers; eventual next-generation ILS systems should be a boost for assessing cost and usage data.

Assessing the material/resource budget will continue to be a fundamental responsibility of acquisitions and collections; specific reviews of fund expenditures by vendor, publisher, and platform, subdivided by subject discipline, will increase in importance as resources are added or discontinued from the collections.

Acquisitions and collections, often in conjunction with e-resources units or departments, will conduct increased numbers of usability and user studies, surveys, and other qualitative studies; for example, academic libraries will participate in more national group enterprises such as the Charlotte Initiative for e-books.[9]

Cataloging and Metadata

This area of operations might be renamed "Discovery and Access," as libraries veer from established cataloging conventions to better organizing and improving the discovery and access to online resources; consequently, usability studies on how users discover and access the resources will become an essential factor in developing original catalog records and enhancing them.

What about shared metadata for resources?!

Digital and Preservation

Assessment projects will continue to involve the digitization of native resources, including developing parameters and assigning priorities for scanning materials and creating or enhancing collections; developing user surveys and studying the usage of institutional repositories and in-house resources will become more commonplace.   *hypocritical compared to what the ch. says*
Efforts to reduce print holdings on campus will continue, as will assessing collections for decisions on what is scanned for the institutional repositories, or transferred to off-campus or consortial repositories.

Future assessment studies will concentrate on providing information and options to resolve the problem of the long-term preservation of library-owned digital resources, as well as maintaining long-term access to commercial content that is no longer supported by a publisher or vendor.

E-Resources and Serials

Assessing budgetary allocations and expenditures, particularly by subject disciplines, will continue as libraries communicate to stakeholders.

Libraries and e-resources staff will develop more enhanced and sustainable assessment procedures that will include overlap content analysis in order to avoid or reduce duplication.

Libraries will continue to assess fund and usage data in order to determine value for a host of expensive licenses for online databases, e-journal subscriptions and packages, and e-books; the information from assessment will help administrators negotiate licenses and make more informed decisions on retaining or discontinuing e-journal packages and databases.

Due to the importance and expense of online resources, libraries will see a growing need to track user access and research collaboration in different ways; for example, incorporating data from altmetrics and other advanced citation tools.

Assessing resources that are not directly purchased will also continue to grow in importance as libraries offer more online collections to users, including open access, HathiTrust, and other venues that ultimately challenge the notion of what constitutes a library collection.

Final Thoughts

It is clear that the online environment has had an enormous impact on library assessment in technical services. Libraries have had to add numerous statistical categories for collections, develop new projects that incorporate a variety of data and formats, and completely revitalize their goals and priorities. The challenge of assessing user services, collections, staffing, and workflows that encompass both print and online resources will continue for some time in the future. It is probable that administrators will place emphasis on evaluating the more expensive online resources, such as large e-journal packages licensed from publishers. It is also probable that studies once traditionally conducted by collection management librarians—such as assessing citation analyses or reviewing the feedback gleaned from qualitative surveys—will often be conducted by technical services in conjunction with librarians and staff from collection management, reference, and assessment committees. The information gathered and compiled from such studies can help libraries make informed decisions on maintaining, acquiring, or weeding online resources. Assessment in technical services and across the library is also an ongoing activity and should focus attention on how library services and operations can be improved.

good takeaway

CASE STUDY

The University of Mississippi Library

Institutional Setting: The University of Mississippi (UM) has a main campus in Oxford with a medical–health sciences branch located in Jackson. In 2016, the university achieved the prestigious R-1 Carnegie Classification. This classification, along with an increased rate of growth over the past few years, is setting an exciting new trajectory for the university, while also intensifying the need for the library to strengthen its resources and user services.

Type of Institution: Public academic

Size/Students: The university is a large research institution; the main campus boasts over 20,000 students and almost 900 faculty.

Memberships: ASERL (Association of Southeastern Research Libraries)

Consortia: LYRASIS; Mississippi Academic Library Consortia (MALC); Mississippi Research Library Group

Colleges/Academic Institutes and Programs/Research Centers: 15 academic schools and colleges; 21 academic institutes and programs; 37 research centers

Library Instruction: The library offers classes in basic library use and navigation, as well as research and research consultations. The value and effectiveness of the classes are measured by survey responses that are collected from students at the end of each semester.

History of Library Assessment: Like most academic libraries, the UM Libraries have a long history of collecting metrics and conducting intermittent assessment projects. Most library assessment to date has revolved around determining usage and user satisfaction through classroom surveys or more formal surveys such as ARL's LibQUAL.[10] Quantitative metrics, feedback, and other information gathered by the library from LibQUAL and other survey tools are reported annually to university administrators and faculty as required by the university's strategic plan. Beyond assessing user services, the majority of

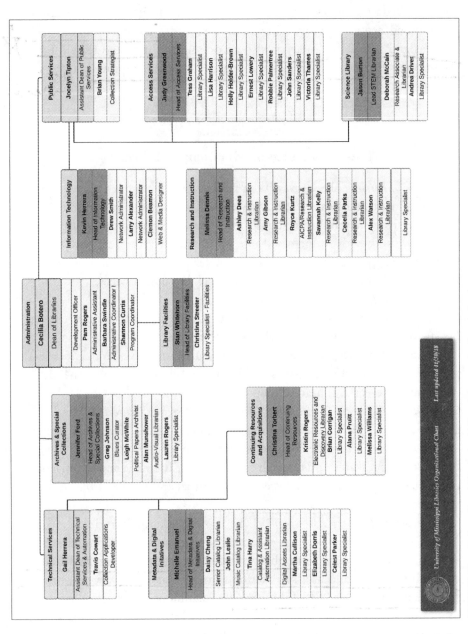

FIGURE 1.1 • University of Mississippi Libraries organizational chart

assessment projects have been conducted by individuals, groups, or departments but were seldom part of a comprehensive library strategy.

Library Organization

Technical Services: The division of Technical Services and Automation consists of Acquisitions, Cataloging and Metadata, and Federal Documents, with a future plan to incorporate Digital Services with a newly created Institutional Repository. The library does not have a separate collections department, with collection liaisons primarily reporting to Reference and Instruction. However, the materials budget and the bulk of collection analyses are performed in Technical Services. Electronic Resources and Discovery Services are also housed in the division, which includes performing online troubleshooting and links resolving. These technical service activities are integral to library operations at UM, and are thus essential to assessment.

Assessment Committee: The Assessment Committee was revamped and enlarged in 2017 to include representatives from all library departments. The committee is composed of librarians from various departments and is responsible for compiling and reporting standard collection, budget, and usage metrics to the university, to collection programs such as the Integrated Postsecondary Education Data System (IPEDS), and to library organizations (e.g., the Association of Southeastern Research Libraries). The committee also conducts user surveys.

Background for the action plan: Despite notable efforts by librarians and staff to perform user surveys and create evaluative projects, the Assessment Committee and administrators determined that assessment endeavors were too often being conducted in silos across the departments and units. An action plan was conceived by the group to develop a library-wide assessment strategy and develop or revise collection and research procedures as part of a long-term project.

Goals of the action plan: A new and still ongoing library-wide assessment action plan was launched with several goals:

- Develop an assessment strategy that is clear, comprehensive, and purposeful; and launch a comprehensive assessment action plan that requires participation by all departments and units, yet is not overly labor-intensive for staff.
- Centralize and coordinate all metric collection and assessment projects.

- Review existing assessment and metric collecting activities and determine what to continue or discontinue.
- Identify untapped and potentially valuable assessment studies or metrics that are not currently being gathered, and then develop new projects and collection procedures.
- Create a methodology for organizing, compiling, and reporting the statistics and assessment studies undertaken each year or by project, making both the outcomes and raw data available to all library personnel.
- Centralize an online database or statistical warehouse where the results of all statistics compiled and surveys conducted can be easily accessed by all library faculty and staff to use for assessment projects, grant-writing, and so on.
- Determine methods and opportunities to communicate noteworthy assessment results and statistics to library stakeholders.

Action plan launch: In 2017, the library embarked on a long-term project to establish library-wide assessment and metrics. The group set out to devise a strategic and comprehensive assessment plan. As a foundation for developing an overall assessment program, the core library functions were identified and organized into three areas: User Services, Spaces, and Collections. Committee members will take these three areas and define the objectives, methodology, and reporting structure for these projects with the goal of establishing a baseline in each area. The baseline will vary in each area but will concentrate on performance level.

Phase 1. Centralizing metric collection: The Assessment Committee reviewed the metric categories and the methods for stats collection in the library, and then created a statistical inventory. The results of the inventory were then matched with the statistics needed for reporting to the university, various library associations (e.g., the Association of College and Research Libraries), and other academic or accreditation organizations. The assessment group next established a "standard statistics sheet" to include only those metrics requested specifically by reporting agencies. Included on the form were categories for the metrics that are requested frequently by departments, faculty, and so on, such as the number of seats or computers available in the library. The committee next made decisions on each category—whether to continue or discontinue collecting the statistics being taken, while also adding new categories for metrics not being

does not provide mtext crtatrons

compiled. This centralized sheet also noted the specific department and unit responsible for harvesting and compiling the various metrics.

Phase 2. Establishing baselines: The committee established a baseline for future assessment activities in each of the three core areas—User Services, Spaces, and Collections. Although the technical services are not designated a core area, the information and statistics gathered from various technical services units are paramount to assessment at the UM Library. Once a baseline is in place for each core area, the library will then use metrics and assessment tools to measure success in meeting both the short- and long-term goals set for the library. Each baseline will define the current metrics and status of activities ongoing in that core area and will be used as a method to measure growth and as a foundation for making future improvements. Using established baselines, the committee can better assess the strengths and weaknesses of library operations and services and offer recommendations to actualize the full potential of the library. Baselines will help the library not only fulfill its role within the university, but can be used as comparison to peer libraries.

Future directions: Moving forward, there are many areas yet to be explored. The newly revised master sheet for the collected library statistics currently resides on a SharePoint site requiring a sign-on and is not readily available. Ideally, all assessment and statistical information compiled by the library should be open and easily accessible to all staff. Developing a centralized, user-friendly, web-based warehouse or database containing library statistics and assessment projects would not only allow the information to be used as a foundation for future projects, it would help staff ensure uniformity in metrics collection. In addition to building an assessment portal for staff, library statistical and assessment information should also be made available to the university community.

good point - support better decision-making

Establishing the baselines of core functions should provide an improved environment of evidence-based information for presentations to key stakeholders. Collection managers can use targeted metrics and assessment results in their presentations on the current state of a specific subject collection to faculty, students, and researchers. For special collections, assessment information can be used to develop short- and long-term goals and what it would take to reach those goals; relaying this information in presentations to donors would offer excellent opportunities for library development.

The Assessment Committee, working with library administrators, is developing important focal points and strategies for the assessment program. One major future goal of the library is to collect and compile user information and usage statistics mined from university and library online integrated systems in order to determine how library resources and services affect student success and research activities. Another main goal will be to develop a methodology for applying assessment results to validate library staffing and budget expenditures to university administrators.

Lessons learned: (1) It took a substantial amount of time for the library's Assessment Committee to coordinate the establishment of an assessment program. The committee members had to review and revise statistical categories and methods for collection; disseminate information and incorporate feedback from each department; and develop a system for managing and centralizing assessment projects. All this required time from librarians and staff across multiple departments. So in order to be successful, a library must recognize the need for establishing a program, give it high priority, and provide staff with the time required for the initiative. (2) For staff, collecting statistics is often an individual or intradepartmental responsibility; simultaneously, working on assessment projects even in small groups can be an insular activity. An element not to be overlooked in developing an assessment program is obtaining buy-in from staff and librarians on the necessity of unifying assessment efforts and relaying this information to stakeholders. With more participants on board, the net results of library-wide assessment will be far more effective and robust.

Unifying assessment

CONCLUSION

For many decades, the numerous statistics collected in technical services were reported to library organizations or were used by the library for grant activities. The statistics also fueled various in-house projects conducted by technical service staff that were centered on specific evaluations of workflows and staff assignments. But assessment activities were not routinely included in larger library assessment strategies. Going forward, statistical gathering in technical service areas needs to be performed with clear goals and sound reasons for the metrics being collected. The metrics collected should continue to address all aspects of technical service operations for reporting purposes, but also be applicable to larger library assessment strategies and data-driven decision-making. Assessment projects and activities should also be goal-oriented and launched within the larger strategies of the library. The ultimate objective of collecting statistics and metrics is assessment; the ultimate goal of assessment is to make

good takeaway

informed and better choices in budget deployment and collection development decisions, and to improve the services provided to users.

As we learned from the case study being conducted at the University of Mississippi Library, establishing a library-wide assessment program is both challenging and time-consuming, especially at the start-up. But once the library's assessment program is developed, staff should not have to spend an inordinate amount of their assignments devoted to assessment activities, although the members of the Assessment Committee should have their important roles and contributions noted in annual evaluations. In addition to working cross-departmentally in the library to collect and preset statistical and assessment information, assessment librarians and committees must also work closely with the college or university in general. Many universities have departments or units dedicated to collecting university-wide statistics and performing large assessment projects that are designed to measure instruction and student success. Libraries need to be an integral part of these activities.

Assessment in libraries is more essential than ever. In a world where users want libraries to offer innovative services, spaces for study and collaboration, and collections that include both online resources and traditional print materials, it is imperative that libraries make the most efficient use of their budgets, operations, and staff. Assessment is crucial to libraries because it provides evidence for better decision-making, and it provides information to relay to stakeholders in the community. Libraries must develop sustainable assessment strategies and create well-designed and useful projects that can be accomplished without overburdening the staff. With collections and budgets managed predominately by staff in acquisitions and e-resources, technical services will only grow as an area targeted for future library assessment.

NOTES

1. Association of Research Libraries, "ARL Statistics," www.arlstatistics.org/home.
2. M. F. Tauber, *Technical Services in Libraries: Acquisitions, Cataloging, Classification, Binding, Photographic Reproduction, and Circulation Operations* (New York: Columbia University Press, 1954).
3. Association for Library Collections and Technical Services, "Sections," www.ala.org/alcts/about/sections.
4. Ibid.
5. Association for Library Collections and Technical Services, "Collection Management Section (CMS)," www.ala.org/alcts/mgrps/cms.

6. Stephanie Wright and Lynda S. White, *Library Assessment,* SPEC Kit 303 (Washington, DC: Association of Research Libraries, 2007).
7. Association for Library Collections and Technical Services, "Turning Statistics into Assessment: How Can Technical Services Measure the Value of Their Services?" August 22, 2012, www.ala.org/alcts/turning-statistics-assessment-how-can-technical-services -measure-value-their-services.
8. Keith Webster, "Leading Technical Services in the Future," February 1, 2017, hosted by the ALCTS, www.ala.org/alcts/confevents/upcoming/webinar/020117.
9. J. Murrey Atkins Library, University of North Carolina at Charlotte, "The Charlotte Initiative," http://charlotteinitiative.uncc.edu/.
10. Association of Research Libraries, "LibQUAL+ Charting Library Service Quality," https://www.libqual.org/home.

REFERENCES

Association for Library Collections and Technical Services. "Sections." www.ala.org/alcts/ about/sections.

———. "Turning Statistics into Assessment: How Can Technical Services Measure the Value of Their Services?" ALCTS E-Forum. www.ala.org/alcts/turning-statistics -assessment-how-can-technical-services-measure-value-their-services.

Association of Research Libraries. "ARL Statistics." www.arlstatistics.org/home.

———. "Collection Management Section." www.ala.org/alcts/mgrps/cms.

———. "LibQUAL + Charting Library Service Quality." www.libqual.org/home.

J. Murrey Atkins Library, University of North Carolina at Charlotte. "The Charlotte Initiative." http://charlotteinitiative.uncc.edu/.

Tauber, M. F. *Technical Services in Libraries: Acquisitions, Cataloging, Classification, Binding, Photographic Reproduction, and Circulation Operations.* New York: Columbia University Press, 1954.

Webster, Keith. "Leading Technical Services in the Future." ALCTS Webinar. www.ala.org/ alcts/confevents/upcoming/webinar/020117.

Wright, Stephanie, and Lynda S. White. *Library Assessment.* SPEC Kit 303. Washington, DC: Association of Research Libraries, 2007. https://doi.org/10.29242/spec.303.

ADDITIONAL SOURCES

Canepi, Kitti. "Work Analysis in Library Technical Services." *Technical Services Quarterly* 25, no. 2 (2007): 19–30. http://dx.doi.org/10.1300/J124v25n02_02.

Chang-FitzGibbon, Kerry, and Jianrong Wang. "In the Spotlight: Technical Services Professionals in Library-Wide Assessment." *Technical Services Quarterly* 34, no. 2

(2017): 157–73. doi: 10.1080.07317131.2017.1286845. http://dx.doi.org/10.1080.0731 7131.2017.1286845.

Dragon, Patricia, and Lisa Sheets Barricella. "Assessment of Technical Services Workflow in an Academic Library: A Time-and-Path Study." *Technical Services Quarterly* 23, no. 4 (2006): 1–16. doi: 10.1300/J124v23n04_01. http://dx.doi.org/10.1300/J124v23n04_01.

Mugridge, Rebecca L. "Technical Services Assessment: A Survey of Pennsylvania Academic Libraries." *Library Resources and Technical Services* 58, no. 2 (2014): 100–110.

Mugridge, Rebecca L., and Nancy M. Poehlmann. "Assessment Strategies for Technical Services." *University Libraries Faculty Scholarship* 5 (2014). (University at Albany, State University of New York). http://scholarsarchive.library.albany.edu/ulib_fac_scholar/5.

ASSESSING COLLECTIONS HOLISTICALLY
A Behind-the-Scenes Approach

Madeline M. Kelly and Stephanie S. Smith

Collections assessment is often thought of as the purview of the subject specialist. After all, specialists know the content and the constituents of the collection, so it makes sense that they would be responsible for assessment tasks such as poring over title lists and usage spreadsheets. However, as the stewards of most library collections data, collection development and technical services departments are also well situated to spearhead collections assessment work. Especially when assessment is approached holistically and comprehensively—beyond a single subject or format—technical services staff can leverage subject specialist expertise strategically while driving the overall assessment program centrally. Within this arrangement, technical services staff can serve as the assessment experts, planning, implementing and maintaining a holistic assessment program and involving others as needed.

This chapter is informed by the authors' experiences with collections assessment at George Mason University (hereafter "Mason"). Located in Fairfax, Virginia, Mason is a large public university with a total enrollment of nearly

35,000 students (about one-third of whom are graduate students) or 28,000 FTEs.[1] Established as its own institution in the 1970s and perceived for many years as a "commuter school" for northern Virginia suburbanites, Mason experienced a period of rapid growth starting in the mid-2000s. As the university's full-time enrollment grew—a 40 percent increase over ten years[2]—the University Libraries (the Libraries) experienced a corresponding time of plenty. Collections, which had once been modest and largely print-based, mushroomed to include nearly 2 million print volumes, thousands of electronic journal subscriptions, and over 800 databases. Faced with this pace and scale of growth, librarians found it increasingly difficult to retain any sense of the collection as a whole. Thus, in 2013, the Libraries implemented a comprehensive collections assessment program to begin answering the question of what there was and why. While this chapter will touch on aspects of the Mason program as an illustration, those looking for a thorough case study of the approach may also wish to refer to the article "Applying the Tiers of Assessment: A Holistic and Systematic Approach to Assessing Library Collections" published in the *Journal of Academic Librarianship* in 2014.[3]

THE WHAT AND WHY OF ASSESSMENT

Collections assessment can be defined in any number of ways. At its simplest, assessment is "an organized process for systematically analyzing and describing a library's collection."[4] Some definitions push beyond simple analysis and into qualitative human judgment and decision-making; others emphasize the element of meeting specific objectives or needs.[5,6] Whatever the exact definition, collections assessment goes beyond simply gathering data, to actually doing something with it. As part of the "cycle of active engagement," collections assessment is an integral part of library decision-making and outreach.[7]

In today's changing library landscape—which includes both shrinking budgets and increased stakeholder expectations for accountability—libraries can use collections assessment to fulfill a variety of needs. From an external perspective, assessment can help define (and defend) the collection's value to stakeholders, including administrators and funding bodies. However, assessment can be just as useful internally. Collections assessment can help libraries act strategically rather than simply responding to external stimuli. Collections assessment can help establish a baseline for the collection's holdings, suitability, and performance; determine whether and how the library meets its patrons' needs and its parent organization's goals; and respond to immediate challenges like funding or space shortages. Lastly, collections assessment can foster familiarity with the collections in a way that intuition and anecdotal accounts cannot. In short, collections assessment is a foundational activity and can be well worth the investment of time and energy if implemented strategically.[8]

CHALLENGES OF COLLECTIONS ASSESSMENT

In spite of the many benefits of collections assessment, libraries may still struggle with even ad hoc assessment projects, let alone the implementation of comprehensive assessment programs. Assessment remains a challenge, due in large part to complications and difficulties inherent in the broader library landscape. These factors, which are well covered in the literature, include:

- the proliferation of electronic formats
- the rise of shared collections
- the variety of acquisitions models available
- the increasingly interdisciplinary nature of research
- the unpredictability of aggregator e-resources
- the shift toward user- and outcomes-centered metrics
- reductions to library budgets[9, 10]

Building library collections in this context requires new approaches; similarly, assessing collections in this environment requires a new set of skills.[11] With regard to collections assessment specifically, Harker and Klein surveyed seventy-one Association of Research Libraries (ARL) member institutions about their collections assessment goals and practices.[12] Of the responding institutions, 23 percent identified consistency and quality of data as a major challenge for collections assessment, while 27 percent cited staffing, time, and cost as challenges; 20 percent cited staff expertise as a problem; and 5 percent mentioned feeling overwhelmed by the content to be assessed.[13] Harker and Klein also asked institutions that were not conducting assessments to describe why, and the same issues emerged: challenges involving staff, time, technical infrastructure, funding, and skills.

These assessment challenges boil down to a few major themes. First, there is the intimidation factor. Assessment is thought of as something labor-intensive—a difficult process that is likely to raise new questions and generate "unwelcome surprises."[14] Today's library collections are vast and diverse, making it more daunting than ever to assess them in a meaningful way. There is also a perception that assessment requires advanced data or technological skills. But while some level of skill in working with data is necessary, assessments and analyses can be performed using standard, familiar tools. For example, Melissa J. Goertzen, the collection development analysis and support librarian at the Columbia University Libraries, supports analysis for twenty libraries using only Microsoft Excel for the majority of her work.[15] In addition to Excel, there is an increasing variety of easy-to-use free (or low-cost) data-processing tools that librarians can learn,[16] aided by a corresponding proliferation of online tutorials and user guides. Assessment need not be an onerous, insurmountable task.

Along with the perception that collections assessment is intimidating or overwhelming, there are additional obstacles to undertaking a dedicated, long-term collections assessment project or program. There is the precision factor, or the sense that many library data sources, tools, and methodologies are inadequately reliable for making sound decisions. There is the inertia factor, or the sense that even with assessment, nothing will change. Lastly, there is the human factor. In many libraries, there are simply not enough staff to tackle collections assessment. At smaller institutions, technical services and collection development staff may fill many roles, and adding collections assessment responsibilities to the mix may seem impractical. On top of that, high turnover rates and staff burnout may further erode support for assessment projects, even in cases where a library can manage to put one in motion. Taken together, all of these factors too often spell the doom of collections assessment in libraries. For an assessment plan to be successful, it must address these issues explicitly.

HOLISTIC COLLECTIONS ASSESSMENT

Within the universe of collections assessment, there are a variety of general approaches. Speaking broadly, assessment can either be comprehensive, and planned as an all-encompassing and ongoing process; or it can be ad hoc, designed on the fly to address a specific question or challenge. Within these two approaches, assessment can be further segmented—by subject, format, location, language, user, and so on—to make projects more focused, finite, and manageable. Assessment can also look through a wider lens, using a mixed-methods approach involving many of the above segmentations to build a well-rounded and rich picture of the collection. This chapter will address this latter, holistic model, outlining a subject-by-subject, comprehensive approach to collections assessment.

Until recently, the assessment literature tended to focus on one tool or format at a time, rather than taking a holistic view. However, there is a growing literature in favor of the holistic approach. In 2004, Nicholson proposed a "framework for holistic measurement and cumulative evaluation," emphasizing the need to combine a variety of measures in order to better understand the library as a system and make better-informed decisions.[17] Since then, at least a half-dozen articles and presentations have struck upon this same concept. Bodi and Maier-O'Shea outline three steps for flexible and holistic assessment, including "breaking down assessment by subject . . . when necessary" and "blending a variety of assessment tools appropriate to the discipline."[18] Borin and Yi propose a framework that incorporates a variety of collection indicators such as usage, users, subject-specific standards, and others, and recommend attention to collections ratios as much as to objective measures.[19] Wilde and Level introduced the concept of "transferable outcomes," or the idea that collections data should be compiled from a variety of sources and perspectives on an ongoing basis, and then harnessed for a variety of outcomes.[20]

In addition to these theoretical frameworks, several libraries have implemented holistic collections assessment programs. Wilde and Level developed a program at Colorado State University that incorporates data from a variety of sources to support ongoing comprehensive and ad hoc assessment and decision-making.[21] At James Madison University, Duncan and O'Gara employed mixed methods to evaluate database and e-journal subscriptions and generate subject-specific collection "snapshots."[22] In their analysis of circulation and interlibrary loan data, Knievel et al. found that "the overall most important factor demonstrated by [their] study [was] the importance of combining different sources of data for collection development decisions."[23] Lastly, at George Mason University, the authors developed a holistic collections assessment program based on tiered subject-by-subject assessment.[24] In this program, specific subject collections are assessed using a portfolio of tools that can be expanded or contracted; low-tier assessments involve fewer metrics, while high-tier assessments involve at least a dozen data sources, methodologies, and tools.

advocating flexibility in assessment based on what type of library is being managed

THE BENEFITS OF HOLISTIC COLLECTIONS ASSESSMENT

While the holistic approach is more involved than a one-dimensional assessment, its benefits make the extra planning and time worthwhile. Holistic collections assessment has the potential to mitigate many of the assessment challenges listed above. For example, using a variety of data sources mitigates the precision problem. As each tool, method, or data set is added to the mix, it can provide a check on the rest of the data, or an illumination of a previously unexamined piece of the collection. Ultimately, the library can triangulate the end result based on consensus among the sources and measures chosen; taken cumulatively, the data become more credible.[25] The mixed methods approach also makes it possible to evaluate the full range of library resources, regardless of subject, format, language, and so on. Table 2.1 provides some examples of managing the "precision problem."

The use of multiple data sets, methodologies, and tools enables the holistic approach to be infinitely flexible and customizable. Metrics can—and indeed, should—be mixed and matched based on discipline, format, and medium. The approach also accommodates logistical flexibility; libraries can expand or contract their portfolio of tools based on their staffing, budget, timeline, priority, infrastructure, goals, available data, and more. Assessments can be segmented by subject, format, or user; they can even be adjusted to respond to a variety of stakeholder interests. Within this adaptable structure, assessment projects—or even full-scale programs—become as manageable as they need to be, and can evolve over time to meet the library's changing needs. This flexibility mitigates both the intimidation factor, especially with regard to labor and scope, and the human factor. Assessment is no longer a behemoth, but rather a flexible tool that can be trimmed or adapted to whatever the moment requires.

TABLE 2.1 • Examples of mitigation of the "precision problem" in holistic collection assessment

Monograph circulation has been decreasing over the last three years . . .	. . . but e-book and other electronic resource usage has been increasing.
Collection size data indicates the collection is small in relation to peers . . .	. . . but user surveys indicate they prefer a targeted collection, and generally have what they need.
Cost-per-use for a given electronic resource increased sharply last year . . .	. . . but acquisition data reveals a growing user population bumped the library into a new pricing tier.

Further information on selecting metrics is included later in this chapter.

Beyond directly mitigating the major challenges of collections assessment, the holistic approach also has strategic value for the library. As Johnson notes, "assessment for everyday collection management and assessment for strategic planning do not have to be, and are often not, completely separate."[26] Because it is intrinsically high-level, holistic assessment provides a range of long-term benefits. First, it establishes benchmarks for future evaluations of the collection. It is also a useful orientation for new subject librarians, libraries experiencing collection "growing pains," and faculty.[27, 28] It allows libraries to monitor not just absolute numbers, but key ratios, as well—ratios like print versus electronic, journal versus monograph, local versus consortial, and so on.[29] Holistic assessment allows us to see the library collection as a system, acknowledging the interconnected (and interdependent) nature of information.[30]

In a similar vein, another major benefit of the holistic approach is its potential to make the library more agile and responsive. Laying a foundation of continuous, holistic assessment enables the library to better respond to ad hoc assessment demands. For example, at Colorado State University, Wilde and Level designed an ongoing data collection program that supports holistic collections assessment and other data needs.[31] Based on this data, they generate subject-specific collections reports on an ongoing basis, as well as fielding requests for accreditation data, new program support, and so on.[32] Duncan and O'Gara argue similarly that "building a rich dataset of quantitative and qualitative information is critical to the success of collections assessment."[33] Luther expands on these sentiments, identifying three layers of data collection and analysis: hard-wired data collection, routine assessment, and intensive assessment.[34] With a holistic framework, all three layers are in place in case they are needed; or, as Luther puts it, "one stone, multiple birds."[35]

One last major benefit of holistic assessment is that by virtue of being flexible and adaptable, it encourages continuous, cyclical improvement. Johnson notes that collections assessment is an "ongoing process" rather than a moment in time.[36] Yes, each individual assessment project is valuable, but without trends—both across the collection and through time—the snapshot is meaningless. Thus, holistic collections assessment requires iterative analysis of collections data—and an iterative evaluation of the assessment process itself. If the goal of holistic assessment is to "[reach] a state of wellness for the entire library," then the process cannot be completed in a single go.[37]

BUILDING THE ASSESSMENT FRAMEWORK

Identifying Institutional Goals and Stakeholders

In designing a holistic assessment program, it is important to start by identifying the goals for the program. Assessment is not one-size-fits-all; it should be adapted to meet local needs. The program goals identified at the outset will shape the data, methodologies, and tools that are applied—not to mention the research questions and the resulting action items. Examples of goals might include:

- determining whether the philosophy collection meets the needs of the philosophy department
- developing an appropriate approach to e-book collections
- reducing the library's subscription commitments by 5 percent
- identifying areas for focused collection development
- determining how best to reduce the physical collection's footprint by 10 percent

Goals can be internal to the library or tied to the mission of the parent institution. Whatever the goal—even if it is purely exploratory—it must be explicit at the start of the planning process.

Similarly, it is important to identify stakeholders. Stakeholders include anyone who will have to help with the assessment, anyone whose work will be impacted by the results, and anyone whose authority (and buy-in) are required to implement any recommended actions. They can be internal or external, and at any level of the organization. Identifying stakeholders up front will go a long way toward helping anticipate potential sticking points and negotiating mutually agreeable solutions. Stakeholders can even be involved in the planning stages of an assessment project, thereby facilitating early buy-in.

Beyond identifying goals and stakeholders, there are other considerations that can help in developing an assessment program. The following questions may be useful:

What assessment—or data collection—is the library already doing? It's possible that existing data and analysis workflows can be repurposed with only minor adjustments.

Is the program intended to be comprehensive? Ongoing? Ad hoc? Knowing how long an approach must be sustained and how broad its scope will be can significantly reshape a project.

What challenges are likely to hinder assessment efforts, and what measures can be taken to mitigate these problems? Issues like staff time, technical expertise, funding, or even an individual predisposed to resist assessment can all hinder a project. They can't be ignored, but they can be managed.

What resources are available to support assessment? Leveraging existing assets can often help overcome any potential hurdles.

What kinds of actions does the library or department hope to be able to take in the end, based on the assessment? Are these actions realistic? If the outcomes are unrealistic, it might be wise to revisit the goals and develop a more actionable plan for assessment.

What is in or out of scope for the project? Where are its boundaries? It will be tempting to pull on every loose thread—but are these in-depth, granular analyses part of the assessment or a separate project altogether? If they are part of the assessment, how will that affect its timelines?

When is the project considered "finished"? What are the anticipated "deliverables"? What is the timeline? If you don't know how to tell when you're finished, the project will never end.

The literature is replete with general guidance for planning a collections assessment. Common themes include balancing numerical data with anecdotal or other community input, limiting analysis to relevant or actionable data, targeting efforts carefully, implementing results, and coordinating efforts across the library.[38, 39] Numerous articles emphasize not reinventing the wheel, and relying instead on existing data, methodologies, and tools.

In addition to theory, there are concrete examples in the literature of institutions that have shaped assessment programs according to their organizational goals. At Colorado State University, Wilde and Level needed a way to assess the collections comprehensively and satisfy other ad hoc data needs like accreditation reports. The resulting assessment program was broad in scope, collecting enough data to support both goals in an agile and flexible way. At James Madison University, Duncan and O'Gara took their cue from the university's mission, which is undergraduate-focused. Based on that institutional goal, they decided to "weight collection use higher than collection size and depth—measures potentially more important for a research institution."[40] Lastly, in developing a rubric for assessing consortial e-resources, the Virtual Library of Virginia's Value Metric Task Force took into account the goals of

Shaping assessment according to org. goals

the consortium's member libraries, as well as the consortium's own overarching values.[41] The resulting assessment mixed quantitative measures like cost and use with values like "supports open access." These three examples represent not only a range of assessment goals, but a range of approaches to holistic collections assessment itself: a subject-segmented approach (Colorado State), a mix of subject and format segmentation (James Madison), and a format-segmented approach (Virtual Library of Virginia).

Choosing Data Points, Methodologies, and Tools

In libraries, data are plentiful. Library staff in technical services settings, who work with data on a daily basis, may be tempted to incorporate every data point available into an assessment program. This is one of the major potential pitfalls of holistic assessment—when trying to paint a big picture, it is tempting to include everything. Nevertheless, it is vital to be thoughtful and selective in choosing data points during the planning process; otherwise, libraries risk developing an unsustainable program. If the volume and diversity of data is so great that collecting and assessing it becomes unmanageable, then the assessment program will never be effective.

When selecting data for holistic assessment, the types of data should be distributed across the many facets of a library collection. One of the most basic divisions between metrics is that between traditional metrics and user-centered metrics. As one might guess in this comparison, traditional metrics don't rely on direct user or patron input; user-centered metrics, on the other hand, seek the input of users (or patrons, students, faculty, clients, etc.) to discover more about the value of a collection.[42] Traditional metrics generally rely on back-end library systems, and are therefore internal to the library. Use- and user-centered metrics are necessarily external to the library itself. An example of a traditional metric might be a title list or expenditure report, while a user-centered metric could be a user survey about the use of and preferences for a collection.

In 2008, Borin and Yi provided a more detailed framework for collections assessment, with six general divisions rather than two: general capacity, subject standards, scholarly publishing, usage, users, and environmental factors.[43] General capacity, long relied on as a backbone of collections assessment, examines the quantity of materials, their age, and how the collection has grown. Ideally, studies of capacity are specific to the needs of the home library, rather than focusing on growth and size as intrinsic indicators of quality. The second set of criteria, subject standards, varies among subject areas, but can frequently be addressed via accreditation standards or other expert recommendations. Related to this is the third indicator, scholarly publishing, which involves surveying the landscape of published materials, including authoritative lists, publishing volume, and average costs within the subject area. In the last three dimensions, Borin and Yi's framework splits users and usage into two categories, emphasizing a difference between users' direct input (surveys, interviews, etc.) and indirect input that libraries can largely gather themselves (COUNTER usage, citation counts, etc.). The final metric, the environmental factor, is also externally focused. This indicator involves examining data on the parent institution or surrounding community and their areas of focus, along with budgetary considerations, peer institutions, and more.

With six dimensions, Borin and Yi's approach can be overwhelming. Other models strike a balance between two dimensions and six. For example, Kelly and O'Gara present a model describing four broad groups of data: collections data, user information, usage data, and citation data.[44] In developing Mason's assessment program, the authors worked off models like that of Borin and Yi, as well as a four-quadrant framework adapted from Matthews's *The Evaluation and Measurement of Library Services*.[45] Collections indicators were mapped out into four basic categories: first, at a high level, as user-based or collection-based. Within these two divisions, indicators were divided between quantitative and qualitative methodologies. Finally, metrics were mapped to three "tiers of assessment," which were used to mark the intensity of a given assessment. Nicholson summarizes a variety of other frameworks, providing yet more models that can be adapted to suit any scenario.[46] Ultimately, there is a wide range of options for categorizing library data as collections indicators. Consider the four models outlined above—and summarized in figure 2.1—and the variety of ways that even ten collection metrics could be mapped across them. The key point in holistic assessment is to achieve balance among whatever categories are used, and to "mix, match and choose factors according to [the] purpose and needs" of each institution or project.[47] Metrics should capture and highlight the many nuances of a library collection—whatever that means given the context.

Being open to creative data points during collections assessment can lead to new discoveries or understanding. For example, it can be just as important to know what is not used as what is.[48] The analysis of standard usage reports like the COUNTER JR1 report (full-text journal article requests) may leave out titles with zero use, which can be vital information for library decision-making. Similarly, the analysis of granular data like that found in the COUNTER JR5 report can reveal gaps in usage based on title or year. Other unconventional *specific data strategies*

1. Nicholson two-category model

1. Title count	Traditional (Internal)	User-Centered (External)
2. User survey		
3. Institutional demographics	1, 3, 7, 8, 9, 10	2, 4, 5, 6, 9, 10
4. Citation analysis		

2. Borin and Yi indicators

1	Capacity	Subject Standards	8
7	Scholarly Publishing	Environmental Factors	3
	Users	Usage	
	2	4, 5, 6, 9, 10	

5. COUNTER usage
6. Proxy logs
7. Reputable bibliographies
8. Accreditation standards
9. Circulation
10. ILL logs

3. Kelly and O'Gara model

1, 7, 8	2, 3
Collections Data	User Information
Citation Data	Usage Data
4	5, 6, 9, 10

4. Matthews quadrants

1, 9	2, 4, 5, 6
Collections: Quantitative	Users: Quantitative
Collections: Qualitative	Users: Qualitative
7, 8, 10	2, 3, 4

NOTE: The arrangement of the ten collections metrics within each model is intended to be illustrative, rather than prescriptive. Which category a metric "belongs to" can be open to interpretation; for example, circulation could be considered traditional or user-centered, depending on whether you are looking at the source of the data (an internal library system) or its subject matter (uses of physical items by users).

FIGURE 2.1 • Ten example collections metrics and conceptual frameworks for organizing them

assessment data includes anecdotal feedback. The Princeton Theological Seminary Library began compiling anecdotal feedback in a systematic way, and found that these "micro-assessments" provided a "simple, quick, and shareable" snapshot of library value.[49] This feedback may be insufficient for major library decision-making, but it can provide valuable context for quantitative findings.

In terms of where to find usable data, much of what the assessment staff might want to compile and analyze is readily available, whether freely on the Web, included as part of a subscription or purchase, or something the library already collects or stores itself. Some examples include:

- title lists from publishers or vendors
- subject-relevant associations' bibliographies
- COUNTER usage from vendor administration platforms
- files of repository title commitments such as LOCKSS or Portico
- impact factor or similar bibliometrics as published on journals' web pages or in title lists (though these may not be current)
- cost data from a library's own fiscal records
- citations from locally hosted theses or dissertations
- circulation data from the integrated library system

TABLE 2.2 • Collections assessment data and methods in use at George Mason University

TIER 1 General Assessment	TIER 2 Moderate Assessment	TIER 3 Thorough Assessment
• Approval data	• Comparison with peer libraries: language	• Combined dissertation-journal citation analysis
• Collections counts	• Database cost-use analysis	• Dissertation citation analysis
• Comparison with peer libraries: size, age	• E-resource ratings	• Faculty and researcher publishing outlets
• Circulation rates	• Faculty survey	
• Modified brief test of collection strength	• Graduate student survey	• JR5 analysis of journals
• Monograph expenditures	• ILL statistics	• Portico commitments
• Overlap with Outstanding Academic Titles	• Journal citation analysis	• Turnaway analysis
• Overlap with Resources for College Libraries	• Journal cost-use analysis	
• Peer e-resource overlap	• Monograph use analysis	
• Program demographics		
• Subscription expenditures		
• Uniqueness vs. WorldCat		

For peer comparisons (except perhaps for special or corporate libraries), a wealth of data is available through peer institutions' discovery systems via broad searches for overall trends, or title list spot-checks; this is one instance where paying for a commercial overlap tool can save considerable time and labor. Similarly, database lists, which can be easier to check systematically than discovery systems, are also sources of valuable comparison data. To give a sense of some of the sources available, a list of the data and assessment methods used at Mason—divided across three tiers of assessment—is given in table 2.2.

The assessment program at the authors' institution has changed over time through regular review cycles, and the data and methods listed in the above table have not always been in place in this exact configuration. Some examples of adjustments and the reasoning behind them include:

> "Comparison with peer libraries: language" was moved from Tier 1 (General) to Tier 2 (Moderate). Mason's process for comparing the languages of peer institutions' collections is more labor-intensive than other peer comparison metrics (age and size), and feedback from user surveys indicated that faculty and students' interest in foreign-language materials was not enough to justify including this time-consuming metric in every single assessment.

"Peer e-resource overlap" was considered for Tier 2, since comparing the e-resources held among peers is often time-consuming. However, because of the applicability of this metric in virtually every subject area, and the importance of e-resources in the Libraries, it was left at Tier 1, ensuring that every assessment would include this essential information.

"Dissertation citation analysis" replaced an earlier metric, "Monograph citation analysis" (using monographs held at the Libraries). The move to analyzing citations from Mason doctoral dissertations was due in part to a desire for institution-specific data. Additionally, monograph citation analysis was causing workflow bottlenecks at the point of selecting appropriately broad yet scholarly monographs for analysis.

[handwritten margin note: recognizing bottlenecks and alternatives]

To guide the selection of data and tools, especially when first setting up an assessment program, collection development and technical services staff should refer to the goals and stakeholders identified during the early planning stages of the assessment. Goals and stakeholders are the foundation of assessment, and subsequent decisions should grow naturally from that starting point. One strategy for identifying useful data points is to focus on the questions that must be answered in order to meet the assessment goals, and then identify the most concise way(s) to answer them. Examples of how goals can lead to data points are shown in table 2.3. If nothing else, one key question to keep in mind is "What is sustainable and meaningful?"[50] If a program overburdens the

TABLE 2.3 • Examples of how to select assessment data points based on project goals

GOAL	QUESTIONS	DATA POINTS	MOST USEFUL AND SUSTAINABLE*
To determine whether the philosophy collection meets the needs of the philosophy department.	What philosophy materials do we have?	Item count by call number; E-resource count; Age distribution of philosophy materials; Language distribution of philosophy materials	Item count by call number; E-resource count
	What existing materials get high use? Low use?	Citation counts; Circulation count by call number; E-resource usage statistics	Circulation count by call number; E-resource usage statistics
	What formats do philosophy scholars prefer?	Citation counts; Circulation counts by call number; E-resource usage statistics; User surveys	User surveys; E-resource usage statistics; Circulation count by call number

GOAL	QUESTIONS	DATA POINTS	MOST USEFUL AND SUSTAINABLE*
	What gaps are there in our holdings?	Interlibrary loan reports; Peer overlap analysis; Item count by call number; Curriculum analysis	Interlibrary loan reports; Curriculum analysis
	What languages do our philosophy users prefer?	Citation counts; Circulation counts by language and call number; User surveys	Circulation counts by language; User surveys
	What do our philosophy users want?	User surveys; Focus groups	User surveys
To develop an appropriate approach to e-book collections.	Which subject areas use e-books?	E-resource usage statistics; E-resource turnaway data; User surveys	E-resource usage statistics; E-resource turnaway data
	What are the preferred platforms?	E-resource usage statistics; User surveys; Focus groups	E-resource usage statistics; Focus groups
	What publishers do we consistently buy in print, and would they be appropriate in e-format?	Item count by publisher; Circulation counts by publisher	Item count by publisher
	How do current e-book holdings perform?	E-resource usage statistics	E-resource usage statistics
	How are e-books used on campus?	User surveys; Focus groups; Curriculum analysis	Focus groups
To reduce the physical collection's footprint by 10%.	How would our users react to compact shelving or off-site storage?	User surveys; Focus groups	User surveys
	Which subject areas receive the lowest print use?	Circulation counts by call number	Circulation counts by call number
	Which subject areas might be most open to an e-preferred collection?	E-resource usage statistics; Circulation counts by call number; User surveys; Focus groups; Curriculum analysis	E-resource usage statistics; Circulation counts; User surveys
	Are there low-use or duplicate titles that could be culled from the collection?	Circulation counts; Duplicate title lists	Circulation counts; Duplicate title lists
	Can print journals or microforms be replaced with electronic content?	Title lists; Lists of Portico (or other) preservation commitments; E-resource usage statistics; Circulation counts by format and title	Title lists; Circulation counts by format and title
	Are there materials that can be borrowed easily from peer libraries?	Peer overlap analysis; Analysis of WorldCat uniqueness; Interlibrary loan statistics	Peer overlap analysis

*These selections are for illustration only; what is useful and sustainable will vary depending on the institution.

organization or yields results that are not actionable, it cannot be considered successful.

Previous ad hoc assessment coverage may also provide guidance in planning an assessment program. If the technical services or collection development department has fielded one-off assessment requests, it may be worthwhile to reuse those tools and data sources. Staff can work to streamline these formerly ad hoc processes so that they can be leveraged for holistic assessment, ultimately saving time in the long run. Examples of ~~repurposed data or workflows~~ could include: *repurposing data & workflows*

- exporting approval plan reports for all subjects/funds by fiscal year for central storage and quick access, rather than on-demand for single projects/selectors
- adding a subject field to annual e-resource usage spreadsheets for easy parsing into individual subject assessment reports
- incorporation of collections questions into regularly scheduled user surveys
- compiling cost-per-use for all subscriptions annually, rather than as needed, for quick reference and incorporation into assessments
- converting a particularly impactful report into a template for future use

This quick repurposing of existing data workflows can be the simplest and most sustainable way to set up a holistic assessment framework—fast.

Once the appropriate data points have been identified, there are numerous methodologies for assessment, most of which are well covered in the library literature. These approaches include overlap analysis, citation analysis, cost or use analysis, turnaway analysis, user surveys, focus groups, and more. A brief overview of selected methodologies can be found in the next section. There are also myriad tools available to support assessment, ranging from the basic (e.g., spreadsheet software) to the specialized (e.g., OCLC Collection Evaluation) to the robust (e.g., Tableau). While costly assessment tools aren't necessary—as discussed earlier in this chapter, Goertzen conducted sophisticated e-book analysis using little more than Excel[51]—they can save significant time and labor, especially if an institution lacks the internal technical savvy to automate data analysis. That said, the costs of these tools should be weighed carefully against their benefits. Consider what "acceptance criteria" will be used to evaluate tools; for example, DePope suggests that assessment tools should be easy to learn,

TABLE 2.4 • Collections assessment tools used at George Mason University since 2013

TOOL	USE
Bowker Book Analysis System	Automated overlap analysis against Resources for College Libraries
Gold Rush Decision Support System	Overlap analysis of databases and journal packages
Microsoft Access	Data cleaning, manipulation, analysis
Microsoft Excel	Data cleaning, manipulation, analysis, visualization
Microsoft Publisher	Reports
Microsoft Word	Documentation, reports
OCLC Collection Evaluation	Automated overlap analysis against Outstanding Academic Titles, WorldCat, and peer libraries
OpenRefine	Data cleaning
PiktoChart	Basic infographics
Qualtrics	Survey administration
Sustainable Collection Services Green Glass	Automated overlap analysis against peer libraries and WorldCat
Tableau	Robust data visualization
Web of Science	Impact factor and faculty publication data

allow for full data extraction, be technologically sustainable, and save staff time.[52] If the learning curve is too steep, the use too restricted, the software too high-maintenance, or the process too convoluted, a tool may not be worth it. As illustration, a list of assessment tools used by Mason (as a formal part of ongoing assessment or as part of ad hoc efforts) since 2013 is given in table 2.4, though it should be noted that this is not an endorsement of any particular tool, nor is it a comprehensive list of what is available. For institutions with limited resources that are struggling to implement or sustain assessment, it may be best to start with versatile, ubiquitous, and/or freely available tools, and then transition to more specialized (or costly) tools later, as needed.

Selected Methodologies

Although providing detailed procedures for each method listed in this chapter would overwhelm the reader, the following selective step-by-step guide may provide clarification or a jumping-off point for library staff who are looking for a place to start. These instructions are provided as examples of how one institution worked with the skills and tools available, and they are certainly not the only way to approach the question. These instructions are also not intended as endorsements of any particular software or tool.

Comparing Local E-Resource Holdings against Those of Peer Institutions

[handwritten annotation: only good for public / academic libraries]

1. Identify peer libraries. Staff may wish to select current peers as well as peers that are considered aspirational. Depending on the type of library, these selections can be informed by conversations with subject specialists, lists of educational institutions available on state websites, constituent demographics, published lists of university rankings, and so on.

2. Visit the website of each peer library and locate its database list. If possible, narrow the scope of the list. For example, for subject-specific assessments, locate the appropriate subject guide or other subject portal (if available).

3. Using spreadsheet software, record the relevant databases listed on the peer library's database list, subject guide, or website. Repeat for each peer library and for the home library. For an example of the file layout, see table 2.5.

4. Once the list of databases is complete, go back and check it against each peer library's full listing of databases. Note which libraries are subscribed to each database. Because e-resources often change names or are packaged in varying ways, this step may take some time to complete. For a true comparison, it is best to remove open-access resources from the list.

5. Useful data points to consider for inclusion in assessment reports are:
   a. Total resources held across all peer libraries
   b. Total resources held by the home institution
   c. Average number of resources held at each peer institution

TABLE 2.5 • Example of Peer E-Resource Analysis Data Collection File

RESOURCE	PROVIDER	PEER 1	PEER 2	PEER 3	HOME LIBRARY	TOTAL LIBRARIES
Database 1	Provider 1	X	X	X	X	4
Database 2	Provider 2	-	-	-	X	1
Database 3	Provider 2	-	X	-	-	1
Total Databases Held		1	2	1	2	

    d. Unique or uncommon resources held by the home library

    e. Common resources not held by the home library

Analyzing a Print Collection's Circulation

Note: At the time this chapter was written, the authors' institution was in the early stages of migrating from an ILS to a next-generation library services platform (LSP); therefore, these processes may be less applicable for libraries that have already made the move to an LSP.

1. Request or generate data files from the ILS or LSP. At the authors' institution, exporting data on the entire physical collection is an extensive process, and Collection Development requests the data once a year, storing the files for use as needed. Valuable data points include:
   a. Title and publication information (title, author, publisher, publication date, format, purchasing fund)
   b. Various ID numbers (ISBN or ISSN, OCLC number, ILS IDs such as bib ID, holdings ID, item ID, bar code)
   c. Call number (both the "display" number as well as a normalized version, if possible)
   d. Location information
   e. Circulation and browse counts
   f. Charge, discharge, and due dates
   g. Status and suppression information
   h. Record update dates, if possible

2. Due to the large amount of data, it will likely be delivered in several files. Depending on each assessment's needs, you should copy chunks of the data and trim or compile it as appropriate (by call number, date, location, fund source, etc.).

3. Before starting to work with the data, some issues should be considered. Depending on how reports are generated, staff may need to spend some time planning for:
   a. Lost, missing, withdrawn, and/or suppressed items; libraries may wish to exclude these from the main analyses.
   b. Multiple statuses for individual items, which may create multiple rows per item, and artificially inflate circulation counts.
   c. Circulating status.

4. Because these can be large files of data, it's helpful to use data-summarizing features in software like Excel and Access. Figures 2.2 and 2.3 demonstrate how a list of item and circulation counts by location can

	A	B	C
1	Item Status	(Multiple Items)	
2	Bib Suppressed	N	
3			
4	**Row Labels**	**Count of ItemID**	**Sum of Circ Count**
5	ACL CD-ROM	1	2
6	ACL Stacks	113	1926
7	FEN Folio	19	65
8	FEN Oversized Folio	2	0
9	FEN Stacks	8136	93549
10	FEN Stacks (SD)	8	0
11	JCL CD-ROM	5	0
12	JCL Dvd	9	54
13	JCL Multimedia	1	0
14	JCL Stacks	431	6921
15	JCL Videotapes	55	324
16	MER Dvd	1	0
17	MER Stacks	271	2894
18	**Grand Total**	**9052**	**105735**

Drag fields between areas below:

▼ Filters	▦ Columns
Item Status ▾	Σ Values ▾
Bib Suppressed ▾

▥ Rows	Σ Values
Location Name ▾	Count of ItemID ▾
	Sum of Circ Count ▾

FIGURE 2.2 • Microsoft Excel example using a pivot table build

Field:	Location Name	ItemID	Circ Count	Item Status	Bib Suppressed
Table:	CircData	CircData	CircData	CircData	CircData
Total:	Group By	Count	Sum	Where	Where
Sort:					
Show:	☑	☑	☑	☐	☐
Criteria:				Not Like "*missing*"	"N"
or:					

Location Name ▾	CountOfItemID ▾	SumOfCirc Count ▾
ACL CD-ROM	1	2
ACL Stacks	113	1926
FEN Folio	19	65
FEN Oversized Folio	2	0
FEN Stacks	8136	93549
FEN Stacks (SD)	8	0
JCL CD-ROM	5	0
JCL Dvd	9	54
JCL Multimedia	1	0
JCL Stacks	431	6921
JCL Videotapes	55	324
MER Dvd	1	0
MER Stacks	271	2894

FIGURE 2.3
Microsoft Access example using a summary query

be generated (while including limiting criteria on item status and bib suppression) using a pivot table in Excel and a summary query in Access.

5. Useful data points to consider for reports include:
   a. Total collection size and circulation
   b. Average circulations per title
   c. Average circulations per title circulated (e.g., circulations among only titles that have ever circulated)
   d. Total or average circulations by location, subject, age, fund, and so on

Analyzing the Cost and Use of a Journal Package

1. Gather title lists for each "Big Deal" journal package held by the home library. These can be requested from the vendor, or generated from an internal source like the electronic resource management system.

2. Gather journal list prices from each vendor. These are sometimes freely available on vendor websites, or may need to be requested. Acquire them in a spreadsheet or data format like CSV whenever possible, rather than a PDF or word processor format.

3. Gather COUNTER JR1 (title-by-title usage) reports for the appropriate time period. These should be available in the admin portals for the big deal vendors. It is useful to sync the time periods for usage and cost—for example, if payment covers the period of January 1 through December 31, then you should collect calendar-year usage data.

4. Combine the title and price lists, entering prices into a new column in the title list. Repeat for usage, entering the total usage into a new column in the title list. This can be done through manual data entry; by using a tool like Open Refine or Access to match on a unique ID field such as ISSN; or by using the VLOOKUP function in Excel. With any automated process, there will be errors or inconsistences for a small percentage of titles, requiring some manual cleanup. However, the time savings through automation can be significant.

5. Once title, price, and usage are merged, calculate the "list price" cost-per-use and the "institution" cost-per-use—based on the price the institution pays for the package, which is generally less than the sum of the list prices of individual journals—for the package as a whole, and individual titles. These can be calculated in spreadsheet software using formulas.

6. Other useful data points to consider for reports include:
   a. Count of, percentage of package comprising, and total price to subscribe to titles with usage over a set threshold
   b. Percentage of overall use coming from titles with usage over a threshold
   c. Count and percentage of titles that can be subscribed to with half of the package cost
   d. Average use and cost-per-use per title within a big deal

Validity Considerations for Data, Tools, and Methods

In developing a portfolio of assessment methodologies and tools, technical services and collections staff should consider the validity of each measure. While this kind of deliberate examination of metrics may feel abstract or philosophical, Gingras suggests three criteria that can nevertheless be helpful in building an assessment toolkit and evaluating the strength of each metric. Gingras's criteria are the following: the adequacy of the indicator for the object it measures, the sensitivity to the inertia of the object measured, and the homogeneity of the dimension of the indicator.[53] Originally developed to address the validity of bibliometrics for determining faculty promotion, these criteria can be extended to thinking about any kind of evaluation. The first criterion (adequacy) asks that assessment staff understand what a metric is (or isn't) saying. For example, libraries should not mistake COUNTER usage stats for true readership, or raw citation counts for quality. This is one area where the holistic approach is particularly helpful: by not relying exclusively on any one "proxy" metric and instead combining them into a cumulative picture, libraries can lessen the impact of each metric's flaws. It is important to consider each metric critically, and to draw conclusions with a measure of care.

The second criterion, inertia, asks that assessment staff be mindful of what degree of change can realistically be expected in any given area. Some facets of library collections are dynamic, while others are intrinsically slow to change; the metrics—and any conclusions drawn from them—should take this into account. Any metric that shows a dramatic change from year to year should be double-checked if it corresponds to the latter group, as should any metric showing no change where change is to be expected. The question of inertia is another argument in favor of the holistic approach (particularly a subject-segmented approach): because library collections have low inertia (barring major collections-changing events), cycling regularly through each subject area and generating a high-level, holistic snapshot allows for gradual changes in the collection to be captured at the appropriate pace.

Gingras's third criterion, homogeneity, asks libraries to make sure that assessment is comparing apples to apples, one to one—for example, e-journals to e-journals or, more preferably, humanities e-journals to humanities e-journals. Print circulation can't be directly compared to e-book downloads, nor can the cost-per-use of a chemical structures database be compared against the cost-per-use of a social sciences e-journal package. Because the holistic framework allows for many tools and metrics, it is important to keep homogeneity in mind when compiling and presenting assessment results. Each assessment may employ a dozen or more metrics, not all of which will be on the same scale—numerically or in terms of importance or priority. For example, the authors incorporate both the overlap with the authoritative list, Resources for College Libraries (RCL), and the relative collection size versus peers into the Libraries' collections assessments. However, RCL is a relatively small pool of relatively low-level titles, while relative collection size is a much more substantial metric (both in terms of the quantity of titles and their importance to the institution). In light of these qualitative and quantitative differences, 99 percent overlap with RCL is perhaps less a cause for celebration than a relatively high collection size versus peers. Both metrics are informative, but they should not be presented as equivalent in any final report.

IMPLEMENTATION AND DATA COLLECTION

While it may be labor-intensive, implementation is in some ways the most straightforward part of the collection assessment process. Every tool and methodology has its own logistics and idiosyncrasies, but these are worked out easily enough through trial and error or by reviewing the literature (which is replete with case studies). Beyond these specific steps or procedures, overall best practices for going live with assessment include scheduling regular time slots for assessment; tracking (and reporting on) progress; staying focused on the initial goals of the specific project; communicating with stakeholders; and becoming comfortable with messy data.[54] Deadlines, documentation, and data cleanliness are particularly important.

Setting and following deadlines is critical to the success of any project, but assessment—an activity often seen as "optional" or "extra"—is particularly vulnerable to loss of momentum. As part of the planning process, technical services staff should clearly articulate a timeline for assessment, whether it is a short-term ad hoc project or an indefinite, ongoing assessment framework. The timeline should include:

- the assessment goal(s)
- key stakeholders
- specific target dates
- concrete deliverables
- the intended outcomes of the undertaking

If these details are clear from the outset, it will be much easier to stay on course. It can be especially helpful to discuss the timeline with stakeholders outside of technical services whose participation will be needed—for example, subject librarians or other public services staff. Their workload probably follows a different yearly cycle than that of technical services, and it is not inconceivable that a subject librarian's teaching or outreach duties could slow down an assessment project if not accommodated as part of the plan. Once underway, staff should make sure that assessment is a regular part of the collection development or technical services to-do lists and calendar, holding regular check-in meetings to monitor progress. If assessment falls behind schedule, the team can adjust the project timeline as needed—while making sure that assessment remains an explicit part of the ongoing departmental workload.

One way to help assessment run more smoothly is to create and maintain clear project documentation. Throughout the planning stages, the assessment team should document goals, stakeholders, and timelines. Once assessment has started, staff can create a manual outlining the scope and aim of the undertaking, as well as the individual steps necessary to complete each portion of the assessment. This documentation should include screenshots or other illustrations where appropriate, or links to external documentation in cases where it is more complete or current (e.g., for specific software). As assessment continues, staff should update the manual to reflect current processes, and store it in a central location for easy access.

It may also be helpful to create templates for documents, reports, and tools that will be used repeatedly throughout the assessment process or in subsequent projects. Obvious examples include templates for outward-facing reports and surveys, but templates can also be used to guide (and expedite) data collection and analysis. For example, Mason uses a modified brief test involving manual data collection from library catalogs and discovery systems. The data is compiled into a template spreadsheet with built-in formulas, such that no further analysis is necessary to generate the results; a summary table is auto-populated with the numbers. Mason uses templates for a variety of inward- and outward-facing purposes. Outward-facing templates include documents for subject librarians' input into assessment planning, faculty and graduate student surveys, preliminary reports to subject librarians, and final assessment reports. Internal templates include forms, charts, and spreadsheets for citation analysis, collections expenditures, ILL data, overlap analysis versus peers, and faculty and researcher publishing outlets. All of these templates are stored in the collection development department's shared network drive. As documentation is updated, old versions are moved to an archive folder.

One last aspect of documentation is the importance of sharing it with stakeholders. This includes data, preliminary findings, and final reports—that is, the "content" of assessment—as well as process documentation. Stakeholders, particularly collaborators, may be helpful in identifying new approaches, processes, or efficiencies. They may pinpoint weaknesses in the methodology or better ways to visualize results. At Mason, the fourth subject assessment resulted in major changes to the tools used and the presentation of results, all because a subject librarian asked key questions and suggested changes that the assessment staff hadn't thought of. Ultimately, stakeholders will feel more invested in the outcomes of assessment if they are involved in the process.

The final major piece of implementing a holistic assessment project is to set—and adhere to—criteria regarding data cleanliness. In his chapter on evaluating indicators, Gingras comments disapprovingly on the "unwritten rule that *any number beats no number*" when it comes to evaluation.[55] While, as Gingras says, this is certainly a poor rule to live by, at the opposite extreme, there is a point in collection assessment past which the perfect really does become the enemy of the good. In dealing with library collections data, "good enough" should be the goal, meaning that data should be cleaned and standardized to the degree that it is practical, given the goals and scope of the assessment. At the same time, collection development and technical services staff should maintain a realistic sense of how "clean" the data needs to be to support the kinds of decisions they hope to make after any given project.

One simple technique and best practice for cleaning and working with library data is to use (or create) unique IDs for resources whenever possible. This can be the ISBN, ISSN, BIB ID/Item ID, ILS bar code numbers, or OCLC number—though staff should anticipate inconsistencies even among the standard IDs and be prepared for some degree of manual cleanup. These unique IDs should then be included in all data exports and analyses, even if they are not explicitly needed for the task at hand. Unique IDs are frequently useful when included, and are often sorely missed when not—it is easier to hide an extra column in a spreadsheet than it is to rematch data that has been stripped of its identifiers. In addition, when modifying data, staff should update or edit in batches whenever possible to avoid stray errors. Libraries can use simple tools and functions like "Find and Replace" or "Convert Text to Data." Similarly, staff can use filters, pivot tables, or tools like Open Refine to identify anomalies. Libraries should automate as much as possible, and in the end, accept that staff time is finite and that at some point, *something* can in fact be better than nothing.

COMMUNICATING RESULTS

Albert describes communication as a "component of visionary leadership . . . and a strategic way to create loyal patrons and advocates for the library."[56] Communication builds trust, boosts visibility, and generates buy-in; in short, communication is one of the most valuable tools libraries have at their disposal when it comes to showing what they do and why it matters. Unfortunately, communication is also the stage in the collections assessment process that is most frequently rushed—if not overlooked entirely. Especially for technical services or collections librarians, who are generally siloed from external stakeholders and may have less experience in the role of advocates or champions, it is easy to do the work and then assume that the data will speak for itself. In doing so, assessment staff are missing the opportunity to share "the stories that lie in the gaps between the data sets."[57] As part of assessment, it is imperative to find—and tell—those stories.

There are several elements of good communication during an assessment project. The first is timing: communication shouldn't be relegated to the end of the project, but should be incorporated at every stage. Goal-setting, choosing data points, establishing workflows, and analyzing results should all include an element of stakeholder communication. This is especially important for a centralized assessment program. If library administrators, subject librarians, and other public-facing stakeholders are going to act on the results of an assessment, they must buy in to whatever approach the technical services and collections staff are taking. At Mason, for example, the authors involved two members of the Libraries' administrative team in developing the assessment program, then piloted the approach in collaboration with three subject librarians whose input allowed collections staff to fine-tune the program. Now, in the fourth year of running assessments, the Libraries survey the appropriate subject librarian at the beginning of each subject assessment, soliciting input on key resources, call number ranges, peer institutions, and other specialized information. Later in the process, the subject librarian helps collections staff distribute surveys to and solicit feedback from faculty and students. Finally,

once the data has been collected, the subject librarian is involved in evaluating
the results, assigning a final rating to the collection, and making recommendations for future collection development efforts. The subject librarians are not
simply issued a completed report in a vacuum and instructed to take x, y, or
z action. Instead, they are involved at multiple stages of the process—and are
even invited to comment on the process itself.

A second significant dimension to communication is telling a compelling
story. Even to a fellow librarian, assessment data may be meaningless without
context. Before sharing any results, assessment staff should ask: Why am I
sharing this? What conclusion(s) do I want my audience to draw from this?
What action(s) do I want them to take? For example, the authors used to include
uniqueness in WorldCat as one of the Libraries' assessment metrics, until a
subject librarian asked, "What does this mean?" With that question in mind,
collections staff now try to keep the metrics much more clearly informative
and actionable. In addition to these basic, guiding questions (or reality checks),
there are some general best practices that assessment staff should keep in mind
when crafting an assessment story. (Amanda Albert summarizes many of these
best practices succinctly in her article "Communicating Library Value.")[58]
First, staff should think about the big picture, reducing unnecessary "noise"
until the overarching message is clear. Next, libraries should mix quantitative
and qualitative elements to reinforce the story. For instance, one could pair
e-book usage statistics with comments from user surveys—or even anecdotal
comments—in support of e-formats. Reports should include positive feedback, as available, to emphasize what is going well (even as they recommend
improvement in other areas). The message should be simple, in order to avoid
drowning the audience in busy visuals or an overabundance of data. It should
appeal to self-interest (and other emotions); why should the audience care? The
message should be confident—arguing for the library, not against its detractors.
Lastly, assessment staff should personalize the story to the stakeholders. Every
stakeholder is looking for something slightly different, so the same message
won't always work across the board.[59] (Stakeholder targeting will be addressed
in greater detail below.) Taken together, these factors should result in a more
compelling story than numbers alone.

The last—and possibly most challenging—component of communication
is visually presenting the data. Speaking broadly, technical services and collections librarians tend to be comfortable with tabular data and are just as happy
digging through raw data as looking at a pie chart. Unfortunately, tabular data

avoiding "curse of Knowledge" → aware of biases

is often not as easy to digest as a chart. Even a simple visualization—like a bar graph indicating the collection size in each Library of Congress class[60]—can convey meaning in a more impactful way than numbers alone. Assessment staff should think carefully about the story, the data required to tell it, and the visual that will most quickly and clearly convey the message. If the goal is to show relative size, a bar or pie chart might be effective. If the goal is to show a trend, a line graph or scatterplot might be better. For describing the basic makeup of a collection, an infographic incorporating icons for each major format can work. One way to explore the spectrum of visualizations is simply to conduct some research on the open Web for phrases like "library infographic" or "library data visualization." The results will show what is possible, what is effective, and what is not. Figure 2.4 shows some basic visualizations adapted from Mason's assessment report template.

Once assessment staff have determined the story and the basic visuals, it can help to sketch things out—literally. At this stage, it is important to consider branding specifics like font and color scheme (the parent institution may have a style guide that includes official colors), as well as logistics like available software. There are a number of free (or "freemium") online tools for generating infographics, like Piktochart, which can be useful; there are also more

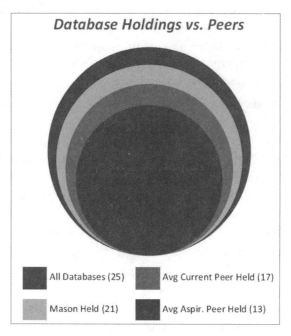

FIGURE 2.4 • Assessment visualizations

sophisticated visualization tools like Tableau, with robust functionality and a correspondingly steep learning curve. In the middle, there are basic tools like Microsoft Excel, Word, and Publisher, all of which are capable of producing tidy and informative data visualizations. Ultimately, the tool is less important than the plan, so thinking through the data, the story, and the stakeholders is the most important part of communicating assessment results visually.

Targeting Your Stakeholders

As mentioned above, library value varies by user. In an academic setting, an undergraduate student's expectations for the library will likely be different from a faculty researcher's expectations—and both will probably diverge from the perspective of a provost or university president. Even within a seemingly homogenous user group—for example, undergraduate students—value can mean many different things. In a 2016 survey, Stemmer and Mahan found that library value changes over the four years of an undergraduate's attendance, shifting from the library as place to the library as resource and service.[61] While this diversity of perspective poses a challenge to assessment and communication, it does underscore the benefits of taking a holistic approach to collections assessment: by using a variety of methods and tools, the library is able to address a wider range of stakeholder interests. One assessment project can be remixed to address the interests of each distinct audience.

The stakeholder groups that collection development or technical services staff are most likely to work with closely are subject or public services librarians. These individuals tend to be close to "the collection," at least in terms of management and decision-making, and will ideally provide some input during the initial stages of any given assessment. However, as discussed earlier in this chapter, the commitment of and expectations for this group can be kept to a minimum. After all, the growing trend for subject librarians is to be pulled in many different directions by an ever-increasing portfolio of responsibilities; at the same time, technical services and collections staff are well-equipped to handle the bulk of assessment data collection and analysis. Subject and public services librarians are good candidates for receiving the most thorough assessment outputs (detailed reports, data files, in-depth interpretations, etc.). It may be helpful to schedule an in-person meeting in order to discuss and interpret the assessment results. The meeting may lead to further action items for the collection development or technical services staff to complete before calling any reports or other documents "final."

Closely related to subject or public services librarians are faculty (or other heavily invested library users). Faculty are likely to be involved in assessment projects, either indirectly (via outreach by a library liaison) or directly (via survey). While not all faculty will care about the "official" results of the assessment, some may be interested in seeing final reports, or even in providing feedback on the assessment process. Where there is interest, this can be a valuable way to build relationships, market the library, and solicit feedback to improve the assessment process. For example, Mason faculty were helpful in revising the Libraries' survey instruments, highlighting questions that seemed innocuous to library staff but were perceived as invasive by faculty.[62] Reports and other assessment documents may need to be revised slightly before they can be distributed to faculty, depending on the library's policy about data-sharing (see below), but at an institution where faculty are heavily invested in the library, it can be worthwhile to develop a faculty-specific report template to fill this need.

The staff who are completing collection assessment may also need to communicate with or provide assessment-related documents to library administrators. It is less likely that much direct back-and-forth will be necessary with this group, but they are likely to require at least some kind of assessment reporting. Library administrators are good candidates for higher-level reports and documents that track and summarize all subject assessments, if for no other reason than as a departmental reporting tool. Placing these documents on an internal web page or shared network drive, where they can be retrieved as needed, makes the process convenient for all.

Other high-level stakeholders include the university administration, governmental bodies, corporate boards, and other funding bodies. These stakeholders will most likely receive their assessment communication from library administrators, and ideally they should receive similarly high-level—and very targeted—information. For these high-level, external stakeholders, it is important to ask: What story do you want these stakeholders to hear? What do you want them to feel? What do you want them to do? Assessment staff should highlight only the most salient data points, and be sure to relate the results closely to user group demographics and outcomes. This is a particularly favorable time to use snippets of user feedback or anecdotes about the user experience. These stakeholders, who are unfamiliar with the internal workings of libraries and are concerned first and foremost with accountability, may be more easily moved by the library's user impact than by spreadsheets and metrics.

One last group with whom the assessment team may communicate during and after an assessment is the users—or in the case of academic libraries, the students. Students are unlikely to be directly involved in collections assessment, except in the case of user surveys, focus groups, or other feedback. Nevertheless, assessment can help identify what matters to users, and certain data and results can in turn be used to market the library to students. For example, if assessment shows that undergraduates strongly favor e-books over print, the library can build—and market—its e-book holdings more concertedly. Or, for instance, if assessment shows that students are having a hard time locating peer-reviewed journals—or really love the leisure reading collection once they discover it—the library can market these resources more directly. Users don't need to know about the formal assessment (though sometimes it doesn't hurt), but they should be made aware that the library is responding to a need.

Ongoing Data-Sharing

As collection development and technical services staff coordinate this variety of stakeholder communications, it is important to establish clear guidelines or policies around the sharing of library data. Some data is regulated explicitly and cannot be shared. Student data is one obvious example, as is vendor-specific data, which is often confidential per license agreements. Peer library data may also be confidential, as in the case of using the OCLC Collection Evaluation tool. Beyond that, assessment staff should consult with the library administration and other stakeholders to determine which levels of information (raw data, aggregate data, summaries, reports, etc.) can be shared, in what form, and with whom. Once basic guidelines have been established, it is relatively easy to develop templates based on audience that exclude or aggregate data to the appropriate level.

WHAT NEXT?

Establishing a Cycle of Assessment

Unless the library is conducting an ad hoc assessment intended to address a one-time, isolated issue, it is useful to think of assessment as an ongoing cycle. This can mean a series of subject-specific assessments that cycle over a period of years; an annual set of format-based assessments (e.g., annual weeding or subscription review projects); a multiyear schedule that addresses a different slice of the holistic perspective each year (e.g., a user survey in year one, an intensive e-resource review in year two, and a print collection assessment in year three); or any other cycle that makes sense given the institution's resources and local needs. Whatever the approach, establishing a clear cycle of assessment will help staff embed assessment into their normal routine, streamline data collection, and refine assessment practices over time.

When structuring the assessment cycle, it can be helpful to set a goal for each year. For example, in a subject-by-subject approach, staff can consider the target for assessing the full collection and use this to estimate an average number of subjects that need to be assessed each year. If the number seems too high, staff can reevaluate either the target deadline or the granularity of each subject, until a feasible schedule can be worked out. At Mason, collections staff found that five subject assessments at a time was too many, and so they scaled back the expected assessment workload to a more modest three.

Similarly, libraries should take into account other constraints on assessment, including other cycles that occur throughout the year. The academic calendar, fiscal year, and volume of other library projects will all impact assessment. For example, user surveys will yield less useful results during times of the year when users are bombarded with other requests for feedback, so assessment staff may want to coordinate with colleagues to make sure that assessment isn't competing with too many other surveys. Subject librarians may be too busy in September and January to provide assessment input. Data availability may also follow certain cycles. For example, COUNTER usage data is not available for a given month or year right away, so assessment may need to accommodate a slight delay in data collection. Similarly, circulation and holdings data may need to be collected strategically, depending on system workload limitations and other library needs throughout the year. Whatever the local limitations, turning a single assessment project into an ongoing assessment program requires thought and planning, but it can ultimately convert the original project's momentum into a valuable—and ongoing—library tool that becomes part of the institutional culture.

Reevaluating and Updating Methods

As assessment becomes an ongoing process, it's advisable to assess the process itself to ensure that it remains sustainable, actionable, and useful. Assessment staff should build a regularly scheduled reevaluation and update period into the assessment cycle, either at the end of every project or at longer intervals (e.g., yearly or even biannually). During the reevaluation, staff can review the validity and usefulness of current assessment methods, asking questions like "what does this tell us?" and "so what?" This is also a useful time to get feedback from stakeholders on both the process and the outcomes. What was confusing, inefficient, or unhelpful? What was easiest, most valuable, or most surprising? What components of the final report(s) could be omitted, and what is missing that stakeholders would really like to know? It is also a good idea to revisit institutional goals, data points, methodologies, and tools to make sure that everything is still aligned. Mason's assessment program was developed in a time of budget growth; now, in an environment of declining funds, the way the Libraries assess collections may need to shift accordingly. Lastly, staff should check the assessment documentation and make sure that everything is up-do-date with any methodological or policy changes. By scrutinizing—and refreshing—assessment practices, approaches, and reports regularly, collections or technical services staff can ensure that collection assessment remains a valuable undertaking for the library.

Taking Action

The last, and perhaps most important, component of collections assessment is to *take action*. Assessment is intended as a means to an end, so every assessment should lead to some sort of decision—even if that decision is to deliberately maintain the status quo. If assessment staff identify a major gap in the collection, the library should develop a plan—or at least an argument—to fill it. If staff identify sorely underused resources, the library can choose to launch a marketing campaign or undertake a round of cancellations. If assessment shows that scholars in a given field are overwhelmingly citing journals, then the library can rebalance its allocations to favor those resources. Whatever the assessment shows, the library should make an effort to act on the results. If action is impossible—if there's no budget, or buy-in, for change—then it may be wise to shift the focus of your assessment to an area where action is more likely.

CONCLUSION

In the end, assessment—even ad hoc assessment—is critical to today's library. Holistic assessment, which harnesses a variety of perspectives to paint a high-level picture of the collection, is one sustainable way for libraries to tackle this necessary challenge. While it takes careful thought and considerable planning at the outset, this preparation pays off when drawing from and leveraging the wide pool of data and analysis tools that collections and technical services staff have at their fingertips. The resulting stories—custom-crafted from a variety of sources—can help constituents ranging from students to board members to subject specialists understand the real scope and value of library collections. Externally, this can mean increased relevance, community support, and even funding. Internally, the resulting assessment framework can serve as the basis for ongoing collections assessment, allowing the library to build and refine local best practices and—in time—establish a stable, robust, and strategic culture of assessment.

NOTES

1. "Office of Institutional Research and Assessment—Course Enrollment (FTE), 2016," George Mason University, Office of Institutional Research and Assessment, https://irr2 .gmu.edu/New/N_EnrollOff/EnrlScsFTE.cfm.

2. "Office of Institutional Research and Assessment—Common Data Set 2016–17: Section B: Enrollment and Persistence, 2017," George Mason University, Office of Institutional Research and Assessment, https://irr2.gmu.edu/cds/cds_new/sec_action .cfm?year=2016–17&sec_id=B.

3. Madeline Kelly, "Applying the Tiers of Assessment: A Holistic and Systematic Approach to Assessing Library Collections," *Journal of Academic Librarianship* 40, no. 6 (2014): 585–91, https://doi.org/10.1016/j.acalib.2014.10.002.

4. "Collection Assessment—UW Libraries Staffweb," University of Washington Libraries, http://staffweb.lib.washington.edu/units/cas/sl-portal/building/collection-assessment.

5. Qiana Johnson, "Moving from Analysis to Assessment: Strategic Assessment of Library Collections," *Journal of Library Administration* 56, no. 4 (2016): 489, https://doi.org/ 10.1080/01930826.2016.1157425.

6. Bart Harloe, ed., *Guide to Cooperative Collection Development* (Chicago: American Library Association, 1994), 21.

7. Amanda B. Albert, "Communicating Library Value—The Missing Piece of the Assessment Puzzle," *Journal of Academic Librarianship* 40, no. 6 (2014): 635, https://doi .org/10.1016/j.acalib.2014.10.001.

8. Ibid., 634

9. Sonia Bodi and Katie Maier-O'Shea, "The Library of Babel: Making Sense of Collection Management in a Postmodern World," *Journal of Academic Librarianship* 31, no. 2 (2005): 143–50.

10. Jacqueline Borin and Hua Yi, "Indicators for Collection Evaluation: A New Dimensional Framework," *Collection Building* 27, no. 4 (2008): 136–43, https://doi .org/10.1108/01604950810913698.

11. Michelle Wilde and Allison Level, "How to Drink from a Fire Hose without Drowning: Collection Assessment in a Numbers-Driven Environment," *Collection Management* 36, no. 4 (2011): 217–36, https://doi.org/10.1080/01462679.2011.604771.

12. Karen R. Harker and Janette Klein, *Collection Assessment*, SPEC Kit 352 (Washington, DC: Association of Research Libraries, 2016), 9, http://publications.arl.org/Collection-Assessment-SPEC-Kit-352/.

13. Ibid., 72

14. Johnson, "Moving from Analysis to Assessment," 90.

15. Melissa J. Goertzen, "Applying Quantitative Methods to E-Book Collections," *Library Technology Reports* 53, no. 4 (2017): 6.

16. Sarah K. C. Mauldin, *Data Visualizations and Infographics,* Library Technology Essentials 8 (Lanham, MD: Rowman and Littlefield, 2015).

17. Scott Nicholson, "A Conceptual Framework for the Holistic Measurement and Cumulative Evaluation of Library Services," *Journal of Documentation* 60, no. 2 (2004): 164–82, https://doi.org/10.1108/00220410410522043.

18. Bodi and Maier-O'Shea, "The Library of Babel," 146.

19. Borin and Yi, "Indicators for Collection Evaluation."

20. Wilde and Level, "How to Drink from a Fire Hose without Drowning."

21. Michelle Wilde and Allison Level, "Adventures in Wonderland: Subject Librarians and Assessment in Collection Development," presented at the Acquisitions Institute at Timberline Lodge (Portland, OR: Colorado State University Libraries, 2008), http://hdl.handle.net/10217/1862.

22. Cheri Jeanette Duncan and Genya Morgan O'Gara, "Building Holistic and Agile Collection Development and Assessment," *Performance Measurement and Metrics* 16, no. 1 (2015): 65, https://doi.org/10.1108/PMM-12-2014-0041.

23. Jennifer E. Knievel, Heather Wicht, and Lynn Silipigni Connaway, "Use of Circulation Statistics and Interlibrary Loan Data in Collection Management," *College & Research Libraries* 67, no. 1 (2006): 47.

24. Kelly, "Applying the Tiers of Assessment."

25. Michael Luther, "Total Library Assessment," *Journal of Library Administration* 56, no. 2 (2016): 158–70, https://doi.org/10.1080/01930826.2015.1116335.

26. Johnson, "Moving from Analysis to Assessment," 495.

27. Wilde and Level, "Adventures in Wonderland."

28. Duncan and O'Gara, "Building Holistic and Agile Collection Development and Assessment."

29. Borin and Yi, "Indicators for Collection Evaluation."

30. Nicholson, "A Conceptual Framework."

31. Wilde and Level, "Adventures in Wonderland."

32. Wilde and Level, "How to Drink from a Fire Hose without Drowning."

33. Duncan and O'Gara, "Building Holistic and Agile Collection Development and Assessment," 75.

34. Luther, "Total Library Assessment."

35. Ibid., 168.

36. Johnson, "Moving from Analysis to Assessment."

37. Nicholson, "A Conceptual Framework," 164.

38. Wilde and Level, "How to Drink from a Fire Hose without Drowning."

39. Lisa R. Carter, "Articulating Value: Building a Culture of Assessment in Special Collections," *RBM: A Journal of Rare Books, Manuscripts, & Cultural Heritage* 13, no. 2 (2012): 92–93, https://doi.org/https://doi.org/10.5860/rbm.13.2.376.

40. Duncan and O'Gara, "Building Holistic and Agile Collection Development and Assessment," 72.

41. Genya O'Gara and Anne Osterman, "Determining Value: The Development of Evaluation Metrics for Shared Content," in *Proceedings of the ACRL 2017 Conference,* ed. Dawn M Mueller (Baltimore, MD: Association of College and Research Libraries, 2017), 179–85, www.ala.org/acrl/conferences/acrl2017/papers.

42. Nicholson, "A Conceptual Framework."

43. Borin and Yi, "Indicators for Collection Evaluation."

44. Genya O'Gara and Madeline Kelly, "Collections Assessment: Developing Sustainable Programs and Projects," in *Racing to the Crossroads: Proceedings of the NASIG 32nd Annual Conference,* forthcoming.

45. Joseph R. Matthews, *The Evaluation and Measurement of Library Services* (Westport, CT: Libraries Unlimited, 2007), 12.

46. Nicholson, "A Conceptual Framework."

47. Borin and Yi, "Indicators for Collection Evaluation," 140.

48. Joy M. Perrin, Le Yang, Shelley Barba, and Heidi Winkler, "All That Glitters Isn't Gold: The Complexities of Use Statistics as an Assessment Tool for Digital Libraries," *Electronic Librarian* 35, no. 1 (2017): 185–97.

49. Jenifer Gundry, "Micro Assessing: Library Impact Story Logs," *College & Research Libraries News* 76, no. 6 (2015): 302–22.

50. Duncan and O'Gara, "Building Holistic and Agile Collection Development and Assessment," 71.

51. Goertzen, "Applying Quantitative Methods to E-Book Collections."

52. Leigh Ann DePope, Rebecca Kemp, Mark Hemhauser, and Diana Reid, "Building a Foundation for Collection Management Decisions," *The Serials Librarian* 66, no. 1–4 (2014): 220–26, https://doi.org/10.1080/0361526X.2014.881204.

53. Yves Gingras, "Criteria for Evaluating Indicators," in *Beyond Bibliometrics: Harnessing Multidimensional Indicators of Scholarly Impact,* ed. Blaise Cronin and Cassidy R. Sugimoto (Cambridge, MA: MIT Press, 2014), 112.

54. O'Gara and Kelly, "Collections Assessment."

55. Gingras, "Criteria for Evaluating Indicators," 111.

56. Albert, "Communicating Library Value—The Missing Piece of the Assessment Puzzle," 634.

57. Gundry, "Micro Assessing," 302.

58. Albert, "Communicating Library Value—The Missing Piece of the Assessment Puzzle."
59. Luther, "Total Library Assessment."
60. Shonn M. Haren, "Data Visualization as a Tool for Collection Assessment: Mapping the Latin American Studies Collection at University of California, Riverside," *Library Collections, Acquisitions, & Technical Services* 38, no. 3–4 (2014): 70–81.
61. John K. Stemmer and David M. Mahan, "Investigating the Relationship of Library Usage to Student Outcomes," *College & Research Libraries* 77, no. 3 (2016): 359–75, https://doi.org/10.5860/cr1.77.3.359.
62. The specific question asked was about areas of research interest, which some faculty with very niche research areas felt qualified as personally identifying information. One option was to make that question optional; however, we elected to drop it entirely, since we had been using that field anecdotally but not conducting significant analysis based on faculty research areas.

REFERENCES

Albert, Amanda B. "Communicating Library Value—The Missing Piece of the Assessment Puzzle." *Journal of Academic Librarianship* 40, no. 6 (2014): 634–37. https://doi.org/10.1016/j.acalib.2014.10.001.

Bodi, Sonia, and Katie Maier-O'Shea. "The Library of Babel: Making Sense of Collection Management in a Postmodern World." *Journal of Academic Librarianship* 31, no. 2 (2005): 143–50.

Borin, Jacqueline, and Hua Yi. "Indicators for Collection Evaluation: A New Dimensional Framework." *Collection Building* 27, no. 4 (2008): 136–43. https://doi.org/10.1108/01604950810913698.

Carter, Lisa R. "Articulating Value: Building a Culture of Assessment in Special Collections." *RBM: A Journal of Rare Books, Manuscripts, & Cultural Heritage* 13, no. 2 (2012): 89–99. https://doi.org/https://doi.org/10.5860/rbm.13.2.376.

"Collection Assessment—UW Libraries Staffweb." University of Washington Libraries. n.d. http://staffweb.lib.washington.edu/units/cas/sl-portal/building/collection-assessment.

DePope, Leigh Ann, Rebecca Kemp, Mark Hemhauser, and Diana Reid. "Building a Foundation for Collection Management Decisions." *The Serials Librarian* 66, nos. 1–4 (2014): 220–26. https://doi.org/10.1080/0361526X.2014.881204.

Duncan, Cheri Jeanette, and Genya Morgan O'Gara. "Building Holistic and Agile Collection Development and Assessment." *Performance Measurement and Metrics* 16, no. 1 (2015): 62–85. https://doi.org/10.1108/PMM-12-2014-0041.

George Mason University, Office of Institutional Research and Assessment. "Office of Institutional Research and Assessment—Course Enrollment (FTE), 2016." https://irr2.gmu.edu/New/N_EnrollOff/EnrlScsFTE.cfm.

———. "Office of Institutional Research and Assessment—Common Data Set 2016–17, Section B: Enrollment and Persistence." 2017. https://irr2.gmu.edu/cds/cds_new/sec_action.cfm?year=2016–17&sec_id=B.

Gingras, Yves. "Criteria for Evaluating Indicators." In *Beyond Bibliometrics: Harnessing Multidimensional Indicators of Scholarly Impact,* edited by Blaise Cronin and Cassidy R. Sugimoto, 109–25. Cambridge, MA: MIT Press, 2014.

Goertzen, Melissa J. "Applying Quantitative Methods to E-Book Collections." *Library Technology Reports* 53, no. 4 (2017): 5–31.

Gundry, Jenifer. "Micro Assessing: Library Impact Story Logs." *College & Research Libraries News* 76, no. 6 (2015): 302–22.

Haren, Shonn M. "Data Visualization as a Tool for Collection Assessment: Mapping the Latin American Studies Collection at University of California, Riverside." *Library Collections, Acquisitions, & Technical Services* 38, no. 3–4 (2014): 70–81.

Harker, Karen R., and Janette Klein. *Collection Assessment.* SPEC Kit 352. Washington, DC: Association of Research Libraries, 2016. http://publications.arl.org/Collection -Assessment-SPEC-Kit-352/.

Harloe, Bart, ed. *Guide to Cooperative Collection Development.* Collection Management and Development Guides 6. Chicago: American Library Association, 1994.

Johnson, Qiana. "Moving from Analysis to Assessment: Strategic Assessment of Library Collections." *Journal of Library Administration* 56, no. 4 (2016): 488–98. https://doi.org/10.1080/01930826.2016.1157425.

Kelly, Madeline. "Applying the Tiers of Assessment: A Holistic and Systematic Approach to Assessing Library Collections." *Journal of Academic Librarianship* 40, no. 6 (2014): 585–91. https://doi.org/10.1016/j.acalib.2014.10.002.

Knievel, Jennifer E., Heather Wicht, and Lynn Silipigni Connaway. "Use of Circulation Statistics and Interlibrary Loan Data in Collection Management." *College & Research Libraries* 67, no. 1 (2006): 35–49.

Luther, Michael. "Total Library Assessment." *Journal of Library Administration* 56, no. 2 (2016): 158–70. https://doi.org/10.1080/01930826.2015.1116335.

Matthews, Joseph R. *The Evaluation and Measurement of Library Services.* Westport, CT: Libraries Unlimited, 2007.

Mauldin, Sarah K. C. *Data Visualizations and Infographics.* Library Technology Essentials 8. Lanham, MD: Rowman and Littlefield, 2015.

Nicholson, Scott. 2004. "A Conceptual Framework for the Holistic Measurement and Cumulative Evaluation of Library Services." *Journal of Documentation* 60, no. 2 (2004): 164–82. https://doi.org/10.1108/00220410410522043.

O'Gara, Genya, and Madeline Kelly. "Collections Assessment: Developing Sustainable Programs and Projects." In *Racing to the Crossroads: Proceedings of the NASIG 32nd Annual Conference.* Forthcoming.

O'Gara, Genya, and Anne Osterman. "Determining Value: The Development of Evaluation Metrics for Shared Content." In *At the Helm: Leading Transformation*, 179–85. Baltimore, MD: American Library Association, 2017.

Perrin, Joy M., Le Yang, Shelley Barba, and Heidi Winkler. "All That Glitters Isn't Gold: The Complexities of Use Statistics as an Assessment Tool for Digital Libraries." *The Electronic Librarian* 35, no. 1 (2017): 185–97.

Stemmer, John K., and David M. Mahan. "Investigating the Relationship of Library Usage to Student Outcomes." *College & Research Libraries* 77, no. 3 (2016): 359–75. https://doi.org/10.5860/crl.77.3.359.

Wilde, Michelle, and Allison Level. "Adventures in Wonderland: Subject Librarians and Assessment in Collection Development." Presented at the Acquisitions Institute at Timberline Lodge, Portland, OR, May 19, 2008. http://hdl.handle.net/10217/1862.

———. "How to Drink from a Fire Hose without Drowning: Collection Assessment in a Numbers-Driven Environment." *Collection Management* 36, no. 4 (2011): 217–36. https://doi.org/10.1080/01462679.2011.604771.

ACQUISITIONS AND E-RESOURCES ASSESSMENT

Trey Shelton and Steven Carrico

⭑ useful for further readings section

Assessment in acquisitions has become imperative. To meet the traditional mission of providing users with innovative services and appropriately sized collections, libraries are now obliged to offer quick, seamless access to an increasing variety of online resources. Many libraries, regardless of their type and size, are struggling with status quo budgets and reductions in staff. The assessment of what libraries acquire, the methods by which the materials are acquired and managed, and how the resources are used can help explain how the library's limited financial and human resources are being utilized. These insights can ideally lead to evidence-based decision-making to improve library services.

Acquisitions is an integral component in the library's daily service mission of providing efficient access to users. Library acquisitions can be defined as the process of purchasing or licensing library materials, and it often involves management of the materials budget. Acquisitions departments may also be responsible for the management of e-resource collections. With most libraries now spending a larger portion of their materials budgets to acquire online resources, acquisitions and e-resources are in many ways becoming synonymous with collection management. In many libraries, the acquisitions department is taking a lead in establishing collections strategies by working with vendors and publishers to increase content while maintaining or reducing costs, and by establishing and maintaining access to e-resource collections.

Traditional assessment activities that occur in acquisitions can be divided into two avenues: (1) gathering and reporting statistics, and (2) documenting and evaluating staff assignments and workflows. Staffing and workflow evaluations are typically focused on internal departmental processes. Today, acquisitions operations have evolved into a more complex, online environment and encompass many initiatives across the library, including:

- Planning and implementing purchasing plans and models
- Negotiating and reviewing license agreements
- Assessing vendor financial stability
- Maintaining access to vendor and publisher content and platforms
- Managing access and discovery systems
- Working in ordering and management systems
- Leading and participating in a variety of collaborative and/or consortial partnerships

In response to these shifts in responsibilities, this chapter addresses the following learning objectives:

- Learn when and how acquisitions and e-resources assessment is performed
- Define the primary areas of assessment within acquisitions and e-resources
- Understand how and what types of acquisitions and e-resources statistics are gathered
- Identify various trends and future challenges faced in acquisitions and e-resources assessment

MANAGING ASSESSMENT

The goals of assessment activities taking place in acquisitions and e-resources should be reflective of the greater strategic direction and mission/vision of the entire library organization. Acquisitions and e-resources staff work collaboratively with every other area of the library, including collection/ subject librarians, access services, outreach/reference services, cataloging/metadata services, branch staff, storage, preservation, central business/accounting offices, and library administration. Therefore, assessing initiatives is frequently a cross-departmental undertaking. Several issues must be addressed when developing both ongoing and one-time assessment initiatives.

[handwritten: different pant from – Ch. 2, which mambms that assessment should be cyclical]

When to Assess

Assessment activities can be grouped by their frequency into one of two types of initiatives: (1) one-time, and (2) ongoing. One-time assessment projects are focused on determining the results or outcomes from a specific resource, plan, or workflow, and often involve more than one department or division. Two good examples are assessing the circulation of books received through an approval plan and the assessment of the cost, usage, and qualitative feedback from users on a database trial. Ongoing assessment, by contrast, involves annual or routine updates for holistic assessment plans and the gathering of statistics for use in reports or institutional surveys. For libraries where specific assessment reporting is required on a recurring basis, developing a calendar or other method of tracking when each report is due and when data collection and other steps in the process should occur may prove useful. Assessment in acquisition, in terms of expenditures, is largely tied to fiscal years, so acquisitions librarians may wish to begin gathering statistics from the prior fiscal year in the first months of the current fiscal year in order to prepare for annual reporting needs. This time of the year may also have a lull in activity before ordering and invoicing ramps up, while libraries wait for institutional budgets to be released.

Whether performing one-time or ongoing assessment, those responsible for the oversight and planning of assessment activities should consider the departments and staff involved. Early in the planning process, staff supervisors should be consulted for feedback and assistance in determining assignments and the time frame required for completion. Assigning roles for small initiatives may prove relatively easy, while larger projects may consume more of a staff person's *[handwritten: time costs]* time than may be delineated in that person's current position description. This is why many administrators and managers in acquisitions units may reorganize their department/unit staffing structures and rewrite position descriptions, so staff and time can be dedicated for assessment and project management.

Library leaders developing more comprehensive assessment plans may wish to form a committee or task force to manage the project.

What to Assess

Many acquisitions or e-resources professionals may be directly involved in traditional collection assessment activities. The measurements related to those types of activities are addressed in the "Statistics and Reports" section later in this chapter. As the ways in which libraries purchase resources and make them accessible continue to change, so will the assessment of these areas. This section discusses several primary areas of acquisitions and e-resources assessment that are prevalent in libraries today. Assessing these workflows is often an intricate task involving focused attention to detail. The following are the standard areas of operations in acquisitions that are routinely assessed:

- Staffing and Workflows
- Materials Budgets and Acquisition Methods
- Publishers and Vendors
- Collaborative Initiatives
- Library Systems
- Each of these areas will be treated in the sections below.

Staffing and Workflows

Staffing and organization are frequent topics of assessment, especially as library budgets shrink. Ensuring the effective use of financial and human resources is imperative if libraries are to succeed. The organizational structure of libraries, even of similar type and size, can vary greatly. While the functions and responsibilities for various areas of acquisitions will have similarities across libraries, who performs or oversees what tasks and how departments are organized will vary. Some positions with similar titles may perform very different tasks or serve different functions. But regardless of organizational structure, workflows will often cross departments or units, and the coordination of the assessment and planning of those workflows is critical.

Materials Budgets and Acquisition Methods

The materials budget is critical to a library's operations, and regular assessment of the budget is needed to ensure that the library's collecting priorities are observed. Frequently, libraries will assess whether their materials budget is sufficient to meet their users' needs in terms of content and cost-per-use. From there, libraries may alter allocations for different subjects, change approval plans, and make cancellation or purchase decisions.

Related to materials budget assessment is acquisitions methods assessment. This type of assessment is performed in order to gain insight into the effectiveness of the methods and practices employed in acquiring resources. Assessment in this area can be used to assess a single acquisitions method or purchasing plan, or to compare methods or plans. Analysis of the subject area of purchases may also play a role in this assessment. Using benchmarks for this type of assessment is critical, whether those are metrics reported by other institutions or local historical purchasing data. The primary methods of acquisition are as follows:

- Firm/one-time orders
- Approval/blanket plans
- Subscriptions and standing orders
- Packages/collections purchases
- Use-driven acquisitions (UDA)
- Patron/demand-driven acquisitions (PDA/DDA)
- Evidence-based acquisition/selection (EBA/EBS)
- Purchase on demand (PoD)
- Pay-per-view (PPV)

[handwritten margin note: no explanation provided – outside scope of book?]

Publishers and Vendors

Since most of the resources that libraries acquire are commercially published, acquisitions departments often play a primary role in developing and maintaining working relationships with publishers, content providers, and vendors. The assessment of products and services provided by these companies and organizations is critical to ensuring that decisions are made that are in the best interest of the library. When evaluating publishers and other content providers, the following areas should be assessed:

- Quality and quantity of content
- Pricing and purchasing models available
- Licensing terms
- E-resource platform functionality and usability
- Inclusion in discovery and access systems

- Quality of customer service and reputation
- Invoicing/account management
- Financial stability

Most libraries work with at least one primary book vendor or dealer. Larger book vendors can provide not only firm order services, but also approval/slip and user-driven acquisition plans. The assessment of book vendors should include the quality and quantity of material available as profiled against an approval/slip/user-driven acquisition plan, as well as the speed and efficiency of ordering and any discounts or other financial incentives that are offered. The features and usability of the vendor's ordering website/database should be considered, for both acquisitions staff and others who may use the system, such as subject librarians. The technical service functions that libraries outsource to vendors are also critical to efficient library operations and are thus worthy of assessment. The consistent quality of physical processing and/or the quality of metadata provided are examples of outsourced services that should be assessed.

Subscription agents are another type of vendor that is critical to most library operations. These third-party service providers help libraries track and manage subscriptions and standing orders for journals and other serials and continuations. Subscription agents maintain relationships with both libraries and publishers/content providers, and they can assist a library that may not have the staff to handle billing transactions for potentially hundreds or thousands of different publishers. Subscription agents charge libraries service fees, and this is a primary factor for consideration and assessment. As with book vendors, the features and usability of a subscription agent's online ordering database are critical to workflow efficiencies.

[handwritten in left margin: lack of focus on library users]

Collaborative Initiatives

Collaborative efforts are another area of assessment to consider. Libraries frequently engage in shared acquisitions and collection-building agreements with partner libraries and consortia. These shared models have the potential to benefit libraries through reduced costs, increased negotiation leverage, or the streamlining/simplification of purchasing processes. Common types of shared collection-building plans include:

- Big Deal journal packages
- Buying clubs/volume discounts
- Group purchasing of packages/collections/plans
- Shared services and systems

Some collaborative initiatives may include assigning or assuming responsibility for in-depth or comprehensive collection in a particular subject area or even for particular titles or publishers. It is also common for consortia or other library organizations to provide shared services and systems that may very well impact acquisitions and e-resources, for example, shared integrated library systems, discovery and access systems, and the related management and maintenance of those systems. Though primarily a topic related directly to collections, collaborative interlibrary services or agreements may also impact acquisitions. For example, acquisitions may not automatically process lost replacements for titles held at other libraries on the agreement. Libraries must consider not only the benefits of the actual shared purchase, service, or system, but also their relationship with the coordinating organization, along with the technical and system requirements, processes, and resources involved to support the collaboration.

Library Systems

The library systems covered here include integrated library systems (ILS), electronic resource management systems (ERMS), and access and discovery systems. Though addressed separately here, these systems may be stand-alone or integrated. The features of all these systems will impact one or more of the following: workflows; user discovery and access; and the ability to assess acquisitions and/or e-resources.

The library systems market has changed drastically in the past several years. Breeding's annual "Library System Reports"[1] provide excellent insight into the changes within this market. In the past, most libraries used a patchwork of systems from multiple providers to acquire, manage, and make library resources discoverable and accessible. The advent of next-generation ILS and library service platforms (LSPs),[2] which merge traditional ILS functionality with e-resource management (ERM) and/or access and discovery system functionality, has become an important trend.[3]

One of the primary acquisitions features within ILSs are related to fund accounting. Being able to structure and track collections expenditures in multiple ways allows libraries to fully assess their materials expenditures. Flexibility in fund structure/creation and fund code designation can allow a library to control and assess the materials budget at the level appropriate to its circumstances. How the system's accounting features handle accounting activities, as listed below, as well as how the system may interface with vendor systems and local enterprise financial systems, will have a significant impact on workflow. How well the system is able to track and report financial-related activities will impact the library's access to collections budget acquisitions assessment data. At a minimum, the following basic accounting functions should be assessed for their functionality and their impact on workflow:

- Invoicing
- Allocations
- Encumbrances
- Free balances
- Fiscal years

Because library collections are built through acquisitions work, the following all play a role in a library's workflow and ability to assess acquisitions methods and practices:

- How ILS order or purchase order (P.O.) records are created/ structured
- How order records are linked to bibliographic records and item/ holding records, or other record types
- What nonbibliographic metadata, such as order details, can be associated with a record
- How the creation and updates of these records, and the impact of those updates on user discovery displays, should be factors to consider when assessing such systems

For example, how the user display changes as a physical item moves from acquisitions to cataloging and then to the shelf, can impact user services. Integration with vendor systems should also be a consideration in assessing ILSs. For a traditional ILS, the ability to upload electronic data interchange (EDI), machine-readable cataloging (MARC), and other formats suitable for data interchange from a vendor in order to create or update bibliographic records, orders, invoices, and claims should be considered standard. Newer LSP systems typically include features comparable to the above and may also include application programming interface (API) integration with material vendors/ subscription agents and/or integration with other library system or content providers. Such integration can help to automate the workflow significantly and should be assessed accordingly. LSPs should also be evaluated on how their acquisitions and financial accounting functionality is tied to ERM and discovery and access functionality.

While bibliographic, holding, and items records are traditionally the domain of cataloging and metadata professionals, many acquisitions and e-resources professionals may also work with these areas of the system. How these record types are created, batch-imported, and managed will impact a variety of workflows. Many batch-order creation activities are tied to importing bibliographic records, which may also create items and holdings. Shelf-ready and vendor MARC/metadata services may be managed by acquisitions departments, usually in coordination with cataloging departments and library branches. Therefore, the way that provisional or order-level bibliographic records are overlaid with full level bibliographic records may be critical to acquisitions workflows. While the assessment implications of how an ILS links with various records types may be wide-ranging, the impact for acquisitions and collections assessment includes how a library is able to reconcile expenditures and order data with bibliographic/holdings and circulation data.

Electronic resource management systems vary greatly in their functionality, their interoperability with an ILS, and their integration with discovery and access systems. Most commercial ERM systems include integrated knowledge bases (KBs) and access and discovery systems, though most open-source or homegrown ERMs may rely on customized automation workflows, or, increasingly, APIs to sync data between systems. KBs typically facilitate direct or indirect integration with access and discovery systems and may also serve as the basis of resource/title records for the ERM system. At a minimum, an ERM will provide the ability to create or select a record that represents an e-resource from the KB. Metadata is then associated with that e-resource record to represent its description, licensing terms, holdings, and access information. Vendor contact and administrative account information are additional standard ERM features. The integration of order and cost data, either through system integration or manual upload, may also be present. Usage data, storage, and analysis tool integration may also be useful functions in an ERM. How ERM systems integrate with access and discovery systems, including link-resolvers, web-scale discovery services, A-Z lists, authentication systems, and MARC record services for use in library catalogs, will impact library workflow. ERMs and KBs can provide extremely useful data for use in assessment. E-resource collection counts are routinely supplied through the analysis of ERM records and KB holdings. The analysis of license terms or other data elements stored within the system may also be possible.

Systems designed to gather, store, and analyze e-resource usage data may be integrated with ERMs or subscription agent sites and platforms. Most systems are designed to work with COUNTER reports, though not all systems may support COUNTER reports or releases. Usage data is either manually uploaded by e-resource professionals or by the service provider's support representatives, or is automatically retrieved using the ANSI/NISO SUSHI standard.[4] The usage of individual titles, databases, platforms, publishers, and resource types can be assessed, including usage for the same title or resource when it is available from multiple sources. This last may be especially useful for database/platform overlap comparisons. Most systems are capable of ingesting cost data to calculate cost-per-use metrics. Cost-per-use calculations will vary by system, so it is critical to understand how usage is calculated across different systems when making comparisons. Limitations on how cost-per-use is calculated may make assessment for some formats and acquisitions methods or sales models challenging. Usage-gathering and assessment systems can reduce the burden on staff who are responsible for gathering usage data and may enhance assessment for collections decision-making.

Discovery and access systems are the primary way in which libraries ensure that users can identify, locate, and access the materials and resources within their collections. Print and electronic resources may be made discoverable via a traditional OPAC or a web-scale discovery system, or in some cases libraries may utilize systems (often locally developed) to aggregate search results from multiple types of discovery systems (catalog/OPAC, web-scale discovery indexes, A-Z lists, and others) in order to provide users with a bento box search results set.[5] Once a user finds a search result that is useful, they must be able to locate and access the associated resource. Regardless of the type of discovery and access system being evaluated, the primary areas of assessment are as follows:

- Usability of interfaces (public and staff)
- Functionality/features
- Content/resources included
- Integration with other systems the library currently is using or investigating (from the same provider, from a different provider, or homegrown)
- Cost

The flexibility in the design and operability/features of the user interface, as well as any user privacy concerns, should also be considered. The assessment of access and discovery systems is a complex topic, and local circumstances will greatly determine the type and extent of assessment performed. The following is a list of the access and discovery system types that may need to be assessed:

- Web-scale discovery system
- OPAC
- A-Z database list
- A-Z journal list
- Link resolver
- Authentication system(s)
    - ◊ Proxy servers
    - ◊ Institutional single sign-on system integration
    - ◊ OpenAthens[6]
    - ◊ RA21[7]

Assessing library systems from an acquisitions and e-resources perspective must involve a holistic, multifaceted approach. A library must assess what users' needs are, determine if a given system or systems meet those needs, and then compare systems in order to determine how effective each system is at meeting those needs. A request for proposal (RFP), an invitation to negotiate (ITN), or other formal bidding processes managed by the central purchasing office may also be involved. While a formal bidding process can potentially complicate or delay purchasing decisions, this process should be viewed as an opportunity to document a formal assessment of the competing products or services; this allows libraries to express their needs and wants in a system, ensure competition in the marketplace, and provide legally binding documentation holding both parties accountable.

How to Assess

The methods and processes for the assessment of any given area of acquisitions or e-resources will vary widely based on the focus of the assessment and local circumstances, such as the amount of staff expertise and time dedicated to assessment activities, data availability, and other factors. Readers interested in a more detailed exploration of the various areas of acquisitions and e-resources assessment should consult the literature listed in the "Further Readings" section at the end of this chapter.

Assessment in acquisitions may involve evaluating staff positions, work-flows, and material budget expenditures. It may also include a wide range of projects, ranging from comparing the cost-per-use of several journal packages,

not focusing on users

to examining the discovery and access issues for licensed resources available on the library's web page. Most assessment efforts taking place in acquisitions fall into one of three types: (1) gathering and compiling statistics and various metrics; (2) merging or comparing this data using reports or spreadsheets; and (3) applying both quantitative and qualitative measures in a project that provides a comprehensive review of a library initiative or resource.

Quantitative assessment in acquisitions relies heavily on pulling reports, such as title lists or expenditure reports. Reports may be obtained from both the library and those managed by the service providers. In this context, a "report" refers to an automated utility or application that is offered by an integrated library system (ILS), e-resources management system (ERM), or a vendor or publisher's platform. Reports may come in a variety of formats and then need to be cleaned or manipulated and then merged or combined with data from other reports for analysis. Even if only one data set is being utilized, the raw data or canned system report will often need to be reviewed for accuracy and likely manipulated to create a report suited for the analysis in mind. If multiple reports request the same or similar data, librarians may wish to construct a common data set of statistical data that is granular enough to meet the needs of multiple reports. The data can then be mixed and matched in different ways to meet the needs of each report. Analyzing expenditures by format is a common method of assessing a materials budget, and a library may need or wish to report these expenditure figures by combining different sets of format and acquisition method categories.

The native reporting capabilities, or canned reports, of some library or third-party systems may be insufficient for even basic reporting needs. Frequently, the need to compare and merge data from multiple sources or systems will arise. Most libraries rely on spreadsheet software, such as Microsoft Excel, and many systems offer the ability to download data in an Excel spreadsheet. If in-house expertise exists, libraries may employ relational databases, like Microsoft Access or other SQL databases, to build homegrown data repositories and build complex reports from multiple data sources. Some libraries are also exploring the use of statistical programming languages, such as R, to manipulate, analyze, and visualize ILS and e-resource usage data.[8]

Some reports are prefabricated, or canned, and are made available either on a system's menu or on a vendor's website. Some reports can be customized by choosing from a suite of fields and options that are readily available on the system or vendor's website. An example of a simple prefabricated or devised report might be a report from a book vendor on the titles ordered in a given

chapter suffers from lack of specificity

period, or a report from an ILS order that provides the invoice details of every order paid on a particular budget in a given fiscal year. Some vendors and service providers are capable of creating customized reports. Customized reports usually involve more complex data fields and often merge complex variables. An example would be a customized report from a publisher that includes complex e-book usage covering multiple years organized by subject, purchased and not purchased, and/or method of purchase.

Collecting and analyzing both quantitative and qualitative data may be necessary for comprehensive data-driven or evidence-based decision-making. Though used less frequently than quantitative methods, qualitative methods can also play an important role in acquisitions assessment. For example, librarians' and users' perceptions of library systems and/or publisher platforms, particularly for user interface and usability assessment projects, will be key.

Communicating assessment outcomes and their impacts is often as challenging as the assessment itself. Many levels of stakeholders may be involved, from upper-level management and governance boards to colleagues and library users. Reports and other communications constructed in-house should take their audience into account. Mid-level managers may need detailed or even raw data to determine patterns and make recommendations, while high-level administrators may only be interested in the conclusions drawn from that data and the options available. Reports, especially for external consumption, should be polished and easily interpretable. Tableau and other data visualization software suites can be used as tools for analyzing statistics and communicating findings. Due to the sensitive nature of assessment in acquisitions, it is also important to keep in mind that some assessment outcomes may be limited to internal audiences.

The following sections will provide general information about how assessment is accomplished within each of the standard areas of acquisitions as defined in the section above. In the previous section, Materials Budgets and Acquisitions Methods were combined in order to emphasize their relation to each other. Here these areas are separated to address the unique methods of assessment for each.

Staffing and Workflow   Whe m ch. 2

One method of assessing the staffing size and structure of a library is to compare it to the size and structure of other peer organizations. This may be accomplished through the analysis of organizational charts. Libraries may also wish to formally or informally interview or survey librarians at the organizations they are comparing themselves with, in order to understand the nuances of the organization and structure at that library in comparison to their own. Administrators and managers should consider examining the percentage breakdown of responsibilities and job duties assigned to each staff and/or unit in order to better plan workflow, position description updates, and reassignments.

Assessing workflow is important to making staffing decisions, but it also serves to understand complex processes and increase efficiencies. Workflow will often cross departments or other organizational units, and the coordination of assessment and planning of those workflows is critical. Workflow assessment may utilize quantitative data on the volume, frequency, or speed of certain tasks, but often qualitative assessment methods, particularly staff interviews, may be as much or more useful in determining the effectiveness of certain processes. Managers may wish to visualize the workflow using flowcharts to more easily understand processes and facilitate discussions on possible revisions. After assessing staffing and workflow it is prudent to review and update position descriptions, department and unit organizational charts, and annual goals and objectives set for each staff person, as appropriate.

Materials Budget

There are a multitude of methods for assessing a materials budget. The most common is a comparison of materials budgets to relevant peer institutions, comparing expenditures across fiscal years, as well as comparing how initial allocations compare to final expenditures. Often, peer libraries may post some version of their materials budget online, but detailed information sufficient for true comparison may need to be directly requested from the peer institution. In many cases, statistical surveys completed by both the library and its peers, and later published by an organization or government entity, may provide the most comparable data set.

Most libraries extract budget data from their ILS, ideally utilizing established fund structures organized by specific funds, subject disciplines, and/or material or resource formats. To extract budget and expenditure data, it is best to use the canned reports offered by the ILS or vendor systems, and then manipulate the data using spreadsheets or other applications for analysis and reports. For example, an ILS report might provide the total funds spent on e-books purchased by firm order in the sciences, but to determine the annual funds spent on both e-books and print books in the sciences requires additional steps and calculations using spreadsheets or alternative applications.

Acquisition Methods

There are several methods of acquiring materials, and each has its own nuances when it comes to assessment. The scope of assessment for any given acquisition method will depend on the question the library is attempting to answer or the issue it is attempting to understand through assessment. The number of items purchased, the cost of those items, the cost-per-use of those items, and the subject and format of those items are all common to almost all assessments of acquisitions. The sections below treat several of the most frequently used methods of acquisitions and a few recommendations on how to perform basic assessment.

Firm/One-Time Orders

Firm orders include all print books and tangible materials, but they also include e-books, and they may also include the one-time purchase of e-resource collections or archives. Although some libraries may still use the paper or spreadsheet methods of manually ticking or counting print and tangible material acquisitions as they arrive to ascertain the number of items ordered, most libraries employ some type of automation to track these statistics. Usually the statistics are generated by format using reports based on the order and invoice records in the ILS, though order reports from vendor websites or title lists from publishers' websites may also be useful, especially for e-resource purchases. Most ILS and certainly vendor systems provide reports that contain the number, format, and cost of the items, as well as the fund code used to purchase them. Libraries' fund structures based on subject areas and/or formats may also be able to utilize expenditure reports to retrieve data. Subject areas information can also be pulled from the bibliographic/holdings/item records associated with the order record. Circulation or usage information will need to be combined with the cost information for each item or resource in order to produce a cost-per-use figure.

Approval Plans, Blanket Orders, and Standing Orders

In general, the tactics used for firm order assessment also apply to the assessment of materials purchased via approval plans, blanket orders, and standing orders. These types of plans should be reviewed on a regular basis, ideally no less than annually. The assessment of approval plans will focus primarily on the quality and appropriateness of the content with regard to the profile that

plans should be refreshed annually

drives the plan. Some libraries may wish to track the titles coming in on an ongoing basis, especially if a new approval profile has been implemented, at least until the library is satisfied that the particular profile or plan is effective. Often, assessing the effectiveness of a profile is best done through vendor reports, since these reports will contain more information directly related to the profile settings than most ILS reports. For example, a library may use an ILS report to determine the subject areas, based on call number, of a set of purchases. However, if the library has assigned a call number different from the one the vendor used to match a given title to a profile, the vendor report would provide the information most useful in adjusting the plan settings. How well the plan covers the publishers that a library is interested in collecting should also be assessed. Lists of publishers covered by the vendor's profiling service, as well as back-run or retrospective approval plans reports, which are designed to show what content would have matched the profile in the past, are also useful in assessing approval plans. The content received through blanket or standing orders is generally dictated or agreed upon by the library and the vendor/publisher, so the assessment of these types of plans primarily focuses on how effective those purchases are in meeting users' needs.

focus on meeting users needs

Serials and Continuations

The assessment of serials and continuations tends to focus on the number of subscriptions and titles actively received in the library, as well as the annual cost and cost increases of those subscriptions. Subscription agents' canned reports may be very useful in assessing subscriptions, especially when a library has all of its subscriptions and continuations with one or more agents. Subscription journal packages, including "Big Deal" packages, provide their own challenges in gathering data, especially if they are not invoiced at the title level but instead the package or component level. Very often, staff will have to merge the data received from the vendors or publishers into spreadsheets or other software in order to review in detail the cost-per-use and other title-level information such as indexing or impact factors. Though the cost-per-use of subscription resources is primarily used for e-resource assessment, it is also possible for the assessment of print materials. Calculating title-level costs for packages not invoiced at the title level can be accomplished by using the list price, if available, for that title and calculating what percentage of the total package or component cost the list price represents. Subscriptions for databases and other e-resources should also be assessed in ways similar to e-journals, though the

need to transfer data from multiple sources

subject assessment may be more in-depth. For databases and other resources, cost data can be gathered from the ILS, but assessment of the content of the database may rely on vendor/content provider reports and title lists. In some cases, knowledge base holdings can be utilized for database content analysis.

? ch. has uneven explanations

Use-Driven Acquisitions

data exists in multiple sources, how m ch. d

Most use-driven acquisition (UDA) plans are established to offer and purchase e-books (PDA/DDA, EBA, PoD), but there are other formats made available in UDA, including plans to offer access to articles in journals (PPV) and streaming videos (PDA/DDA, EBA). In some cases, print resources are also purchased by these plans (PoD, PDA/DDA). Most UDA publishers or vendors offer tailor-made reports that will provide much of the information needed for assessment, including the number of titles, cost, use, and subject area. However, library staff may still find a need to manipulate and merge the data from canned vendor reports for assessment purposes. Some PDA/ DDA e-book plans utilize a profile that is similar to an approval profile, so *need* some of the assessment techniques applicable to approval plans may be used *to* to evaluate UDA plans. As with approval plans and blanket orders, it is wise *manipulate* for the staff working with collection managers to conduct qualitative reviews *data* of the content received.

Vendors and Publishers

Libraries should assess the performance of the vendors they use on a routine basis. For monograph and e-book vendors, reviewing the turnaround time for orders submitted and received, the discounts offered, the customer and technical support provided, and the navigation and functionality of the vendor system are all relevant. Much of this can be assessed using the vendor's own canned reports, but ILS reports may also provide the same or similar information. For example, reports from either system should contain the order date and either the shipping date (vendor report) or the arrival date (library report). Assessing customer/technical support and the functionality of the vendor's system will require a qualitative approach, since staff and collection managers' input should be surveyed. As with assessing monograph vendors and publishers, evaluating subscription agents' performance is a crucial component to acquisitions. The exact service fee charged by a serial agent should be monitored and compared from year to year, and compared with other subscription agents if the library is searching for the lowest-cost provider. As with monograph or e-book vendors,

→ correlates to experience of Evidence

a serial agent's customer service and the features and usability of their online ordering database are all critical issues to assess through qualitative surveys and frequent staff discussions. When assessing the outsourced services provided by vendors, libraries typically will assess the quality and consistency of the service provided, as well as comparing the cost of the service to the cost of performing the task in-house or outsourcing it to a different vendor. For example, if a monograph vendor is providing MARC records and/or shelf-ready services for materials ordered, then the accuracy of the files provided and the quality of metadata and/or physical processing should be assessed at the start of the service and at regular intervals, perhaps yearly. In this example, coordination with cataloging may be needed, depending on the structure and division of duties in a particular library.

Finally, when evaluating publishers and content providers, there are several areas to assess: the quality and quantity of content, pricing and purchasing models available, licensing terms for e-resources, e-resource platform functionality and usability, inclusion in discovery and access systems, quality of service, and reputation. Most content and pricing assessment can be performed using data provided by the publisher, though historical pricing information from the ILS should also be consulted. Purchasing models should be compared across publishers and content providers, within the same content categories. Licensing terms can be compared to the license terms negotiated within other licenses held by the library, or to model licenses or licensing guidelines adopted by the library. Platform functionality and usability will typically involve some sort of user-testing, either by the librarians or by actual library users, and may utilize a qualitative or mixed-methods approach. Librarians may also wish to determine whether a publisher or content provider's content is included, or indexed, within a discovery system. Since libraries would typically only be concerned if the resource(s) in question were indexed in their current access and discovery systems, the question is frequently to what level the content is indexed. For example, are only title-level or article-level metadata available, or is the entire full text of the resource also indexed?

Collaborative Initiatives

The methods for assessing collaborative acquisitions are not much different from those for assessing individual library acquisitions. However, assessment becomes a little more complicated when it involves multiple library partners. Developing shared review guidelines and determining who will handle the assessment are imperative tasks. Usually a committee or task force is formed by the library group or consortium to handle assessment projects. In addition, libraries should individually assess the pros and cons of their participating in the collaborative initiative itself. Determining whether the benefits of participation outweigh the financial and human resource costs may save the library time, effort, and money.

Library Systems

The assessment of library systems and platforms is somewhat subjective and is always relative to the circumstances, needs, and desires of the library. Purchasing or subscribing to a system because others have positively evaluated it, or are using it, will not guarantee that a local implementation will be successful. However, being aware of others' opinions of the system(s) in question can be highly valuable, and librarians should consider holding interviews with librarians who are currently using the systems being evaluated. These interviews may bring to light features or functionality that had not been considered. The basics of system assessment include listing all the features and functionality a library requires or desires in a system, along with any relevant details, and then evaluating how the system does or doesn't meet the criteria. Rating or ranking systems may be employed to score each function or feature of a system or competing systems, and should include descriptive text of the library's evaluation of each feature to justify the assigned score. The level of complexity for such an evaluation can vary based on the needs and resources available, in addition to any requirements imposed by formal bidding processes. As with vendor platforms, usability testing can also be employed.

STATISTICS AND REPORTS

The vendor and ILS systems discussed in the preceding sections are used to manage and provide access to print and electronic resources, and they play a leading role in acquisitions assessment. These systems are often designed to generate reports and facilitate the extraction of the raw data that is used in assessing acquisition methods, collection strategies, and resource use and usability. Often the resulting statistics and metrics are used to build more comprehensive, meaningful reports that can be used to communicate assessment outcomes to stakeholders at all levels. This section will discuss the statistics, reports, and other data that are typically available to acquisitions professionals.

The gathering of statistics is a time-consuming and often challenging exercise. Cobbling together those statistics to generate metrics for assessment can be even more time-consuming. While acquisitions and e-resources departments or units may track metrics for their own internal purposes, most metrics tracked are intended for organization-wide reporting efforts or, at the very least, have broader implications for collections, access services, and other operational areas of the library.

Many libraries participate in annual institutional surveys that cover multiple operational areas, including acquisitions and e-resources. These surveys are intended to assess and compare libraries nationally by library type. Libraries may find the statistics gathered for the surveys useful in local assessment, advocacy, and marketing efforts. Typically, acquisitions or e-resources professionals report these figures to a central position in the library responsible for submitting survey responses, such as an assessment librarian or, in some cases, the library director.

Academic libraries with expenses over $100,000 at federally funded institutions are required to submit their responses to the annual Integrated Postsecondary Education Data System (IPEDS) survey conducted by the National Center for Education Statistics within the U.S. Department of Education's Institute of Education Science.[9] Conveniently, the results from the Association of College and Research Libraries' (ACRL) Academic Library Trends and Statistics Survey can be used to populate IPEDS responses.[10] Members of the Association of Research Libraries (ARL) also participate in the ARL's annual statistical surveys.[11] For public libraries, the Institute of Museum and Library Services' (IMLS) Public Libraries Survey is a comparable statistical gathering tool,[12] but the data for this survey is centrally reported to the IMLS by the state library or equivalent which serves as a state data coordinator.[13] Additionally, other national, regional, and state library organizations and consortia may also have similar annual statistical reporting surveys or requests for libraries to respond to one-time, project-driven questionnaires.

Statistics and metrics are also used for a variety of purposes beyond institutional surveys. This information can be used by libraries in marketing materials, internal and external reports and presentations, accreditation, new degree certification, and grant-related documentation. Examples of marketing and promotional uses include touting that the library offers x number of e-books or databases, provided access to x number of articles, added x number of new

*having assessment data on hand
to support new initiatives*

items to the collection, or even touting the amount that a library spends annually on a particular type of resource or in total. Administrators and managers may wish to track these statistics for budget request justifications or any number of ongoing or project-based collection and technical services assessments. In academic libraries, most accreditation and new degree certification documents require that information related to the library's collections be included. The information requested for these documents may be generalized, but in many cases it can be quite specific. Volume and title counts and funds expended for a particular subject area, as well as analysis of the breadth and depth of the collection in that subject area, may be required. In addition, some grants related to library collections may also require similar information. Regardless of the purpose, most acquisitions and e-resources statistics and metrics fall into four basic categories:

- Expenditures
- Material counts
- Circulation and usage
- Discovery and access

Expenditures

The ARL, IPEDS/ACRL, and IMLS surveys all include questions concerning materials and materials-related service expenditures, though each survey is structured slightly differently. Depending on the survey, expenditure information may be grouped by commitment type (one-time vs. ongoing expenditures) or by medium (print vs. electronic). In some cases, format types (monographs, serials, e-books, and e-journals) may also be incorporated. The totals for the subcategories are typically summed to generate a total library materials expenditures figure. For example, the ARL[14] and ACRL/IPEDS[15] surveys both request information on one-time resource expenditures and ongoing/subscription resource expenditures, with ACRL/IPEDS incorporating more detailed format questions in order to determine the amounts spent on e-books and e-journals. By contrast, the IMLS survey requests expenditures for print, electronic, and other materials in order to calculate a total amount spent on the collection for each library administrative entity within a state.[16] Libraries may also wish to track materials expenditures at a higher level of detail than is required by any institutional surveys. For example, they may track expenditures for format categories that are lumped into "other materials" categories, or track expenditures by acquisition method such as approval, firm, PDA/DDA, subscription, or standing order. This type of data-gathering allows for the local assessment and longitudinal tracking of expenditures, which can impact overall collection development strategies, help determine appropriate staffing levels, report on the library's financial support for a given subject area or branch location, or be used to build a case for a funding request.

A library's ability to retrieve and organize expenditure information in order to fulfill its reporting requirements will vary depending on the financial

TABLE 3.1 • Material expenditure tracking data elements

MATERIALS EXPENDITURES TRACKING DATA ELEMENTS	DESCRIPTION
Title/Name	title or name of the item, product, service
Amount Paid	cost
Shipping/Postage	charges for shipping/postage
Taxes Paid	if applicable
Service Fees	charges for vendor service/handling fees
Medium	print, electronic, microform, realia, etc.
Format	monograph, periodical, other serials, DVDs, CDs, music scores, etc.
Subject Area	may be broad (fiction/nonfiction; humanities, social sciences, STEM, health/medicine) or specific (anthropology, art, religion, history, engineering, chemisty, dentistry, etc.); consider approaching the level of specificity around institutional structure, academic libraries may track based on support at the college/school or department/center level, while public libraries may focus on adult, teen, and children services.
Purchasing Method	P.O. number/invoice; credit card; prepay/deposit
Acquisitions Method	firm order, approval, subscription, standing order, DDA/PDA, etc.
Vendor	the company/entity being paid
Budget/Fund	the fund code used to encumber and/or pay for the materials
Source/Type of Funds	appropriation, grant, endowment, carry-forward, etc.
Fiscal Year	the fiscal year in which the expenditure occurred
Quantity	number of copies/volumes ordered and received
Branch/Collection	information about which branch and/or subcollection for which the materials were ordered

tracking systems being used, how materials budgets and funds are structured, and what level of detail is kept in regard to the format of each expenditure. Typically, a library's materials budget(s) are structured by the source of funds. A library may receive one or multiple "pots" of funds from a parent organization or governing entity and have one or more grants or endowments relied upon for materials purchases. These funds may or may not be designated solely for materials purchases. Some funds devoted to materials may have restrictions on the types of materials, subjects, and acquisitions methods that can be applied to those funds. Libraries that use an ILS to interface with or shadow an enterprise financial accounting system used by their parent administrative organization often have some flexibility in structuring funds and assigning multiple types of codes to orders as a means to track resource type and format. See table 3.1 for a listing of elements that are useful in expenditure reporting. Each library should consider the use-case scenario and cost-benefit ratio of both tracking and reporting on the data element.

Material Counts

Libraries may determine the statistical counts of various material categories for use in assessment or other purposes. Almost all institutional library surveys contain categories related to volume and/or title counts, and frequently include one or more counts by medium and format. Frequently, the total volume count is calculated by adding any volumes/titles added to the collection in the past fiscal year to the prior year's response. These figures are often calculated by cataloging departments or units, especially for print materials, though e-resources professionals are often called upon to provide definitive counts for electronic materials. In cases where acquisitions departments or units are involved in the cataloging of materials, either print or electronic, coordination among areas is necessary to ensure that the final counts are not duplicated and are inclusive of the appropriate resources. For accurate bibliographic counts, a deep understanding of how resources are cataloged, and in some cases how e-resources are managed in discovery systems, is necessary to produce accurate figures. Some libraries may also rely on physical inventory counts instead of bibliographic counts.

Although cataloging professionals typically report volume/title counts for print materials, it is not uncommon for acquisitions personnel to also be responsible for copy cataloging and/or batch record-loading activities. In these scenarios, it is critical that procedures for tracking the number of physical volumes added parallel or complement the procedures in other departments and across workflow streams. The creation and/or update date of either the bib, item, or holdings records in the ILS can be useful in determining how many volumes or titles were added in a given year. Log files from batch MARC record loads may also be useful.

Information from multiple systems may be needed to accurately count e-resources. The most common e-resource counts reported are the number of e-books, number of e-journals, and number of databases. As newer electronic formats become more popular, such as streaming videos and digital objects/ images, libraries should include separate counts for these items as well. Catalog records within the ILS may be useful if a library consistently catalogs all or a subset (e-books, for example) of its e-resources for discovery within the OPAC. However, e-resources professionals may also rely on data in an ERMS,[17] web-scale discovery system and link resolver KB, or other e-resource listings, such as A-Z journal and database lists. Depending on the integration of the ERM into the ILS or KBs the library utilizes, the ERM may be able to provide counts for all e-resource formats. Again, native reporting capabilities vary by system, and some counts may require exporting and manipulating raw KB data for the library's holdings. These raw data reports are often filled with duplicate entries due to titles being represented in multiple databases or due to poor metadata quality. Extensive manipulation and de-duplication of the KB exports is required to produce accurate counts. Though somewhat dated, the document "ARL Statistics Best Practices for Deduplicating Serial Titles"[18] can still be useful in understanding the issues surrounding e-resource counts

TABLE 3.2 • E-resources count data elements

E-RESOURCES COUNT DATA ELEMENTS	DESCRIPTION
Title/Name	title or name of resource
Format	e-book, e-journal, database, streaming video, digital object/image, datasets, etc.; remember that titles within databases should also be counted, depending on the metric being gathered, separate lists for each type of count or format may be necessary
Access/Ownership	perpetual ownership; licensed access; open access/OER; consortially provided
Subject	the subject area supported by the resource
Paid by	It is useful to be able to report by funding source when dealing with a library system or a library with multiple funding streams.

derived using KBs, and it can be adapted and updated based on the systems or reports used at a given library.

For print resources, most ILS systems include mechanisms to track materials added to locations or collections, but e-resources are typically only tracked at an institutional level. Similarly, most ILSs include call numbers and subject headings which can be used to determine subject area, though this information may not be as readily available for cataloged e-resources due to variations in metadata quality across e-resource MARC record providers.[19] Again, ERMS and KB data may be available as a substitute for traditional ILS data to determine the subject area for e-resources. See table 3.2 for a listing of the elements that are useful in reporting e-resource title counts.

Circulation and Usage

The ARL, ACRL/IPEDS, and IMLS statistical surveys all require libraries to report total print circulation figures and aggregated e-resources usage figures. In some cases, particularly with e-resources, figures may be broken down by format, such as e-books, e-journals, and databases. While circulation data is primarily tracked by circulation and/or access services departments, e-resource usage data is almost invariably gathered and analyzed by e-resource professionals. Both circulation and e-resource usage data can be instrumental in acquisitions and e-resources assessment. Circulation and usage data can be combined with expenditure data to calculate a return on investment (ROI) for a particular purchase or set of purchases, expressed as cost-per-use (cost/use). For example, a book or other one-time purchase that cost $100.00 and was circulated 50 times to date has a cost-per-use of $2.00. As time passes, the book could likely circulate more times, and the cost-per-use would decrease. However, a one-time purchase made years or decades ago may not bear the same weight in assessment priority as more recent or ongoing purchases. While such historical data is useful in retrospective or long-term assessment projects, many libraries may not have the luxury of spending time on such projects and will instead focus on circulation and usage data for the assessment of current purchasing methods.

For subscription or continuing resources, circulation or usage data is typically limited to time frames associated with the subscription or access period, especially for e-journals and databases. The circulation or in-house use of print periodicals is often problematic. Depending on the practices of each library, unbound and bound journals may or may not circulate. Tracking the in-house use of items is challenging, especially if the items are not bar coded, or patrons reshelve the items instead of having library staff count the items removed from shelves before reshelving them. This method is typically fraught with accuracy issues,[20] but it can provide some insight into how print materials are being used.

The level of detail within circulation records will vary by system, and any steps taken to scrub user data due to privacy concerns or regulations may further reduce the level of detail available. For example, academic libraries often wish to know the status of a user (faculty, staff, student, or other), and most libraries may be interested in how an item circulates over time. But even if such information is tracked within the ILS, this data may be removed to protect the privacy or intellectual freedom of users, leaving only the total number of circulations. For volume sets purchased for a single price, a library may wish to aggregate usage for the set to get an accurate ROI. It may be difficult to associate which monographic volume sets were purchased together or separately after the fact, or to link any purchases to individual item records if that information is not actively and consistently tracked within the ILS. If such ILS functionality does not exist, staff may need to manually associate orders with items in the catalog. Just as the circulation policy for bound and unbound print serials varies by library, so do bar coding practices. Without a complex tracking system, the in-house use of un-barcoded items may only be easily tracked at the title level.

Ideally, e-resource usage should be reported using COUNTER[21] compliant reports that are available from the content provider. In some cases, the usage for all of a library's purchases across a single publisher or platform may be represented in one usage report, and it may be necessary to manipulate those reports to separate or distinguish that data based on the purchasing method or collection, especially if this usage data will later be used to calculate cost-per-use metrics. In addition, monthly usage data from multiple COUNTER reports may need to be compiled if reporting or subscription periods cut across calendar years. Smaller libraries with limited e-resource collections may have to pull usage reports from only a small number of providers, but larger institutions often deal with hundreds or thousands of providers, and the staff time needed to consistently gather the usage for every platform may be daunting. Some ERMS contain features that utilize the SUSHI[22] protocol developed by the National Information Standards Organization (NISO),[23] which can automate the gathering of usage data from some providers. However, some smaller e-resource providers may not offer COUNTER-compliant usage reports, if usage reports are provided at all. A listing of COUNTER-compliant providers can be found on the Project COUNTER website.[24] Understanding the differences and nuances of each type of COUNTER report is critical in being able to assign meaning to the numbers and to produce accurate statistics. Particularly useful in quickly gaining a basic understanding of COUNTER reports are Dunkley's 2016 *Friendly Guide to COUNTER Journal Reports: A Guide for Librarians*[25] and his accompanying guides for COUNTER Book[26] and COUNTER Database reports.[27] In addition to Dunkley's guides, the "Hints and Tips" section of the Usus website[28] lists many other information resources that are useful in understanding usage reports. Librarians should also review the current COUNTER Code of Practice,[29] which governs how publishers and content providers determine uses in usage reports. This code also explains the differences between report types. Project COUNTER issues updates to the Code of Practice on a regular basis, with Release 5 of the COUNTER Code having become effective in January 2019.[30] As the Code of Practice changes, so do the reports and the methods used to gather the data, so reports from different codes of practice may not be entirely comparable. No one publisher or vendor will offer all possible COUNTER reports. For example, a publisher of only journals will not provide e-book statistics. In other cases, reports are optional for COUNTER compliance certification. Additionally, some reports consist of a subset of data contained within other reports. For example, the Journal Report 1 GOA and Journal Report 1a reports both contain usage data that is also contained within the Journal Report 1 report. Frequently, COUNTER report names are abbreviated (Journal Report 1 becoming JR1), and some vendors may not provide details on what usage each available report may represent. Learning the lingo will save time and effort for staff and help those who are assessing to know what usage data is available and what reports should be requested for specific assessment projects.

Table 3.3 lists the report name, common abbreviation, and description for the COUNTER reports that are most frequently made available by content providers. The information in this table was adapted from the report listing of Release 4 of the COUNTER Code of Practice.[31] At a minimum, libraries will want to track JR1, BR1 and/or BR2, as well as DB1 and/or PR1 reports to gain basic insight into e-resource usage. COUNTER reports that show "access denied" statistics, often called "turn-away" reports, can be useful in determining which resources a library might consider for purchase from a given provider.

TABLE 3.3 • Common COUNTER reports

COMMON COUNTER REPORTS	COMMON ABBREVIATION	DESCRIPTION
Journal Report 1	JR1	Number of successful full-text article requests by month and journal
Journal Report 1 GOA	JR1 GOA	Number of successful gold open access full-text article requests by month and journal
Journal Report 1a	JR1a	Number of successful full-text article requests from an archive by month and journal
Journal Report 2	JR2	Access denied to full-text articles by month, journal, and category
Journal Report 5	JR5	Number of successful full-text article requests by year-of-publication (YOP) and journal
Database Report 1	DB1	Total searches, result clicks, and record views by month and database
Database Report 2	DB2	Access denied by month, database, and category
Platform Report 1	PR1	Total searches, result clicks, and record views by month and platform
Book Report 1	BR1	Number of successful title requests by month and title
Book Report 2	BR2	Number of successful section requests by month and title
Book Report 3	BR3	Access denied to content items by month, title, and category
Book Report 4	BR4	Access denied to content items by month, platform, and category
Multimedia Report 1	MR1	Number of successful full multimedia content unit requests by month and collection

Not surprisingly, these reports are frequently used by publishers and vendors to market and sell their products to librarians.

Access and Discovery

Libraries expend considerable funds and considerable effort to maintain their discovery and access portals. Entire departments are dedicated to maintaining the accuracy of the catalog/OPAC. Web-scale discovery services, such as Primo or EBSCO Discovery, and link-resolvers, such as SFX and Full-Text Finder, are typically maintained by e-resource professionals and are used to help users find and access library materials. Other online listings of a library's e-resources may also be of interest for assessment. Institutional surveys may ask about a library's discovery and access systems, but most libraries will be interested in more detailed usage metrics of these systems in order to gauge user satisfaction with or the effectiveness of these services. Libraries may be interested in several different types of statistics for access and discovery services, some of which may be similar to the metrics used to assess databases. The number of searches, number of record views, and/or full-text accesses facilitated by the system are the primary focus of statistics in this area.

Most OPAC and web-scale discovery services are able to provide statistics on the number of searches executed or performed by users in a given time period, or on how many unique user sessions were established. This can provide libraries with both a total number of searches as well as the average number of searches-per-session. A high number of searches-per-session may indicate issues with users needing to reformulate query terms multiple times before locating information resources. A detailed discussion of user query formulation in discovery services, among other assessment topics and their impact on search success, can be found in Niu, Zhang, and Chen's 2014 study on user searching of discovery services in academic libraries.[32]

Some statistics from these services may also be used to estimate some e-resource usage data. For example, link-resolver "click-through" statistics for journals, though not a one-to-one comparison, have been found to be a reasonable substitute for COUNTER reports in most circumstances due to the high correlation of the two data points.[33] This is particularly useful for estimating the use of open-access resources included in a library' e-resource access systems, since traditional usage reports for these materials may not be available from some publishers. Low link-resolver statistics may also point to issues with the metadata, or lack thereof, in the discovery service or the link setup in the link-resolver for that resource. Libraries may also utilize proxy server logs to perform an analysis of usage trends.[34]

The search queries that users submit in discovery services are another potential area that is ripe for assessment. In addition to insights on topics and subjects that are of interest to users, this information can be used to identify what types of non-topical information users are searching for, which may lead to the addition of this information into the service. For example, some discovery services allow for the addition of library hours, events, database listings, and other nonmaterial-related metadata. Most discovery services are also able to provide a listing of the most popular search terms submitted by users. Libraries may be interested in trending the topics that users are interested in so they can

Using technical service "back-end" activity Stats to guide "front-end" activities (see next page)

customize their instructional or outreach services or programs. Also, libraries may find value in using the search queries to run and evaluate test searches in evaluations of new products.

FUTURE TRENDS AND CHALLENGES

With users expecting innovative services and access to an ever-growing portfolio of web-based resources, libraries must continually evaluate their operations in order to determine best practices for achieving long-term organizational goals and objectives while still meeting users' immediate needs. Assessment activities and projects in acquisitions will continue to grow in importance as administrators and librarians try to make better-informed, evidence-based decisions on collections, budgets and online resources.

Collaborative Assessment

Trend

Library assessment is moving toward a comprehensive model. As such, assessment plans and projects are directed by administrators and are coordinated by collaborative, interdepartmental groups, such as assessment committees. A large assessment project in acquisitions may require input and staff collaboration from collection development, systems or information technology, the budget office, and other departments across the library.

Challenges *determining man-hours*

Determining staff roles and the number of hours to be spent on any given assessment project are issues that libraries must anticipate. Having a central assessment group or committee assist in these multi-departmental projects could be helpful to the management and reporting processes. The managers in departments engaged in cross-departmental assessment must be ready and willing to allow their staff to participate for an agreed-upon amount of time per project. Retaining and developing staff expertise in acquisitions and e-resource assessment will be another challenge. Often, acquisitions assessment projects require knowledge and skills in multiple areas of the library and/or multiple systems that are used to gather, manipulate, and report data. Developing training programs to address these gaps in staff knowledge and skills can free key people for other projects and empower staff to use their newly gained skills.

Budgets and Collections

Trend

As the percentage of a library's collection budget devoted to the purchase and license of increasingly expensive online resources continues to expand, acquisitions assumes some responsibility for collection management. Specifically, acquisitions becomes an integral part of providing efficient online service to users, since so often acquisitions must resolve access issues and problems directly with vendors, publishers, and other content providers.

Challenges

Beyond analyzing the simple but important cost and usage metrics of various online products, it is important to consider the qualitative aspects of resources and how they support the institution's mission. In-depth collection and budget assessment will involve both qualitative and quantitative analyses and ideally should be approached as a collaborative partnership between collection managers and acquisitions. Extracting data from some systems in a useful format can be problematic, and since many library systems are not fully integrated with each other, linking or comparing data across systems can be time-consuming. As the library systems market continues to consolidate, native system integrations may ease this burden.

Vendor/Publisher Relations

Trend

Virtually all libraries rely on vendors and publishers to provide online content and associated services. Assessment reports, however, can vary widely from one vendor to the next. The costs for these resources also continue to increase, and negotiating licensing agreements that represent the interests of both parties continues to be a challenge.

Challenges

While most vendors offer usage reports, few provide assessment reports that include cost, cost-per-use, and subject analysis. To perform a complete assessment, libraries must merge data from multiple systems and reports. Libraries must also assess the price they are paying for resources, and communicate with publishers and vendors about resource affordability, especially when usage is factored in.

Merging Data

Trend

The reality of today's complex library world is that there are an amazing number of software and systems being employed across departments that enable data to be extracted and compiled, often from a variety of platforms, in order to perform assessment. The need for powerful analytics and statistical software and for an understanding of the principles of quantitative and qualitative assessment is continually increasing. Also increasing is the consolidation in the library systems market. While this consolidation brings system integration, it also has the potential to decrease the competition in the market.

Challenges

To perform any in-depth assessment of data extracted from more than one source often necessitates merging the information and data from more than one system or software. More often than not, staff must merge the siloed data by their own labor and methods. Training programs on the software and skills needed for advanced data manipulation and the effective use of assessment methods are needed to update technical skills and elevate the level at which assessment takes place. Libraries must also pay attention to the systems currently being offered in the market. Due to the rapid pace of change the market has experienced, it may be difficult to keep track of what is offered and by whom. Libraries must advocate that the systems they are considering or have already purchased include or are enhanced to include the tools and features needed to both increase workflow efficiencies and perform advanced assessment.

Project Management Software and Approaches

Trend

Libraries are increasingly using project management software. These tools, such as Teamwork, BaseCamp, and Trello, are designed for managing projects with multiple people sharing the workload. As libraries conduct assessment studies across departments and divisions, having a centralized tool that provides staff options regarding assignments and schedules, data warehousing, file-sharing, report generation, and instantaneous communication will be extremely helpful going forward. Even using a comparatively simple Gantt chart to organize and maintain the deadlines for each step in an assessment project can prove beneficial. How the management of a project is approached can also impact the success of the project. Libraries are further borrowing from the information technology industry through the use of Agile and other related project management principles to facilitate the efficient management of projects.[35]

Challenges

Determining the right project software tool from a wealth of choices in the market requires a systematic and comprehensive review. Before selecting the method or project tool to use in an assessment project, libraries must also decide if it is worth the time needed for multiple staff to learn a new software or application, and the cost of the software, if any. Libraries conducting numerous and cross-departmental assessments, or that are involved in an assessment project that is large and comprehensive, may find such project management tools useful. Otherwise, it might be easier and faster for library staff to use more customary approaches, such as a shared server space or cloud storage, to store and retrieve data. *not overthinking the wheel*

Communicating the Results of Assessment

Trend

For an assessment project to be truly successful, the librarians and staff will have to parlay the results into a clear, concise message that tells a meaningful story to colleagues, faculty, administrators, and other stakeholders of the library. Data visualization tools can be employed to make the data meaningful and easy to review.

Challenges

Within the library, the hurdles for relaying information to colleagues and administrators are usually associated with synthesizing data and simplifying the technical aspects of a project. Many assessment projects entail tools and reports that are very intricate and delve deep into integrated library systems and software applications, or that involve highly technical terms and methodologies. Using data visualization tools to report on assessment activities provides a way to quickly explain and communicate results.

CONCLUSION

The assessment of acquisitions and e-resources continues to evolve in function and relevance, especially as acquisitions and e-resource departments take on more collection development and strategy roles. Effective assessment can succeed if there is collaboration within and across library departments. Leveraging the knowledge, skills, and expertise held by acquisitions, collection development, and e-resource professionals will ensure that these collaborative efforts are successful. While many of the traditional library statistics and metrics are still collected and relevant to assessment, many new activities taking place in acquisitions and e-resources are now critical to library success. Dedicated staff time and assessment training programs to boost the staff's assessment skills will be necessary to meet these challenges. Though the multifaceted nature of acquisitions and e-resource assessment may be overwhelming, there are basic metrics that can be produced to assess key areas. While some of these metrics may feed into annual statistics surveys, others may be useful for internal assessment projects. As discovery and management systems for online resources continue to grow in complexity, future assessment activities should address these systems' functionality for both library staff and users. New systems must effectively deliver content to users while also efficiently providing control to staff over the management of resources and related data. While there are many challenges in assessing acquisitions and e-resources, the associated opportunities and results from assessment activities offer libraries the potential to improve a wide range of library services and operations that ultimately benefit the users.

NOTES

1. Marshal Breeding, "Library Systems Report 2018: New Technologies Enable an Expanded Vision of Library Services," *American Libraries,* May 1, 2018, https://americanlibrariesmagazine.org/2018/05/01/library-systems-report-2018/.
2. Marshall Breeding, "Library Services Platforms: A Maturing Genre of Products," *Library Technology Reports* 51, no. 4 (2015), http://dx.doi.org/10.5860/ltr.51n4.
3. Peter McCracken, "Current and Future Library Catalogs: An Introduction to FOLIO," *Against the Grain* 30, no. 1 (February 2018): 12–16.
4. "Standardized Usage Statistics Harvesting Initiative (SUSHI) Protocol (ANSI/NISO Z39.93–2014)," NISO, https://www.niso.org/standards-committees/sushi.
5. Emily Singley, "To Bento or Not to Bento—Displaying Search Results," *Usable Libraries* (blog), January 4, 2016, http://emilysingley.net/usablelibraries/to-bento-or-not-to-bento-displaying-search-results/.

6. "OpenAthens," OpenAthens (part of Eduserv), https://openathens.org/.

7. "RA21: Resource Access for the 21st Century," International Association of Scientific, Technical, and Medical Publishers (STM) and the National Information Standards Organization (NISO), https://ra21.org/.

8. Clarke Lakovakis, "Introduction to R for Libraries," Association of Library Collections and Technical Services, webinar, May 9–30, 2018, www.ala.org/alcts/confevents/ upcoming/webinar/IntrotoR.

9. "Academic Library Information Center," IPEDS, National Center for Education Statistics, https://nces.ed.gov/ipeds/report-your-data/resource-center-academic -libraries.

10. "ACRL Academic Library Trends and Statistics: Annual Survey—Instructions and Definitions," Association of College and Research Libraries, revised August 2017, https://acrl.countingopinions.com/docs/acrl/2017Instructions_12_07_17.pdf.

11. "ARL Statistics: Annual Library Surveys," Association of Research Libraries, https:// www.arlstatistics.org/home.

12. "Public Libraries Survey," Institute of Museum and Library Services, https://www.imls .gov/research-evaluation/data-collection/public-libraries-survey.

13. "State Data Coordinator Directory," Public Library Survey, Report Your PLS Data, Institute of Museum and Library Services, https://www.imls.gov/research-evaluation/ data-collection/public-libraries-survey/report-your-pls-data/state-data-coordinators.

14. "ARL Statistics 2016–2017 Worksheet," Association of Research Libraries, https:// www.arlstatistics.org/documents/admin/17arlstatistics.pdf. See questions 7, 7a, 7b, and 7c.

15. "2017 ACRL Survey Form," Association of College and Research Libraries, https://acrl .countingopinions.com/docs/acrl/ACRL2017SurveyForm.pdf. See questions 20, 20a, 21, 21a, 21b, 22, and 23; note that only 20, 21, and 22 are summed in order to provide the total expenses for materials and services.

16. "FY 2017 Public Libraries Survey, PLS Web Portal User's Guide, Appendix A: Survey Instrument," Institute of Museum and Library Services, p. 45, https://www.imls.gov/ sites/default/files/pls_users_guide_fy2017.pdf.

17. An ERMS may be stand-alone or incorporated into some next-generation ILS or library services platform.

18. "ARL Statistics Best Practices for Deduplicating Serial Titles," Association of Research Libraries, last updated December 4, 2008, www.libqual.org/documents/admin/dedupe _best_practices.doc.

19. David Van Kleeck, Hikaru Nakano, Gerald Langford, Trey Shelton, Jimmie Lundgren, and Allison Jai O'Dell, "Managing Bibliographic Data Quality for Electronic Resources," *Cataloging & Classification Quarterly* 55, no. 7–8 (2017): 560–77, https://doi .org/10.1080/01639374.2017.1350777.

20. Some users cannot resist reshelving items, or they may unintentionally ignore signage asking them to leave materials on a table or cart.

21. "Project COUNTER," COUNTER, https://www.projectcounter.org/.

22. "SUSHI for Librarians," National Information Standards Organization, https://groups .niso.org/workrooms/sushi/librarians/.

23. "NISO Homepage," National Information Standards Organization, https://groups.niso .org/home.

24. "Registries of Compliance," COUNTER, https://www.projectcounter.org/about/ register/.

25. Mitchell Dunkley, *Friendly Guide to COUNTER Journal Reports: A Guide for Librarians* (COUNTER, 2016), https://www.projectcounter.org/wp-content/uploads/2016/03/ Journal-pdf.pdf.

26. Mitchell Dunkley, *Friendly Guide to COUNTER Book Reports: A Guide for Librarians* (COUNTER, 2016), https://www.projectcounter.org/wp-content/uploads/2016/03/ Library-pdf.pdf.

27. Mitchell Dunkley, *Friendly Guide to COUNTER Database Reports: A Guide for Librarians* (COUNTER, 2016), https://www.projectcounter.org/wp-content/uploads/ 2016/03/Database-pdf.pdf.

28. "Hints and Tips," USUS: A Community Website on Usage, www.usus.org.uk/hints -tips/.

29. "COUNTER Code of Practice: General Information," Release 4, COUNTER, https:// www.projectcounter.org/code-of-practice-sections/general-information/.

30. "COUNTER Code of Practice: Abstract," Release 5, COUNTER, https://www.pro jectcounter.org/code-of-practice-five-sections/abstract/.

31. "Release 4 COUNTER Code of Practice, Usage Reports, List 1: List of COUNTER Usage Reports," COUNTER, https://www.projectcounter.org/code-of-practice -sections/usage-reports/.

32. Xi Niu, Tao Zhang, and Hsin-liang Chen, "Study of User Search Activities with Two Discovery Tools at an Academic Library," *International Journal of Human-Computer Interaction* 30, no. 5 (2014): 422–33, https://doi.org/10.1080/10447318.2013.873281.

33. Sandra L. De Groote, Deborah D. Blecic, and Kristin Martin, "Measures of Health Sciences Journal Use: A Comparison of Vendor, Link-Resolver, and Local Citation Statistics," *Journal of the Medical Library Association* 101, no. 2 (2013): 110–19, https:// dx.doi.org/10.3163%2F1536–5050.101.2.006.

34. Jean Barron, "Why and How to Measure the Use of Electronic Resources," *LIBER Quarterly: The Journal of the Association of European Research Libraries* 18, no. 3–4 (2008): 459–63, http://doi.org/10.18352/lq.7944.

35. Michael Perry, "Work Smart: Applying Project Management Techniques to Library Projects," Library Leadership and Management Association webinar, August 24, 2016, www.ala.org/llama/sites/ala.org.llama/files/content/8–24–16%20Slides%20-%20 Project%20Management%20for%20librarians.pdf.

REFERENCES

Association of College and Research Libraries. "ACRL Academic Library Trends and Statistics: Annual Survey—Instructions and Definitions." Revised August 2017. https://acrl.countingopinions.com/docs/acrl/2017Instructions_12_07_17.pdf.

———. "2017 ACRL Survey Form." https://acrl.countingopinions.com/docs/acrl/ACRL2017SurveyForm.pdf.

Association of Research Libraries. "ARL Statistics: Annual Library Surveys." https://www.arlstatistics.org/home.

———. "ARL Statistics 2016–2017 Worksheet." https://www.arlstatistics.org/documents/admin/17arlstatistics.pdf.

———. "ARL Statistics Best Practices for Deduplicating Serial Titles." Last updated December 4, 2008. www.libqual.org/documents/admin/dedupe_best_practices.doc.

Barron, Jean, "Why and How to Measure the Use of Electronic Resources." *LIBER Quarterly: The Journal of the Association of European Research Libraries* 18, no. 3–4 (2008): 459–63. http://doi.org/10.18352/lq.7944.

Breeding, Marshall. "Library Services Platforms: A Maturing Genre of Products." *Library Technology Reports* 51, no. 4 (2015). http://dx.doi.org/10.5860/ltr.51n4.

———. "Library Systems Report 2018: New Technologies Enable an Expanded Vision of Library Services." *American Libraries*, May 1, 2018. https://americanlibrariesmagazine.org/2018/05/01/library-systems-report-2018/.

COUNTER. "COUNTER Code of Practice: Abstract." Release 5. https://www.projectcounter.org/code-of-practice-five-sections/abstract/.

———. "COUNTER Code of Practice: General Information." Release 4. https://www.projectcounter.org/code-of-practice-sections/general-information/.

———. "Project COUNTER." https://www.projectcounter.org/.

———. "Registries of Compliance." https://www.projectcounter.org/about/register/.

———. "Release 4 COUNTER Code of Practice, Usage Reports, List 1: List of COUNTER Usage Reports." https://www.projectcounter.org/code-of-practice-sections/usage-reports/.

De Groote, Sandra L., Deborah D. Blecic, and Kristin Martin. "Measures of Health Sciences Journal Use: A Comparison of Vendor, Link-Resolver, and Local Citation Statistics." *Journal of the Medical Library Association* 101, no. 2 (2013): 110–19. https://dx.doi.org/10.3163%2F1536–5050.101.2.006.

Dunkley, Mitchell, *Friendly Guide to COUNTER Book Reports: A Guide for Librarians.* COUNTER, 2016. https://www.projectcounter.org/wp-content/uploads/2016/03/Library-pdf.pdf.

———. *Friendly Guide to COUNTER Database Reports: A Guide for Librarians.* COUNTER, 2016. https://www.projectcounter.org/wp-content/uploads/2016/03/Database-pdf.pdf.

————. *Friendly Guide to COUNTER Journal Reports: A Guide for Librarians.* COUNTER, 2016. https://www.projectcounter.org/wp-content/uploads/2016/03/Journal-pdf.pdf.

Institute of Museum and Library Services. "FY 2017 Public Libraries Survey, PLS Web Portal User's Guide, Appendix A: Survey Instrument," p. 45. https://www.imls.gov/sites/default/files/pls_users_guide_fy2017.pdf.

————. "Public Libraries Survey." https://www.imls.gov/research-evaluation/data-collection/public-libraries-survey.

————. "State Data Coordinator Directory." Public Library Survey, Report Your PLS Data. https://www.imls.gov/research-evaluation/data-collection/public-libraries-survey/report-your-pls-data/state-data-coordinators.

International Association of Scientific, Technical, and Medical Publishers (STM) and the National Information Standards Organization (NISO). "RA21: Resource Access for the 21st Century." https://ra21.org/.

Lakovakis, Clarke. "Introduction to R for Libraries." Association of Library Collections and Technical Services webinar, May 9–30, 2018. www.ala.org/alcts/confevents/upcoming/webinar/IntrotoR.

McCracken, Peter. "Current and Future Library Catalogs: An Introduction to FOLIO." *Against the Grain* 30, no. 1 (February 2018): 12–16.

National Center for Education Statistics. "Academic Library Information Center." IPEDS. https://nces.ed.gov/ipeds/report-your-data/resource-center-academic-libraries.

National Information Standards Organization. "NISO Homepage." https://groups.niso.org/home.

————. "Standardized Usage Statistics Harvesting Initiative (SUSHI) Protocol (ANSI/NISO Z39.93–2014)." https://www.niso.org/standards-committees/sushi.

————. "SUSHI for Librarians." https://groups.niso.org/workrooms/sushi/librarians/.

Niu, Xi, Tao Zhang, and Hsin-liang Chen. "Study of User Search Activities with Two Discovery Tools at an Academic Library." *International Journal of Human-Computer Interaction* 30, no. 5 (2014): 422–33. https://doi.org/10.1080/10447318.2013.873281.

OpenAthens (part of Eduserv). "OpenAthens." https://openathens.org/.

Perry, Michael. "Work Smart: Applying Project Management Techniques to Library Project." Library Leadership and Management Association (LLAMA) webinar, August 24, 2016. www.ala.org/llama/sites/ala.org.llama/files/content/8-24-16%20Slides%20-%20Project%20Management%20for%20librarians.pdf.

Singley, Emily, "To Bento or Not to Bento—Displaying Search Results." *Usable Libraries* (blog), January 4, 2016. http://emilysingley.net/usablelibraries/to-bento-or-not-to-bento-displaying-search-results/.

USUS: A Community Website on Usage. "Hints and Tips." www.usus.org.uk/hints-tips/.

Van Kleeck, David, Hikaru Nakano, Gerald Langford, Trey Shelton, Jimmie Lundgren, and Allison Jai O'Dell. "Managing Bibliographic Data Quality for Electronic Resources." *Cataloging & Classification Quarterly* 55, no. 7–8 (2017): 560–77. https://doi.org/10.108 0/01639374.2017.1350777.

FURTHER READINGS BY TOPICAL AREA

Staffing and Workflow

Anderson, Elsa K. "Workflow Analysis." In *Electronic Resource Management Systems: A Workflow Approach, Library Technology Reports*, no. 3 (April 2014): 23–29. https:// journals.ala.org/index.php/ltr/article/view/4491.

Bazirjian, Rosann. "After Assessment: Application of the Results of an Acquisitions Teams Survey." *Library Collections, Acquisitions, & Technical Services* 25, no. 4 (winter 2001): 371–87. https://doi-org.lp.hscl.ufl.edu/10.1016/S1464–9055(01)00223–8.

"Core Competencies for Acquisitions Professionals." Education Committee of the Acquisitions Section of the Association of Library Collections and Technical Services, a division of the American Library Association. 2018. http://hdl.handle.net/11213/9058.

"Core Competencies for Electronic Resources Librarians." NASIG. 2016. www.nasig.org/ site_page.cfm?pk_association_webpage_menu=310&pk_association_webpage=7802.

Garza, Lanette. "The E-Resources Playbook: A Guide for Establishing Routine Assessment of E-Resources." *Technical Services Quarterly* 43, no. 3 (2017): 243–56. https://doi.org/10 .1080/07317131.2017.1321373.

Hamlett, Alexandra, "Keeping Up with the Flow: Electronic Resource Workflow and Analysis." *The Serials Librarian* 70, no. 1–4 (2016): 168–74. https://doi.org/10.1080/036 1526X.2016.1159434.

Hart, Katherine A., and Tammy S. Sugarman. "Developing an Interdepartmental Training Program for E-Resources Troubleshooting." *The Serials Librarian* 71, no. 1 (2016): 25–38. https://doi.org/10.1080/0361526X.2016.1169569.

Miller, Laura Newton, David Sharp, and Wayne Jones. "70% and Climbing: E-Resources, Books, and Library Restructuring." *Collection Management* 39, no. 2–3 (2014): 110–26. https://doi.org/10.1080/01462679.2014.901200.

Mugridge, Rebecca, and Nancy M. Poehlmann. "Internal Customer Service Assessment of Cataloging, Acquisitions, and Library Systems." *OCLC Systems & Services: International Digital Library Perspectives* 31, no. 4 (2015): 219–48. https://doi.org/10.1108/OCLC -12–2014–0037.

Stouthuysen, Kristof, Michael Swiggers, Anne-Mie Reheul, and Filip Roodhooft. "Time-Driven Activity-Based Costing for a Library Acquisition Process: A Case Study in a Belgian University." *Library Collections, Acquisitions, and Technical Services* 34, no. 2–3 (2010): 83–91. https://doi.org/10.1016/j.lcats.2010.05.003.

Torbert, Christina, "Cost-per-Use versus Hours-per-Report: Usage Reporting and the Value of Staff Time." *The Serials Librarian* 68, no. 1–4 (2015). https://doi.org/10.1080/036152 6X.2015.1017705.

Budgets

Brillon, Alicia. "Collection Analysis When the Budget Decreases." *Legal Reference Services Quarterly* 30 (2011): 289–98. https://doi.org/10.1080/0270319X.2011.625863.

Catalano, Amy J., and William T. Caniano. "Book Allocations in a University Library: An Evaluation of Multiple Formulas." *Collection Management* 38, no. 2 (2013): 192–212. https://doi.org/10.1080/01462679.2013.792306.

Enoch, Todd, and Karen R. Harker. "Planning for the Budget-ocalypse: The Evolution of a Serials/ER Cancellation Methodology." *The Serials Librarian* 68, no. 1–4 (2015): 282–89. https://doi.org/10.1080/0361526X.2015.1025657.

Enoch, Todd, and Mark Henley. "Finding the Target: An Experiment in Benchmarking." *The Serials Librarian* 70, no. 1–4 (2016): 217–23. https://doi.org/10.1080/036152 6X.2016.1156963.

Ferguson, Anthony W. "Collection Assessment and Acquisitions Budgets." *Journal of Library Administration* 17, no. 2 (1992): 59–70. https://doi.org/10.1300/J111v17n02_06.

Kirk, Rachel, and Kelli Getz. "Accounting Techniques for Acquisitions Librarians." *The Serials Librarian* 62 (2012): 17–23. https://doi.org/10.1080/0361526X.2012.652454.

Lyons, Lucy Eleonore, and John Blosser. "An Analysis and Allocation System for Library Collections Budgets: The Comprehensive Allocation Process (CAP)." *Journal of Academic Librarianship* 38, no. 5 (2012). https://doi.org/10.1016/j.acalib.2012.07.006.

Nabe, Jonathan and David C. Fowler. "Leaving the 'Big Deal' . . . Five Years Later." *The Serials Librarian* 69, no. 1–4 (2015): 20–28. http://dx.doi.org/10.1080/036152 6X.2015.1048037.

Nash, Jacob L., and Karen R. McElfresh. "A Journal Cancellation Survey and Resulting Impact on Interlibrary Loan." *Journal of the Medical Library Association* 104, no. 4 (2016): 296–301. https://dx.doi.org/10.3163%2F1536–5050.104.4.008.

Trail, Mary Ann, and Kerry Chang-Fitzgibbon. "Using Assessment to Make Difficult Choices in Cutting Periodicals." *The Serials Librarian* 65, no. 1–4 (2012): 159–63. https://doi.org/10.1080/0361526X.2012.652931.

Library Systems

Asher, Andrew D., Lynda M. Duke, and Suzanne Wilson. "Paths of Discovery: Comparing the Search Effectiveness of EBSCO Discovery Service, Summon, Google Scholar, and Conventional Library Resources." *College & Research Libraries* 74, no. 5 (2013): 464–88. https://doi.org/10.5860/crl-374.

Belford, Rebecca. "Evaluating Library Discovery Tools through a Music Lens." *Library Resources and Technical Services* 58, no. 1 (2014): 49–72. http://dx.doi.org/10.5860/lrts.58n1.49.

Chickering, F. William, and Sharon Q. Yang. "Evaluation and Comparison of Discovery Tools: An Update." *Information Technology and Libraries* 33, no. 2 (2014): 5–30. https://doi.org/10.6017/ital.v33i2.3471.

Collins, Carol Morgan, and Eliza Fink. "How to Select a New ILS/LSP Vendor." *Computers in Libraries* 38, no. 3 (2018): 4–9. www.infotoday.com/cilmag/apr18/Collins-Fink—How-to-Select-a-New-ILS-LSP-Vendor.shtml.

Deodato, Joseph. "Evaluating Web-Scale Discovery: A Step-by-Step Guide." *Information Technology and Libraries* 34, no. 2 (2015): 19–75. https://doi.org/10.6017/ital.v34i2.5745.

Ellero, Nadine P. "An Unexpected Discovery: One Library's Experience with Web-Scale Discovery Service (WSDS) Evaluation and Assessment." *Journal of Library Administration* 53, no. 5–6 (2013): 323–43. http://dx.doi.org/10.1080/01930826.2013.876824.

Gallagher, Matt. "How to Conduct a Library Services Platform Review and Selection." *Computers in Libraries,* October 2016: 20–22. www.infotoday.com/cilmag/oct16/Gallagher—How-to-Conduct-a-Library-Services-Platform-Review-and-Selection.shtml.

Prommann, Merlen, and Tao Zhang. "Applying Hierarchical Task Analysis Method to Discovery Layer Evaluation." *Information Technology and Libraries* 34, no. 1 (2015): 77–105. https://doi.org/10.6017/ital.v34i1.5600.

Vendors, Publishers, and Content/Service Providers

Anderson, Elsa K., Stephen Maher, and Bill Maltarich, "Evaluating the Consortia Purchase: Journal Usage in a Multi-Institution Setting." *Collaborative Librarianship* 8, no. 3 (2016): 130–43. https://digitalcommons.du.edu/collaborativelibrarianship/vol8/iss3/6.

Besen, Stanley M., and Sheila Nataraj Kirby. "Library Demand for E-Books and E-Book Pricing: An Economic Analysis." *Journal of Scholarly Publishing* 45, no. 2 (2014): 128–41. https://muse.jhu.edu/article/531407.

Busby, Lorraine. "The Business of Serials: Elevating Aggregator Evaluation." *The Serials Librarian* 69, no. 2 (2015): 126–32. https://doi.org/10.1080/0361526X.2015.1074439.

Davis, Susan, Deberah England, Tina Feick, and Kimberly Steinle. "Why Using a Subscription Agent Makes Good Sense." *The Serials Librarian* 70, no. 1–4 (2016): 277–87. https://doi.org/10.1080/0361526X.2016.1157739.

Erb, Rachel Augello, and Nancy Hunter. "Prelude, Tumult, Aftermath: An Academic Library Perspective on the SWETS B.V. Bankruptcy." *The Serials Librarian* 69, no. 1–4 (2015): 277–84. https://doi.org/10.1080/0361526X.2015.1118423.

Lam, Helen. "Library Acquisitions Management: Methods to Enhance Vendor Assessment and Library Performance." *Library Administration & Management* 18, no. 3 (2004): 146–54. *Library Literature & Information Science Full Text (H.W. Wilson),* EBSCOhost.

Pan, Denise, and Yem Fong. "Return on Investment for Collaborative Collection Development: A Cost-Benefit Evaluation of Consortia Purchasing." *Collaborative Librarianship* 2, no. 4 (2010): 183–92. https://digitalcommons.du.edu/collaborativelibrar ianship/vol12/iss4/3.

Zula, Floyd M. "Creative Outsourcing: Assessment and Evaluation." *Library Acquisitions* 21 (1997): 89–91.

Acquisition Methods

Alan, Robert, Tina E. Chrzastowski, Lisa German, and Lynn Wiley. "Approval Plan Profile Assessment in Two Large ARL Libraries: University of Illinois at Urbana-Champaign and Pennsylvania State University." *Library Resources and Technical Services* 54, no. 2 (2010): 64–76. http://dx.doi.org/10.5860/lrts.54n2.64.

Austin, Ronald. "An Evaluation of a Blanket Order Plan for French Publications." *Collection Management* 10, no. 3/4 (1988): 137–48.

Childress, Boyd, and Nancy Gibbs. "Collection Assessment and Development Using B/NA Approval Plan Referral Slips." *Collection Management* 11, no. 1/2 (1989): 137–43.

Dewland, Jason C., and Andrew See. "Notes on Operations: Patron Driven Acquisitions: Determining the Metrics for Success." *Library Resources and Technical Services* 59, no. 1 (2015): 13–23. http://dx.doi.org/10.5860/lrts.59n1.13.

Downey, Kay, Yin Zhang, Cristobal Urbano, and Tom Klinger. "A Comparative Study of Print Book and DDA Ebook Acquisitions and Use." *Technical Services Quarterly* 31, no. 2 (2014): 139–60. https://doi.org/10.1080/07317131.2014.875379.

Goertzen, Melissa J. "Applying Quantitative Methods to E-Book Collections." *Library Technology Reports* 53, no. 4 (2017): 5–31. http://dx.doi.org/10.5860/ltr.53n4.

Herrera, Gail. "Testing the Patron-Driven Model: Availability Analysis of First-Time Use Books." *Collection Management* 40, no. 1 (2015): 3–16. https://doi.org/10.1080/01462679.2014.965863.

Jahre, Benjamin G. "Analysis of the Decision to Implement an Approval Plan at the R.B. House Undergraduate Library at the University of North Carolina at Chapel Hill: A Case Study." Master's thesis, University of North Carolina at Chapel Hill, 2013. https://cdr.lib.unc.edu/record/uuid:445b50e8-ec2a-42ac-bedf-ed2f5e3b293a.

Jones, Elisabeth A., and Paul N. Courant. "Monographic Purchasing Trends in Academic Libraries: Did the 'Serials Crisis' Really Destroy the University Press?" *Journal of Scholarly Publishing* 46, no. 1 (October 2014): 43–70. https://muse.jhu.edu/article/555837.

Ke, Irene, Wenli Gau, and Jackie Bronicki, "Does Title-by-Title Selection Make a Difference? A Usage Analysis on Print Monograph Purchasing." *Collection Management* 42, no. 1 (2017): 34–47. https://doi.org/10.1080/01462679.2016.1249040.

Kerby, Erin E., and Kelli Trei. "Minding the Gap: eBook Package Purchasing." *Collection Building* 34, no. 4 (2015): 113–18. https://doi.org/10.1108/CB-06-2015-0008.

Kohn, Karen. "Worth the Wait? Using Past Patterns to Determine Wait Periods for E-Books Released after Print." *College & Research Libraries* 79, no. 1 (2018): 35–51. https://doi .org/10.5860/cr1.79.1.35.

Mays, Antje. "Biz of Acq—An Environmental Analysis Corroborating PDA and the Winthrop Example." *Against the Grain* 24, no. 2 (2012): 64–67. https://doi.org/ 10.7771/2380–176X.6153.

Pickett, Carmelita, Simona Tabacaru, and Jeanne Harrell. "E-Approval Plans in Research Libraries." *College & Research Libraries* 75, no. 2 (2014): 218–31. https://doi.org/ 10.5860/cr112–410.

Pongracz, Sennyey. "Assessing Blanket Order Effectiveness: A Neglected Task in Collection Development." *Library Acquisitions: Practice & Theory* 21, no. 4 (1997): 445–54.

Sammonds, Laurel Ivy. "Sustainable Collections: The Pay-per-View Model." *The Serials Librarian* 63, no. 2 (2012): 173–77. https://doi.org/10.1080/0361526X.2012.700778.

Sheehan, Beth, and Karen Hogenboom. "Assessing a Patron-Driven, Library-Funded Data Purchase Program." *Journal of Academic Librarianship* 43, no. 1 (2017): 49–56. https:// doi.org/10.1016/j.acalib.2016.10.001.

Spratt, Stephanie J. "Exploring the Evidence in Evidence-Based Acquisitions." *The Serials Librarian* 72, no. 1–4 (2017): 183–89. https://doi.org/10.1080/036152 6X.2017.1321901.

Tucker, James Cory. "Collection Assessment of Monograph Purchases at the University of Nevada, Las Vegas Libraries." *Collection Management* 34, no. 3 (2009): 157–81. https:// doi.org/10.1080/01462670902962959.

Waller, Jeffrey H. "Undergrads as Selectors: Assessing Patron-Driven Acquisitions at a Liberal Arts College." *Journal of Interlibrary Loan, Document Delivery, and Electronic Reserve* 23, no. 3 (2013): 127–48. https://doi.org/10.1080/1072303X.2013.851052.

Zhang, Yin. "Ebook ROI: A Longitudinal Study of Patron-Driven Acquisition Models." *Computers in Libraries,* June 2017. www.infotoday.com/cilmag/jun17/Zhang-Downey —Ebook-ROI.shtml.

Zhang, Yin, Kay Downey, Cristobal Urbano, and Tom Klingler. "A Scenario Analysis of Demand-Driven Acquisition (DDA) of E-Books in Libraries." *Library Resources & Technical Services* 59, no. 2 (2015): 84–93. https://journals.ala.org/index.php/lrts/article/ view/5681.

Statistics, Metrics, and Other Reports

Beile, Penny, Kanak Choudhury, and Morgan C. Wang, "Hidden Treasure on the Road to Xanadu: What Connecting Library Service Usage Data to Unique Student IDs Can Reveal." *Journal of Library Administration* 57, no. 2 (2017): 151–73. https://doi.org/ 10.1080/01930826.2016.1235899.

Borin, Jacqueline, and Hua Yi. "Assessing an Academic Library Collection through Capacity and Usage Indicators: Testing a Multi-Dimensional Model." *Collection Building* 30, no. 3 (2011): 120–25. https://doi.org/10.1108/01604951111146956.

Bucknell, Terry. "Garbage In, Gospel Out: Twelve Reasons Why Librarians Should Not Accept Cost-per-Download Figures at Face Value." *The Serials Librarian* 63, no. 2 (2012): 192–212. https://doi.org/10.1080/0361526X.2012.680687.

Coughlin, Daniel M., and Bernard J. Jansen. "Modeling Journal Bibliometrics to Predict Downloads and Inform Purchase Decisions at University Research Libraries." *Journal of the Association for Information Science and Technology* 67, no. 9 (2016): 2263–73. https://doi.org/10.1002/asi.23549.

Danielson, Robert. "A Dual Approach to Assessing Collection Development and Acquisitions for Academic Libraries." *Library Collections, Acquisitions, and Technical Services* 36, no. 3/4 (2012): 84–96. https://doi.org/10.1016/j.lcats.2012.09.002.

Diedrichs, Carol Pitts. "Making Choices: Vendors and Agents in the Assessment Process." *Library Collections, Acquisitions, and Technical Services* 23, no. 3 (1999): 321–38. http://dx.doi.org/10.1016/S1464–9055(99)00074–3.

Harker, Karen R., and Priya Kizhakkethil. "The Quick and the Dirty: The Good, the Bad, and the Ugly of Database Overlap at the Journal Title Level." *The Serials Librarian* 68, no. 1–4 (2015): 249–54. https://doi.org/10.1080/0361526X.2015.1016858.

Ladwig, J. Parker, and Thurston D. Miller. "Are First-Circulation Patterns for Monographs in the Humanities Different from the Sciences?" *Library Collections, Acquisitions, & Technical Services* 37, no. 3–4 (2013): 77–84. https://doi.org/10.1016/j.lcats.2013.09.004.

Litsey, Ryan, and Weston Mauldin. "Knowing What the Patron Wants: Using Predictive Analytics to Transform Library Decision Making." *Journal of Academic Librarianship* 44, no. 1 (2018): 140–44. https://doi.org/10.1016/j.acalib.2017.09.004.

Rathmel, Angie, and Lea Currie. "'Big Deals' and Squeaky Wheels: Taking Stock of Your Stats." *The Serials Librarian* 68, no. 1–4 (2015): 26–37. https://doi.org/10.1080/036152 6X.2015.1013754.

Scott, Mitchell. "Predicting Use: COUNTER Usage Data Found to Be Predictive of ILL Use and ILL Use to Be Predictive of COUNTER Use." *The Serials Librarian* 71, no. 1 (2016): 20–24. http://dx.doi.org/10.1080/0361526X.2016.1165783.

Sutton, Sarah. "A Model for Electronic Resource Value Assessment." *The Serials Librarian* 64, no. 1–4 (2013): 245–53. https://doi.org/10.1080/0361526X.2013.760417.

Wilde, Michelle, and Allison Level, "How to Drink from a Fire Hose without Drowning: Collection Assessment in a Numbers-Driven Environment." *Collection Management* 36, no. 4 (2011): 217–36. https://doi.org/10.1080/01462679.2011.604771.

Wiley, Lynn, Tina E. Chrzastowski, and Stephanie Baker. "A Domestic Monograph Collection Assessment in Illinois Academic Libraries: What Are We Buying and How Is It Used?" *Interlending and Document Supply* 39, no. 4 (2011): 167–75. https://doi.org/10.1108/02641611111187587.

SERIALS AND CONTINUING RESOURCES

Kristin Calvert and Whitney Jordan

Serials and continuing resources may be the most regularly assessed areas of technical services, certainly in collections. Though the formal vocabulary of assessment may not always be in use, the practice of reviewing, evaluating, and improving serial titles is alive and strong. Subscription resources dominate many library collections' budgets. By their very nature, subscriptions require ongoing care and attention; the simple act of renewing a serial title requires some measure of assessment, even if the only criterion is a price check. Annual serial price increases, especially when library budgets are unable to keep pace with them, make serials review projects a regular necessity for library acquisitions units. Scarce financial resources demand the regular assessment of serials collections by forcing libraries to be more critical of long-standing subscriptions in order to allow for new resources to meet emerging needs. It is incumbent upon librarians to regularly assess serials in order to be good stewards of the collections budget and to ensure that libraries are meeting their patrons' needs.

It is impossible to know how to approach the assessment process for serials without first understanding the reasons driving the assessment. The motivating factors behind the project will shape its scope and depth. Understanding why the assessment needs to happen will help align the review process with the desired outcomes. Four categories of outcomes typically drive the assessment of serials:

1. Achieve cost savings
2. Identify unmet content needs
3. Identify underperforming titles
4. Improve content delivery

Because subscription obligations represent 70–80 percent of most academic libraries' collections budgets, serials and electronic resources are the focus of most collection reviews. Given these rising costs, maintaining journal packages necessitates the allocation of an ever-increasing amount of money to the serials budget. If the budget is flat or slow to increase, libraries face the unpleasant option of either canceling subscriptions or cutting money from monographs; and choosing the latter course places the burden of budget problems on those disciplines that rely primarily on monographs.[1] Thus, cost savings will drive almost every assessment project.

Assessment is a time to revisit existing resources in order to evaluate whether the collection is continuing to meet the needs of the library and the patrons it serves. The second and third categories of outcomes—identifying unmet content needs and identifying underperforming titles—are two sides of that process. The need to identify resources in new collection areas is an excellent reason to undertake an assessment project. Academic programs grow over time, and the curricular or research focus of the department may not look the same as it did ten years ago. Likewise, resources that were seen as essential to the discipline might no longer be so—the library's serials collection often moves more slowly than the speed of innovation and changes in knowledge, and so underperforming titles must be canceled.

Finally, the processes within technical services for serials acquisitions continue to evolve. Consolidation among vendors and subscription agents has brought an upheaval to library business processes. Changes to the landscape of scholarly communications—whether from open access or the rise of academic networking sites like ResearchGate—are challenging the subscription paradigm to defend its role in delivering scholarly resources to patrons. Libraries are looking to new acquisitions models, like article pay-per-view, to provide quick access to research through flexible content delivery. Consequently, assessment can be driven as much by the needs of technical services units themselves as it is by external forces.

This chapter focuses on the main area of assessment for continuing resources: conducting a serials review. The majority of the chapter is given over to describing the process for undertaking large-scale collection review projects. The focus on serials includes journals, periodicals, standing orders, newspapers, and microfilm subscriptions; it omits databases, streaming resources, and other aggregated online research content. Special consideration is given to the review of large packages of e-journals—typically referred to as "Big Deals." The process for a comprehensive collection review of electronic resources (more broadly) is nearly identical to that of a serials review; these different types of assessment typically diverge only in their evaluative criteria and strategies for identifying alternative content.

Despite the overwhelming preference for and predominance of electronic journal content, it would be remiss of us not to devote some time to the management of print journals. The latter portion of the chapter looks at what are being called the legacy services for print serials. Obviously, the volume of print serials in libraries has waned from the height of the serials crisis of the 1990s. Nonetheless, the few that do remain still require staff processing. Assessment for print serials in this chapter encompasses staffing, workflows, and criteria to consider whether in-sourcing, outsourcing, or elimination is the best option for a department.   *against ch. 1*

SERIALS REVIEW PROJECTS

There is no shortage of case studies of libraries that have undertaken major serials reviews. The assessment process described herein reflects the authors' experience conducting multiple reviews, and their knowledge of these published studies.[2] A well-conducted serials review will include every aspect of serials assessment, from needs assessment to identifying cost efficiencies. While most serials reviews will result in cancellations, these approaches can be applied to all collection review scenarios. There are four phases to the assessment project (see table 4.1):

TABLE 4.1 • Project phases and sample project schedule for serials review

PROJECT PHASE	MILESTONE	DURATION	DEADLINE
Planning and Data Collection	Project team assembled		May 1
	Set goals for review	2 weeks	May 15
	Set assessment strategies	2 weeks	May 15
	Data collection and presentation	4–5 weeks	June 21
Stakeholder Review	Subject liaison review	2–4 weeks	July 21
	Faculty review	3–4 weeks	August 24
	Project team compiles feedback	1 week	August 31
Enacting Decisions	Project team prepares list of cancellations, etc.	1–2 weeks	September 15
	Feedback and approval to proceed from administrators	1–2 weeks	September 21
	Finalized list sent to subscription agent	1 week	September 30
	Publicize decisions	Ongoing	October–December
Post-Assessment Review	Track feedback concerning the process, decisions, etc.	Ongoing	January–April
	Monitor demand for cancelled serials from stakeholders or interlibrary loan	Ongoing	January–June

1. **Planning and data collection:** The project team is assembled and charged with determining the scope, goals, and strategies for the assessment; and the data are identified and gathered.

2. **Stakeholder review:** How will feedback be solicited and from whom; how will feedback be considered, and who holds final decision-making authority?

3. **Enacting decisions:** What changes will be made? The project team communicates decisions to patrons, publishers, consortia, or subscription agents; and the changes are reflected in library systems.

4. **Post-assessment review:** Feedback is tracked and integrated into future assessments; and the demand for new and canceled titles is monitored.

Planning and Data Collection

By the end of Phase 1, the aim will be to have assembled the project team, established the goals and strategies for the review, and gathered the data that will be presented to the project stakeholders. Before starting any assessment project, you should include the library administration in the plans. While they won't often be on the project team, their perspectives and support for the project will be invaluable.

While not the longest phase of the project, Phase 1 is the most labor-intensive portion for technical services. It is crucial for the project team to take the time to come to agreement on the broad goals for the review. What gets decided on during this phase, from the data presentation to the choice of metrics, is critical because the targeted outcomes and choice of strategies will have a huge impact on how stakeholders will review and make decisions about titles.

Project Team

Each library will have its own system for managing collection development decisions. Authority may be decentralized, consolidated, or decided collectively. In smaller libraries, one person may manage everything from selection and acquisition to access. In larger libraries, these responsibilities are distributed; data will pass through many pairs of hands throughout the project. Regardless, it is advisable to form a project team to manage the project. A successful team will include people who can gather and provide information on the serials under consideration; people who can provide subject-specific and resource-specific feedback; and serials and acquisitions staff who can act on the decisions. The team should include representatives from technical and public services, and representation from both areas should be sought if they are lacking. You should consider the following questions when drafting people to join the project team:

> Who in technical services needs to be involved, either directly or indirectly? The personnel needs can evolve over the course of the project, since each phase may require a different skill set. The needs of the decision-making phase are different from what is needed to carry out the decisions. Adjust the project team accordingly.

Do people have the requisite skill sets? Important skills include order and subscription knowledge; data management skills, especially with tools like Microsoft Excel or Access; accounting and budget knowledge; administrative perspective; and subject-matter expertise.

Project Goals

As mentioned earlier, review projects can have different triggering events. The trigger fundamentally shapes the scope of the project. One-time serials reviews often accompany tough budget times—either due to a reduction in funds, or because rising journal prices and inflation have outstripped available funding. In these cases, a fixed amount of money must be recouped through cancellations or other cost-saving measures. Serials can also be part of a regular collection review calendar in which portions of collections are reviewed at specific intervals. One advantage of a regular review cycle is the reduced overhead for the project; there are fewer titles to review, and it reduces the number of stakeholders that need to be pulled in for the project.

The first question to ask is: what resources are on the table? A massive budget cut might require a comprehensive approach, and an all-encompassing review. Several years ago, at Western Carolina University (in Cullowhee, North Carolina), the serials review was so extensive that the motto was "everything is on the table—even the TABLE is on the table." When was the last time the collections were closely examined? One can start with making small changes, one year at a time, when renewals are processed.

Selecting Titles to Be Reviewed

When starting a large-scale project, one way to keep the project manageable is to subdivide the project by format. Print journals, e-journals, journal packages, standing orders, newspapers, microforms, and even databases could be potential candidates for a format-specific serials review. Just as with a rolling cycle of review by subject areas, only one specific subcollection might be reviewed each year. Another alternative to a comprehensive review is to divide the work among the project team by subcollection. The timeline for making decisions may vary across collections, which may lend themselves to a staggered timetable; this can reduce the stress of getting all decisions made and processed simultaneously. Here are a few ways to break down a serials review:

- Comprehensive (all current orders)
- By format (e.g., microfilm, newspapers, popular magazines)
- Rolling, annual reviews
    ◊ By academic department or college
    ◊ By subject librarian

There are a few other smaller considerations for what titles to include. E-journal packages are often tied up in multiyear agreements; even if changes to the agreements are desired, it may not be possible to make them in the same year. New resources can also be problematic for serials reviews. A resource that has been recently acquired may not yet generate high use numbers. Depending on which criteria are used for the assessment, the new resource may be at a disadvantage compared to a more established resource. You should consider deferring cancellation decisions for newly acquired resources.

Journal Package Analysis and Assessment

Journal packages come in all different shapes and sizes. Traditionally, packages were set up through an agreement with the publisher in which the library would maintain current subscriptions and then be granted access to previously unsubscribed titles for an additional fee. This deal has often benefited libraries, especially smaller ones, because it offers them a chance to access a larger number of journals for not much more money than they were already paying. Once access to a vast number of journals is gained via a Big Deal, it becomes more difficult to imagine the collection without them.

Thinking about assessing, or even canceling, a large journal package can be daunting. Even discerning how a package is being paid for is not a straightforward process. Payments are often spread across titles, and titles are constantly changing publishers. It is tempting to avoid the headache of reviewing packages, but the cost of maintaining large journal packages will inevitably force libraries to question the sustainability and value of these Big Deals. The need to locate significant cost savings may compel libraries to consider making a change to a package, regardless of whether they want to or not. These packages represent sizable portions of the serials collection (both in terms of dollars and number of titles), and it is negligent to leave them out despite their challenges.

There is a growing body of literature devoted to the cost-benefit analysis of exiting Big Deal journal packages. The results of such exits have been mixed.[3] The breaking point where the benefits of cancellation outweigh the costs of continuing to subscribe to the package will be different for each library. Not only does the library stand to lose access to hundreds of journal titles, but the cost to individually subscribe to a handful of high-use titles often ends up being close to the entire amount of the package. For this reason, journal package assessments deserve to have their own set of outcomes, separate from the general serials assessment. As with other serials, the assessment of journal packages may be driven by budget crises or by routine evaluation.

Before digging in, you should review the license and payment structure for the package. There are many ways for journal packages to be billed, and knowing how titles within the package are structured will make a difference in how the package is reviewed. These questions will help the library know whether the package can be changed, or if cancellation will be an all-or-nothing endeavor. Later sections in this chapter will go into more detail about how these packages can be evaluated, and what metrics to consider. The following are some questions to ask when reviewing a journals package:

- Is the package made up of subscribed titles, access-only, or a combination of both? Many packages are priced based on a list of subscribed titles, plus a package upcharge. Others are priced into one lump sum.
- Is the library locked into a multiyear deal at a high inflation rate?
- Does the license require a minimum spend from the library? These rules limit the extent to which the library can make title-level cancellations.
- Can individual titles be swapped in and out? How much control (if any) does the library have over the title list?
- Are smaller or subject-based subcollections available?
- Is the subscription negotiated through a consortium?

Package cancellations may have broader implications if they were made as part of a consortial deal. These deals, at times, can be contingent upon all participants maintaining their subscriptions. If one library decides to cancel, it may cause the deal to fall apart or need to be renegotiated. It is worthwhile to contact the lead negotiator for these consortial arrangements as part of the data-gathering process. This person should be able to warn the library about the nature of the deal and whether cancellations will impact other libraries.

Project Strategies

At the outset, it is important to identify the strategies the project team will use to guide the review. Strategies and goals comprise the key factors that guide how titles will be targeted for review and which review criteria are used. When facing budget reductions, for instance, a guiding principle is often to do the least amount of harm to the collection, and to try to minimize the impact of cuts on students and researchers.[4] There may be cuts to the collection that can be made easily, without restricting access to needed content, especially if the collection has not been assessed in a while. If there are serials that are not being used, who will even notice when they are gone? While this is not always possible, it is an example of a user-centered approach to collection development. Here are some sample strategies: *user-centered approach*

- Prioritize the alternatives to losing access to content.
- Prioritize minimizing the effect of changes on a specific user-group (e.g., graduate students).
- Prioritize making equal cuts across subjects/collection areas.
- Prioritize protecting underserved or emergent subjects/collection areas.

Alternative Cost Savings (Non-Cancellations)

There are alternatives to cancellations for reducing expenses. For example, one can renegotiate subscription terms with the publisher. Publishers are often willing to be flexible in order to find the price point that will work within the library's budget. The library can also rein in spending by negotiating the inflation rate or extending the length of the contract. Going through a consortium (or other buying club) can provide better business terms because the deal has been centrally negotiated for a much larger group of libraries.[5] The library can also bring a package to their consortium, if it is not currently offered, and seek out other libraries that may be interested in joining.

Often overlooked are the fees charged by subscription agents. The service fees charged by these companies can and should be revisited regularly. A library with a 4 or 5 percent service charge on a Big Deal package may decide to seek cost savings by renewing directly with a publisher. However, working with a subscription agent to manage journal subscriptions provides many benefits, from streamlined invoicing to incentive programs for early payment or pre-payment; Grogg discusses these benefits in detail in an article in the *Journal of Electronic Resources Librarianship*.[6] Deciding to cut out a subscription agent might be monetarily advantageous, but there will be major drawbacks. The management of title lists for e-journal packages is one of the most difficult parts of maintaining access to these collections. The challenges of e-journal packages are discussed in more detail later in this chapter.

Selecting or changing a subscription agent may require initiating a request for proposal (or RFP) process. An RFP is a document with the library's requirements for a service used as a basis for sending a business proposal out to bid. Before sending out an RFP, be sure to check with the financial or accounting departments at the institution or municipality that has administrative authority over the library. There may be policies and price thresholds which govern when the library must send a request out to bid. More information on writing an RFP is available in the "Resources" section at the end of this chapter.

Evaluative Criteria

The decision of which criteria to use when evaluating serials deserves some thought and care. The criteria should be applicable across all serials titles. Consistency ensures that every person uses the same standards to review titles and that every title is judged by the same set of standards. At more than one point in the project, the library will face questions about its decisions and the process. Taking care early on to establish the standards for reviewing serials will make it much easier to defend and justify decisions when they are scrutinized by those outside the library. An excellent starting point is with the survey of cancellation factors conducted in 2006 by Mark Ware for the Association of Learned and Professional Society Publishers.[7]

Be wary of using metrics that are the easiest ones to gather. The criteria chosen should reflect the library's specific needs and be aligned with the project's guiding principles and strategy.[8] The library's collection development policy, strategic plan, and mission statement all inform which criteria are selected and how they are prioritized. The project team should consider the information that reviewers will need in order to evaluate a title. What are the types of decisions they will need to make? What is valued most highly by the library or institution? Not all metrics should have the same weight. The importance of each metric will depend on the project's scope and the institutional mission. For example, journal impact factors or journals in which faculty members' works are cited will matter much more to research-intensive institutions, but may be ignored in other settings.

The measures for evaluating serials can be grouped into three categories: availability, financial, and value.

Evaluative Criteria

I. Availability Measures

Format duplication: Does the library collect serials in multiple formats? In what cases?

Duplicated electronic access points: Is the journal available from more than one online source? Is the coverage comparable?

Embargos: How critical are the most recent issues of a journal? Does this vary across disciplines?

Indexing: Where is the journal indexed? Is it only available through the publisher's platform?

Full-text availability: Does the full text of an e-journal need to be on hand? Or are abstracts through an abstracting and indexing database sufficient?

On-demand availability: How easy is it to get an article through interlibrary loan? What is the typical turnaround time for ILL article requests? Does the publisher participate in any on-demand article service (e.g., Get It Now, Reprints Desk, article tokens, pay-per-view access)?

II. Financial Measures

Cost: This varies by discipline, but in terms of the bottom line, high-priced journals will bear additional scrutiny.

Cost-per-use: This is typically the annual cost divided by the number of uses (or article downloads) in a single year. You should establish a threshold for what a "high" cost-per-use means to the library (or discipline): $25? $50? $75? The number can be compared to the average cost of an ILL article, or the purchase price for per-article charges offered by an on-demand purchase.

Inflation rates: Which titles or packages have higher-than-average inflation rates (e.g., over 6 percent)? Does the license agreement cap these increases?[9]

License terms: Particularly for packages, does the publisher allow the library to swap or cancel titles in a package? (See the section on "Journal Package Analysis and Assessment" earlier in this chapter.) Is the library required to maintain subscriptions when titles transfer between publishers? Or to subscribe to newly launched titles?

Vendor: Is the publisher/vendor easy to work with? How responsive are their customer service reps? Are they able to provide timely invoicing that meets the library's needs?

III. Value Measures

Use: This is the most common metric for demand. Typically these comprise the number of article downloads for e-journals, and circulation/reshelving counts for print journals and microfilm.

Accreditation: Is the journal required for an academic program's accreditation?

Citations: Resources like Journal Citation Reports can provide subscribers with lists of journals where their institution's researchers have been cited.

Journal prestige: Does the institution highly value impact factors, Eigenfactors, or altmetrics to rank journals?

Curricular importance: How important is the journal to student education in the discipline? Is the program growing or declining at the institution?

Research importance: How important is the journal to the research done by scholars at the institution?

Unmet demand: Is there a high demand for the journal or journals in the discipline? Interlibrary loan requests or turn-away reports can demonstrate unmet need at the institution.

When journal packages are part of the review process, they deserve special attention. While the criteria used to assess packages are much the same as for individual titles, there is specific information that should be considered when reviewing these types of subscriptions.[10] Because of this, it is important to identify and separate package titles early on. Two additional categories of evaluative criteria for packages are business terms and license terms. While this section references Big Deal packages, the discussion applies to smaller e-journal packages as well.

There are business terms that put pressure on the library's budget without impacting the patron. This aspect of journal packages can drive decisions, but this behind-the-scenes maneuvering is challenging to communicate to patrons who never experience their impact or see the bill. Business terms vary, but some common themes are:

Inflation caps: Are price increases fixed over the duration of the contract?

Required pickups: Can the library opt out from adding new titles to the package? Is the library required to subscribe to new titles acquired by the publisher? Are these prices capped?

Swap and cancellation allowances: What percentage of the title list can the library cancel or exchange for other titles?

Multiyear licenses: Will the publisher reduce the subscription price or inflation rate if the library agrees to subscribe to a package for more than one year at a time?

Bail-out or hardship clauses: Does the library have a way to cancel before the end of the contract due to changes in its budget?

Nondisclosure agreements: Is the library barred from sharing contract terms or pricing with colleagues?

Aside from cost, there may be other rights and permissions the library is interested in adding to the package. The library's licensing requirements may have changed since the license was first signed. Irrespective of its satisfaction with the business terms, the library may want to inventory and assess what standard rights are included in all licenses. Licenses should be reviewed and updated every few years to ensure compliance with all state or institutional requirements and to ensure that they are meeting the needs of library users. Terms that might be negotiated could include:

- Text and data mining
- Electronic ILL sharing
- Use in coursepacks or in learning management systems
- Perpetual access/post-cancellation access: Will the library retain access to any content paid for during the subscription period?
- Scholarly sharing or self-archiving for authors in a repository

Data Collection and Management

The data used to support the evaluative criteria will come from many sources. Title and order information will come from the library system; usage statistics, indexing information, and online availability will come from publishers' web pages; and qualitative feedback will eventually be provided by faculty and library personnel. Juggling all of this electronic paperwork is one of the most challenging practical aspects of review. You must decide early on who should have responsibility for maintaining the files, and what access other people should have to them. Accidentally deleting data, or even sloppily sorting a spreadsheet, can undo weeks of work. Bear in mind that publishers' contracts may specify that cost, usage data, or both must be treated as confidential. Aspects of the data compiled and used for the serials review may need to be locked down—for instance, behind a firewall in an intranet. The sections that follow recommend some best practices for data management.

Keeping a Master List

You should keep a list of all titles that will be under review for the project. The list should include the minimum amount of bibliographic information needed to be able to locate the title and order information. This information could consist of the title, standard numbers, library system record numbers, format, and any fund codes to indicate which department or subject librarian has a stake in the subscription. This should not be a working list, but it should include a column to indicate a final decision.

Internal and External Data Sources

Reviewers will need information to make decisions based on the criteria and strategies developed for the review. It will not be practical to have reviewers look up information from each source title-by-title. In most cases, it is more efficient to export the data and compile them in a single location. This saves time by providing all the information in one place. It also ensures that the same metrics from the same sources are used for every title. Libraries using an electronic resource management system (ERMS) may be in a better starting position than libraries whose information is disaggregated. The downside to this approach is that it takes time and skill for technical services staff to locate, export, and manipulate the data into a usable form. There are many ways to do this, depending on the resources and skills of the people on the project team. The typical data sources accessed are:

> *Library system:* order and payment information, circulation information (checkouts and internal/in-house use)
>
> *E-journal holdings/A-Z lists:* alternate access online, coverage years, embargos
>
> *Indexing/abstracting information:* Ulrich's Serials Analysis System, or information that is available from subscription agents

Interlibrary loan: the number of borrowing and lending requests for the title

Third-party providers of impact measures: journal citation reports, Scopus, altmetrics, core subject lists, accrediting body requirements

Statistical repository/publisher sites: EBSCO's Usage Consolidation, 360 Counter, and the publisher's COUNTER reports, especially JR1, and JR5 in Release 4

The decision on which solution to use for the data-gathering will be dependent on the total number of serials under review and the tech-savviness of the technical services staff. A small number of titles can be compiled by hand, but the same cannot be said for hundreds or thousands of titles. But it is not only necessary to consider what tools the staff have the skills to work with; one also needs to consider what the stakeholder groups will be comfortable using. Most people are comfortable working with spreadsheets (with varying degrees of sophistication). There are also tools available to assist libraries with preparing data and working with more advanced techniques.[11] This section will briefly touch on several ways to manage storing and presenting data from multiple data sources. You should choose which option(s) work best for your library.

Relational databases (Access or MySQL): These have more sophisticated options for combining data sources and can export reports as PDFs or spreadsheets.

Spreadsheets (Excel): These are ubiquitous, and they include additional features for advanced users.
- The VLOOKUP function can pull information stored in a different table based on a common value.[12]
- Merge macros can be used to combine multiple worksheets.[13]
- Otherwise, you can manually enter data into a single workbook.

Regardless of which approach is chosen, the data will need to be standardized (or cleaned). Each source may use a different piece of information as the main identifier for records. Some may use ISSNs, whereas others may only have titles, and each may format those fields differently. For instance, ISSNs include hyphens (or not), and may be tracked using a print ISSN, e-ISSN, or have both. Title matching is possible, but it can be more difficult to match on text fields and account for the myriad ways that titles can be entered (e.g., initial articles, subtitles, abbreviations).

Specific Data for Journal Packages

When it comes to measuring the value of a journal package, it is difficult to know how to define value. A single journal taken on its own will be either high- or low-performing. But when there are hundreds of titles and years of usage statistics for each package, the value equation becomes more complex. The package is more than a collection of titles; its value is also affected by the terms of the contract governing the deal. Even with a firm understanding of the pricing structure and business terms, it is challenging to know how the package is actually performing and whether the library is getting a good return on investment (ROI). Each library will have a different threshold for what a good ROI entails. This section suggests several metrics that have been useful for drilling down into a package, and even comparing the performance of different packages head-to-head.

The first step will be to get the title lists and the most recent two or three years of usage data. There are three key package-level analytics to calculate. First, there is the cost-per-title, which can provide an average subscription cost for each title. This is especially helpful for packages that lack title-level pricing. Next, you can calculate the cost-per-article download at the package level. Lastly, you can look at the percentage of package titles with zero use. Some subscription agents can provide these package-level analytics as part of their suite of subscription management tools. These key performance indicators (KPIs) are one way to narrow down which of the library's packages, on their face, are underperforming compared to others. Because packages are often large, it is advisable to focus on one or two packages with the worst KPIs per the review.

The second step is to drill down into the title-level performance by looking at the average number of downloads annually for each title. You should decide the baseline for low-, mid-, and high-use. The Commission on New Technological Uses of Copyright Works (CONTU) guidelines typically allow up to five articles from the last five years to be borrowed through ILL without paying copyright charges (often referred to as the "rule of five").[14] Any titles falling in the range of five to ten downloads per year might be designated low-use titles. Using these categories, you can show the percentage of titles in the package for each category (see figure 4.1).

From here, you can compare the cost of the package to the cost of subscribing to the high-use titles. Would there be a savings in moving to a small core of individual subscription titles? Another option is to take the current usage

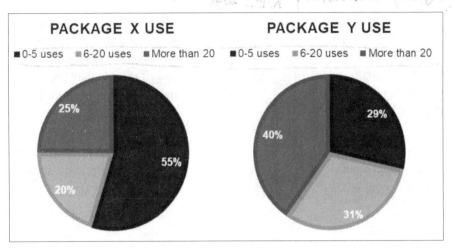

FIGURE 4.1 • Comparing the number of uses per title in two journal packages

figures and the typical cost-per-article for ILL (or some other pay-per-view service) and calculate how much it would cost the library to meet the current demand without committing to an annual subscription.[15]

It is useful to look up sources of alternate access to these titles. For instance, the library may find that there is acceptable (if embargoed) access to the titles through an aggregator database. For titles lacking access to the current year, it is necessary to decide what an acceptable embargo period is. The answer will vary depending on the discipline, but typically, one year to eighteen months is acceptable.[16] One way to help determine if an embargo period is acceptable is to refer to COUNTER report JR5, which breaks down use by publication year. If most of a journal's use is from years where the content is available through an aggregator, it doesn't make sense to pick up a separate subscription to that title.

PHASE 2

Stakeholder Review

With Phase 1 complete and the data collected, it is time to solicit feedback from a wider audience. Serials reviews can be massive in scale and impact, involve a lot of data, and necessitate redundant avenues for communication and feedback. Not every piece of information for every metric can be gathered by the project team ahead of time. It is uncommon for technical services, for

→ Using Community Knowledge

example, to have the most up-to-date information on accreditation or course adoption. Subject liaisons and patrons can provide deep disciplinary knowledge and firsthand testimony about the impact and value of the titles under review.

Additionally, what drives Phase 2 is the need to ensure that the review process is transparent and collaborative. The team should present and defend the process by which they selected the goals, titles, and strategies developed in Phase 1 before presenting the title-level data. At this point, the project team should set the timeline for gathering feedback and be clear about what stakeholders should provide, including who will have final decision-making authority over what actions to take.

Stakeholders

Major serials reviews, particularly when cancellations occur, can be politically fraught. Losing access to titles will often be met by strong emotions, ranging anywhere from disappointment to outrage. Not all of this pushback can be mitigated, but in general, a project will be more successful when the process is transparent and stakeholders are kept informed.[17] You should identify which external stakeholder or patron groups will need to be consulted. For academic libraries, there may be student or faculty advisory committees that can serve as proxies for the larger patron populations. In other situations, the library may rely on subject librarians to know which key individuals to contact. More details on soliciting feedback and announcing decisions are discussed later, as part of managing the assessment project and communicating the results of the assessment.

Timeline

Once the need for a review is identified, begin planning the project. The length of the planning period will vary depending on the number of people involved, the amount of data collected, and the extent of the review done by people outside the library.[18] You need to settle on a date when final decisions will be delivered to the publishers and subscription agents. For calendar year subscriptions, subscription agents prefer to receive this information by the end of September to allow enough time to communicate decisions to publishers. Some publisher contracts specify 30-, 60-, or 90-day notification requirements

Stakeholders

on cancellations. It is unpleasant to undergo review, and identify resources to cancel, but be unable to enact those changes because the notification window has closed.

You should identify key milestones along the way. Build in plenty of time to involve stakeholders in the decision-making process. There is ample evidence in the literature that, regardless of process, serial review projects produce better outcomes when they are done collaboratively with faculty.[19] Information will need to flow from the project team to the library and to institutional stakeholders and back again throughout the process. For academic libraries, faculty are typically not available during the summer. Mid-April is often the latest you can wait before asking them for feedback in the spring. In fall, the window between classes starting, typically in late August, and a late September project end date does not leave much time for faculty to contribute meaningfully to the process. It is helpful to work backwards from these types of fixed dates, since there will tend to be more flexibility internally with serials and acquisitions staff to complete the data-gathering processes than there is on the back end with outside groups. See table 4.1 earlier in the chapter for an example of a project timeline.

Asking for Feedback

You should reach out to all librarians and the stakeholder groups that have been identified early in the assessment project. The goal of this phase should be to gather the qualitative information about serials to complement the quantitative data provided by the project team. The importance of feedback from patron groups cannot be understated. This phase is typically marked by a flurry of e-mails and spreadsheet exchanges. Whether intentional or not, there will be more versions of spreadsheets than desired. Librarians reviewing titles will want their own copies to work from. Rather than fight against this, be clear from the outset how people should submit feedback. The master title spreadsheet could include columns for each reviewer's recommendation, or separate lists could be sent to review. Three things are key to communicate: when the feedback is due, how it should be submitted, and who has final decision-making authority.

Soliciting feedback from library colleagues is a relatively straightforward matter. For external stakeholders, like faculty, a variety of channels for receiving feedback can be used. The most effective choice for a library will depend on how the faculty are consulted in typical collection development decisions.

exclusivity

Much will depend on the relationship between the faculty and the library. The library may rely on a faculty advisory board to review decisions. There may be a faculty representative designated to work with the library on collection issues for their department. The subject librarian may attend the department's (or college's) faculty meeting. The consultation may happen purely over e-mail, or through feedback forms on the library's web page. The form of the consultation need not be the same for every stakeholder group. Use as many channels of communication as necessary to get the responses the library requires to proceed.

A public comment period can be left open for anyone to advocate for a resource on the library's website, or the comments can be submitted through subject librarians. For the former, a feedback mechanism on the website can be created to allow individuals to advocate for a title.[20] However feedback is to be managed, be sure to leave enough time for the project team to review and respond to the feedback before coming to a final decision for each title.

But what does feedback look like? The evaluative criteria selected by the project team is a good place to start. You should refer to the strategies and metrics identified in Phase 1, and identify what information the project team does not have and who can provide it. Subject liaisons possess both deep disciplinary knowledge and an intimate familiarity with library resources. They can help identify whether the content is available elsewhere or the subject matter is adequately covered by another title. Even though usage statistics are helpful in determining need, they are not always the most reliable source of information for demonstrating this need. Often it is up to librarians to assess whether or not a journal is truly vital to support the research interests of students, faculty, and staff at the university. Faculty, on the other hand, are uniquely qualified to provide information on emergent research areas, and changes to curricula. You can ask faculty members to rank titles that are important to their discipline, research, or students; their input may not necessarily match usage patterns.

Stakeholders can provide information to the project team, or they can recommend decisions. The approach to take will depend on who has final decision-making authority. Be transparent about the assessment and keep lines of communication open between the library and patrons.[21]

Stakeholders can:

- Suggest titles to be canceled
- Rank titles by importance
- Provide the context for a title's use
- Comment on the importance of access to the most recent issues of a title

- Suggest alternate titles
- Respond to individual recommendations made by the project team

Acting on Feedback

Once the window for feedback closes, transfer all the information received back into the master spreadsheet, where it will be easier to identify conflicting recommendations. With the project strategies in mind, the project team uses the feedback to finalize a decision for each title. Individual titles may be interdisciplinary and require input from more than one subject area. When there is disagreement about a title, the project team will weigh the provided justifications against the overall project goals. Stakeholder groups will naturally be focused on the titles most important to them. But the project team has an obligation to the collection as a whole, and must make decisions that keep in mind the bottom line and that meet the project's goals.

An example of this can be seen in cancellations of e-journal packages. Often there will be alternative avenues to access titles from database aggregators. When there is no alternative access for a title, the question becomes whether it is necessary to have a separate subscription. Having access to full text is great for patrons; however, if the article is indexed in the catalog and is still findable, relying on ILL or document delivery to fill requests may be an acceptable compromise. A cost-conservative option would be to allow the subscriptions to lapse and judge the true demand for the title through direct faculty requests or ILL requests. Patrons retain access to the content, and the cost savings are in alignment with assessment outcomes.

PHASE 3

Enacting Decisions

Now that Phase 2 is complete, feedback has been gathered and the project team has drafted decisions for each serial title under review. Phase 3 is the time to finalize and act on these decisions. Where the focus in Phase 1 was on the project team and Phase 2 focused on the stakeholders, Phase 3 re-centers the project in technical services. This is also the time to check in one last time with the library administration. When it is time for hard choices to be made, administrators get one last chance to provide their institutional-level, big-picture perspective. They can also help craft messaging.

The goal of Phase 3 is to maintain the transparency built in Phase 2 while acting on decisions and clearly documenting any changes taking place. Since not all decisions made by the project team will go into effect immediately, this section will discuss ways to publicize decisions, and it will reiterate the importance of record-keeping. By keeping the different stakeholder groups aware of what is happening and continuing to foster communication, Phase 3 will have a better chance for success.

Administrative Support

[handwritten: take away - maintaining admin support]

With any major assessment project, the library administration should be kept informed throughout the process. At the outset, and all along the way, the project team should keep the library administration apprised with status reports. This approach provides several benefits. First, administrators can help the project team formulate assessment goals and strategies that align with the library's strategic priorities. Second, they often have close relationships with other administrators on campus and can provide information on the wider budget and political climate. Finally, it is important for the project team to feel confident about the library administration's support of their recommendations, especially when there is pushback from faculty or other patron groups. It is good practice to share any e-mails the project team plans to send out about final decisions with administrators for their review and approval. Because regardless of how the results are communicated, or by whom, many people will contact the library director directly with comments or questions. You should arrange ahead of time what amount of information the director will want to have on hand to field those questions, or if they will simply pass them off to the project team.

Communicating the Assessment Results

The results of the assessment need to be distributed to the library, patrons, and vendors/publishers. Each group will require slightly different data for the titles, and each group will respond to different presentations of the data. The time for major objections to the process and the resources is past. The focus of this phase is to communicate the results, provide justifications, and perform a final check for accuracy. But that is the ideal case. In reality, people will respond most strongly when the cancellation is at hand.

[handwritten: takeaway — last-minute changes]

The key takeaway from this section is that there will always be last-minute changes. It is crucial to build extra time into the timetable to accommodate these delays. There will always be patrons who are unhappy with cancellation decisions. Often, it will be a matter of responding to their concerns with information about the process or providing a justification for the decision. Occasionally, new information is introduced about the resource. For instance, a faculty member may be on the editorial board of a journal. Publishers will often provide counter-offers when the library announces its intention to cancel. They may even contact faculty members directly to drum up support for reversing the decision. Whether the library wants to reconsider the decision when faced with new information, or acquiesce to pressure, is a matter for the project team to decide. You should consider discussing matters with library administrators before moving ahead.

Patrons should be provided with sufficient background information about the assessment project and the list of serials and the action to be taken (i.e., titles to be canceled, format changes, new subscriptions). A good practice is to offer alternate options for accessing the journal—perhaps through an aggregator, or directing people to interlibrary loan. Graphs of declining library budgets paired with the rising cost of journals can illustrate the magnitude of the overall problem and reinforce the reasons behind the cancellations. *[handwritten: user focus]*

Communication Channels

There are a variety of communication channels that can be used to inform people about the assessment's results:

Library website or research guides: Post the information in a prominent place where it will be easy for library staff or patrons to locate. See the "Resources" sections at the end of this chapter for examples from various libraries.

E-mail messages: E-mails can be sent either to the library or to the campus community at large. They can also be customized and targeted towards a department, usually with a subset of serials appropriate for those subjects. Decide whether the e-mails should come from subject liaisons or from library administrators for the most impact.

Library newsletters: If the library sends out a regular newsletter, this can have a blurb about the decisions and can point readers to the library's website or invite them to contact collection development or subject librarians.

Attend departmental meetings: Likewise, information can be shared at academic departmental meetings, which are often held at the end of summer before classes start up. Controversial decisions may require representatives from the project team to attend these meetings and provide additional or background information.

Library signage: This is especially useful for communicating cancellation decisions about popular magazines and newspapers which community members may have come to expect. (See figure 4.2.)

Lists for public service desk staff: Where once public services staff maintained shelf-lists of periodicals, it can be useful to have a paper copy of the cancellation decisions at the desk in case frontline staff need to refer to them easily.

Now begins the long chain of events for serials staff who begin to act on the cancellation decisions. This process is time-consuming and painstaking. Subscription agents, vendors, and publishers need to be contacted directly with cancellation decisions. Be honest with the vendor about why the cancellation is taking place. Once the decision has been communicated, vendors will often try to work with the library to find a compromise that will work within the library's budget. Knowing this is a possibility, it is helpful to know what, if any, pricing would be acceptable to maintain the subscription. For any subscriptions that are licensed consortially, be sure to notify the person responsible about the cancellation. As mentioned earlier, one library's decision to cancel can have cost implications for the remaining subscribers.

FIGURE 4.2 • Signage announcing changes for print newspapers

Useful along w/ workflows

CANCELLATION CHECKLIST FOR SERIALS STAFF

- Communicate the cancellation to the stakeholder

- (Optional) Cancellation notification sent to consortium

- Cancellation sent to subscription agent/publisher

- Update the library system

    - Close the order record

    - Add a cancellation note with the decision date (e.g., "Canceled for CY2019 per serials review")

    - Research perpetual/post-cancellation access

    - Update the holdings

    - (Optional) Update print retention or bindery

Record-Keeping

You should document decisions for posterity in the library system, a spreadsheet, or in an ERMS. Include information about the vendor or subscription agent, renewal dates, and any other notes that could prove helpful. It is important for library staff to feel comfortable justifying each decision when they are challenged by faculty or administrators. After several weeks or months, it will not be enough to rely on one person's memory for how the discussions transpired for each title—especially when there may be hundreds to cancel.

Duplicating this information in multiple places is not necessarily a bad thing. Having this information in multiple places is a better guarantee that subscriptions do not slip through and get paid for another year. It also serves as a reminder that access to titles will soon be lost and to look into what perpetual access (also referred to as post-cancellation access) the library is entitled to. Placing a note in the order record or in an ERMS with standard language provides a reference in the future for the reason the journal is being canceled and when the change will take effect. Using standard language also allows library faculty and staff to run lists or reports for records containing that note field.

PHASE 4

Post-Assessment Review

Phase 4 is the time to tie up loose ends and assess the assessment. Assessment projects often take the better part of a year, and demand a lot of time and attention from everyone in the library—not just the project team. Although the project team might feel dragged down by decision fatigue and ready for the project to be over once the decisions are sent to the publisher, this is the time to review any concerns that were raised during the assessment process and discuss ways to improve it for the next review cycle. It won't be long before another serials assessment project is needed.

This phase will be longer than previous phases, lasting months or even years. Taking a "wait and see" approach to canceled titles requires librarians to continue to track these titles through interlibrary loan requests and through direct patron requests. Monitoring the ongoing demand for titles can provide useful collection development data about actual patron needs versus perceived patron needs.

This phase will also involve following up with vendors about subscription changes and checking for perpetual access. This section will talk about the importance of tracking feedback, enumerate some of the challenges that might be encountered during a serials review project, and offer lessons learned from the authors' previous experiences with serials review projects. What follows are some words of wisdom that have come with the benefit of hindsight.

Tracking Feedback

takeaway - assessing assessments

Assessing the assessment and following up on the cancellation decisions are good practice. First, it is important to assess whether there were any problems in the process, in how feedback was gathered, or in the criteria used to make decisions. It will be inevitable that the process will repeat, and so it is good to learn from past efforts. Following up on demand is another crucial step. The library may have underestimated the use or demand for a journal. Tracking interlibrary loan requests for the canceled titles can be one way to monitor ongoing demand. It is always possible to re-subscribe to titles if demand outpaces what the library can borrow at low cost or for free. Many studies on the impact of serials cancellations on interlibrary loan demand frequently report very modest numbers of requests for canceled journals in the period following cancellations.[22] Often this is an outcome of the assessment strategy: identifying low-use titles or cutting subscriptions to journals but retaining access elsewhere typically results in few or no ILL requests.

Challenges

Too often libraries rely on institutional memory for subscription details. New staff coming in will only have what can be found in order records. For e-journal packages, especially, the payments are not always straightforward in the library system—they may be split across individual titles, with no package-level payments required. At Western Carolina University, there had been considerable turnover in the department prior to a major cancellation project in 2012. The new librarians were unaware that the library had only just moved to a Big Deal package for a major journal provider in January of that year. When they reviewed usage statistics, only a handful of titles that had been part of a smaller subject-specific package showed use. Without knowing the context, it appeared as if the Big Deal was not being well-used and could be safely canceled. Only later, when facing pushback from the faculty, did information about the order history come out. Closer scrutiny of the latest eight months of use then showed extremely high use across the entire package. Needless to say, the package was not canceled.

Packages Are the Worst

All serials, whether print or online, have challenges that require thoroughness and patience to maintain. While not an exhaustive list, here are some challenges that may be encountered when analyzing and assessing journal packages:

- Keeping track of titles the library will retain perpetual access to
- Having little or no flexibility to make changes and lower costs
- Documenting and updating publisher or package changes
- Explaining the cancellation decision to people who may view the package as a database instead of a journal package

takeaway
↳ balancing assessment w/
available manhours

Lessons Learned and Tips/Tricks

Cancellations are never popular. There will never be enough time for patron and faculty feedback. It is important to balance transparency with the necessity to make what, at times, are painful decisions to cancel resources.

You should overbudget how much to cancel in order to meet budget needs. Cutting more than the minimum amount will free up resources to add new titles or to reverse decisions at the last minute. It will also provide a buffer for the next year's inflationary increases.

Take time to get support and buy-in from administrators. Whether it is the library director or the university provost, it is important to keep administrators apprised of forthcoming decisions, especially if they will be unpopular.

Follow up to make sure that changes to subscriptions are actually made. It is easy, especially with a lot of subscription changes, for titles to slip through the cracks. Plan for the serials team to follow up with the subscription agent and confirm that everything has been processed.

directly contradicts ch. 1

EVALUATING LEGACY FUNCTIONS AND WORKING WITH PRINT SERIALS

In many libraries, the question of what to do with print serials has been asked, and answered, ten or even twenty years ago. Economic pressures, workforce reductions, and growing demands for dedicated electronic resources staff have led serialists to address the activities related to print serials: check-in, claiming, and binding. Many articles have addressed individual cases, several of which are cited in the "Resources" section for this chapter. For some libraries, the decision to reduce or eliminate print serials staffing may have been precipitated by financial or institutional crises. In others, similar changes may have waited until key staff members retired and the positions were reevaluated. But while the number of acquired print serials has dropped and workflows have changed, some of these serials continue to be acquired and processed by staff.[23]

Of the types of assessments enumerated for serials in this chapter, dealing with legacy processes has the most significant staffing implications. As with many areas of technical services that are involved in physical item processing, handling print serials is a hands-on process whose importance commanded a sizable cadre of skilled staff to manage at the height of print serials subscriptions in 1990s. While this section will discuss the ways to assess each process within the greater organizational context, the most challenging aspect will be addressing the existing personnel engaged in these activities and managing effective change for them.

Questions to Ask/What to Consider

As with all assessment activities, the choice of assessment strategies for print serials is dependent on the outcomes the assessment is intended to measure and the needs that are driving change in the organization. You will need to consider the forces behind the decision to initiate a review of print serials. For many libraries that have walked through this process before, budget crises and reductions in workforce have already caused reductions in print journal operations.[24] Other libraries have sought time and cost efficiencies by outsourcing many areas of technical services. Now libraries are assessing these activities to determine whether they still provide value to the organization. In an ideal world, libraries would regularly assess the day-to-day operations of their units; in reality, it is much more often the case that departments perform assessments only when tasked to do so by outside events or by administrators. Print serials operations are seen as outdated and outmoded—an area of technical services that is ripe for reallocating resources to emerging areas and resources. Patrons' preference for online journal content has driven most libraries to abandon print subscriptions whenever possible; however, there are still times when print makes sense. Consider the following sets of questions as the scope of the assessment project is developed.

For current print serials:

- How many titles are currently received in print?
- How many print titles did the library receive at its peak?
- Have staffing levels changed since then?
- When was the last time serials staffing was reviewed?
- What competing needs or processes require additional staff in the department/library?
- Are e-journals and other e-resource processes adequately staffed?

The following are considerations for keeping serials in print:

- Does the publisher offer an online subscription?
- Is there a cost differential between the print and online subscriptions?
- Are the authentication options acceptable to the library (e.g., user name/password access, IP authentication)?
- Does the library have existing online access to the title through a journal package or aggregator database?
- Is the title meant for browsing or leisure reading?
- Is the content best viewed in print (e.g., art and design journals)?

The following are considerations for outsourcing/insourcing:

- What technical services processes does the library currently outsource?
- What materials (if any) come shelf-ready?
- What funds are used to pay for these expenses?
- Which resource is more scarce in your organization: staff positions or operating funds?
- Can these tasks be handled centrally (for instance, centralizing processing for branch libraries, or sharing processing staff with consortial partner libraries)?

Depending on the answers to these questions, you may prefer to focus your assessment efforts on either outsourcing or insourcing.

Human Resources

The results of the assessment activity most often will recommend designating fewer positions for print serials. Union contracts and state and local personnel guidelines will dictate how and to what extent existing staff can be reassigned. Understanding the regulations and being attentive to employees' rights early in the process will prevent any sudden surprises down the line. Here are some questions to ask in this regard:

- What guidelines govern reassigning existing staff within the library?
- What skill sets do your staff currently possess?
- Can staff duties be updated without reclassifying positions?
- Will reassigning staff to new or updated positions require salary increases?

Space Planning

Library space considerations also drive decisions regarding long-term journal binding, storage, and retention. The trend to reclaim space from print collections in order to create other library functions can put pressure on serials staff to reduce or eliminate those collections. These pressures should be weighed against the intrinsic scholarly value the collections provide to patrons, and any obligations the library has for the retention of print journals.

- Are bound journals occupying a high-demand footprint of the library?

- What are the competing space needs at the library?
- What possibilities exist for alternative storage locations, either as closed stacks or off-site storage or otherwise?
- How would moving or reducing these collections affect other departments in the library (e.g., ILL, document delivery)?
- Are backfiles of the journal available online?
- Are online backfiles acceptable replacements for the print volumes (e.g. digitized cover-to-cover, adequately reproduced images or graphics)?

Retention

The following are questions to ask with regard to retaining print journals:

- Is the journal widely held within the state/region?
- What are the retention policies for journal titles?
- Is the library involved in a cooperative journal retention program?

These agreements contain stipulations for retaining journals in good condition and making them accessible to partner libraries.[25] Be aware of contractual obligations in these situations and which journal titles are covered by the program. You can save time by removing them from the analysis.

What to Assess—Staff, Skills, Workload, Workflows

Inventory Print Processing

The first step in the assessment process is to perform a self-study of the staffing model for handling print serials. You can begin by determining the amount of time that staff spend on each function; the options for doing so can be scaled to fit your circumstances. Existing job descriptions can be mined for a staff member's assigned duties (e.g., 15 percent claiming print serials) for an aggregate breakdown of total departmental FTEs that are dedicated to processing. Be sure to include student worker or volunteer labor. For detailed processes or per-item information, it will be necessary for staff to report their work. This can occur either through self-reported numbers, or as a time study where each staff member tracks their activities to the minute for a set period, often for a week or two during a representative month.

Next, create an inventory of what processes are carried out with serials staff. What portion of print serials receive processing? Do all serials receive the same amount of processing? Print serials may be checked in, but newspapers are not. What portion of the titles are claimed? How often does claiming result in receipt of the missing issue? Is there a good reason for the claiming? Claiming may be reserved only for titles destined for the bindery, when requested by a patron, or for newspapers that are converted into microfilm. Time studies are beneficial for two reasons: to account for staff work, and to assess the quality of service delivered to the patrons. For the latter, some metrics to consider would be the turnaround time between

- when a serial arrives in the mail and when it is checked in;
- when it is delivered to separate branches; and
- when it is on the shelf, available to patrons.

The inventory process can provide for the qualitative assessment of processes based on staff feedback. Ask staff to report what has worked well and what pain points exist in the system. Additionally, work with the staff to ascertain why certain steps or processes exist. Often, long-standing practices arise from the limitations of earlier systems that have never been revisited—for instance, the manual claiming of titles for which automated processes have since been created (or improved). It is possible to tease out unseen connections with other functions of the library by asking what happens before and after a process is complete, in order to tie print serials activities into the broader work of the department or library. From invoicing to stacks maintenance, a small aspect of these responsibilities may touch other parts of the organization and need to be considered as change is implemented.

Alternatives to In-House Processing

You should investigate the alternatives for processing print serials and determine the combination of options that is most advantageous to your department and your patrons. Generally speaking, the options include (1) scaling back the amount of processing, (2) eliminating some or all of the processing, or (3) outsourcing the processing to a vendor. The questions proffered earlier in this chapter for developing the framework for the assessment project will help you determine which set of options to explore. The external or internal forces which precipitated this review often will dictate the magnitude of the change. The inventory process can also illuminate the value placed on these services by the wider library. Whenever possible, you should query public services staff about which processes provide the most value to them or the library's patrons, and then use their feedback to shape the functional requirements of your solutions.

 User - focus

Consolidation services, or off-site delivery and check-in for serials, have long been offered by subscription agents as a suite of services for shelf-ready serials.[26] For the sizable proportion of libraries that outsource technical service functions—cataloging, shelf-ready books, authority control—adding print serials to the list amounts to only a minor change in their operations. For others, the decision to outsource is a balance of costs, staffing levels, and a negotiation of perceptions of differences in quality. The available services include receipt, check-in, claiming, processing, and shipping the issues to the library. These are accompanied by electronic shipping lists and Electronic Data Interchange for Administration, Commerce and Transport (EDIFACT) files to check in to your library management system. Ask the subscription agent for information on the costs and turnaround time for your title lists.

Staff Skills and Retraining

Earlier, the authors alluded to the impact on personnel as an outcome of print serials analyses. Sarah Glasser's survey on the staffing implications for print serials management queried libraries that had undergone a reassessment of print serials processes, asking what happened to not just positions, but the employees in those positions. A very small percentage of positions were eliminated entirely, and over 80 percent of the individuals in those positions were retained either in repurposed positions in technical services departments or in another part of the library.[27] The implication of these statistics is the obvious, as is the overriding need to retrain existing staff for new positions.

Retraining print serials staff to focus on electronic resources maximizes that staff's existing expertise regarding serials publishing, but it requires additional demands for technological competencies. A comparison of knowledge, skills, and abilities associated with print serials jobs to electronic resources jobs is provided in the "Resources" section at the end of this chapter. Often, the shift to electronic resources requires staff to move away from a production-oriented mindset, with its checklist of operations and routine procedures, towards a problem-solving mindset. E-resources demand an ability to tolerate ambiguity and frequent change.[28] Short of theft or loss, an issue of a print serial, once processed and added to the catalog, will not change—but you can find yourself fixing the same e-journal access issues again and again.

One recommendation is to establish the basic technological competencies expected of each library employee. Combined with the specific needs for the position under review, these competencies form the basis for a gap analysis of existing staff skills. From this will then come a training plan to address any deficiencies. The authors recommend being comprehensive: from training on how to scan documents, how to use features in e-mail programs to send attachments, and training on the basic functions in spreadsheets, to more specialized skills including subscription management tools, e-journal holdings and linking tools, and proxy server customization. A robust training plan for each employee is crucial to the employee's success in the new position.

Communicating the Assessment Results

You can create a workflow process diagram for how print serials are handled. Process mapping is a method for understanding a process with the intention of assessing and improving it. A process diagram closely resembles a flowchart and can be a useful way to document the steps and individuals involved with a process. It can also be used to visualize the changes made to a process as a before-and-after comparison. Swimlane maps can serve much the same purpose, but they are especially advantageous for processes that involve multiple units in order to evaluate their efficiency; a process that bounces between lanes may be a sign that resources are being physically handled by the same people more than once, and time and effort are being unnecessarily expended to transport the material back and forth.

The relative time and costs of processing options are well-suited for presentation as a table. Possible metrics include a comparison of in-house processing versus outsourcing for cost-per-issue (or cost-per-title); the total cost savings in reducing or eliminating processes; and the turnaround time for getting a serial title on the shelf and available to patrons.[29] You should report the aggregate reduction in time spent on print serials functions by staff-hours or by total staff FTEs.

Organizational charts are another tool for reporting staffing changes, especially when positions are reclassified or redeployed to another department. Updated organizational charts, when paired with updated job descriptions and training plans, can be provided to administrators or human resources staff as a road map for managing the personnel changes accompanying the recommendations for changes in the processing of print serials.

Lessons Learned

Staff engagement and involvement is crucial for most assessment processes, and when those assessment activities result in direct changes to those employees' positions and responsibilities, continuing to effectively manage change

emotionality of library assessment

throughout and after the implementation phase is imperative. It is important to focus discussion from the outset on the position or process itself and not the person in the position. Language intended to describe the declining importance of claiming print serials can be misconstrued as describing the declining importance of the individual who does the claiming.

Transparency and involvement in all stages of the assessment project can reduce anxiety over job security. Furthermore, training plans and ongoing development of employees in their new and evolving roles can help build their confidence in taking on new responsibilities. These efforts demonstrate that the library is investing in their success.[30] Validating the transferability of an employee's previous skills can reinforce management's perception of their value to the organization by honoring their history and expertise within the library.

It has not been all that long since print serials check-in was a core service. Staff still remember how important it was for patrons to see that the library had received the most recent issue of a journal. Setting these duties aside can cause morale to drop among staff who may see their importance and value to the organization diminished alongside these changes. You should allow staff the time to mourn these processes while showing them a future where they (and their skills) are still valued.

Staff Qualifications

The knowledge, skills, and abilities needed for work in print serials are:

- Detailed knowledge of and experience with serials subscription and title maintenance, including management of lapses, title changes, cessations, and format and publisher changes
- Ability to perform work requiring accuracy and considerable attention to detail without close supervision
- Prior library experience in serials or technical services; familiarity with an online library catalog; familiarity with e-mail and the use of applications in a networked environment; some accounting experience preferred
- Expert knowledge of the functions involved in serials acquisitions processing, including ordering, receiving, invoicing, and renewals and cancellations within an academic research library

For electronic resources, the knowledge, skill, and abilities required to perform the duties are:

- Ability to work as part of a team in a complex and changing environment
- Familiarity with Windows desktop, word processing, e-mail, and Internet resources and tools
- Familiarity with electronic resources management systems—for example, Serials Solutions
- Experience with an integrated library system—for example, Innovative Interfaces
- Experience with loading vendor-supplied records into an automated library system
- Experience with electronic resources support systems—for example, LibGuides, EZproxy, or Summon
- Experience with a national bibliographic utility—for example, OCLC
- Demonstrated ability to adapt to rapid change and to exercise creativity and initiative

TRENDS IN SERIALS

The shift from print to electronic journal content has done little to challenge the supremacy of the subscription model for serials within libraries. Yet worldwide, the conversations between publishers, researchers, and librarians are dominated by disagreements over publisher profits, open access content, and the viability of Big Deals. Researchers' expectations for freely accessible content continue to rise, while libraries struggle to find practical solutions to keep pace.

Many librarians and academics are advocating to dismantle the paywall that blocks access to articles. Libraries have been promoting open-access publishing by marketing self-archiving in institutional repositories and by mediating, negotiating, or paying for article-processing charges. Academics are heading more often to the Web and the proliferation of sources like Sci-Hub and ResearchGate in order to share articles (legally or otherwise) peer-to-peer.[31] Publishers are fighting back by pursuing legal action against sites for illegally hosting copyrighted material.[32] The antagonism between for-profit publishing and the open access movement is ongoing. Libraries are left to make small, iterative changes to improve access within the limits of budgetary realities and copyright law.

A growing number of libraries and library consortia have walked away, or threatened to walk away, from Big Deals. SPARC, the Scholarly Publishing and

Academic Resources Coalition, has launched a new resource for tracking Big Deal cancellations in order to "detail what specific steps libraries have taken to 'cut the cord'; and to provide practical resources for libraries interested in evaluating collection strategies, honing value-for-money calculations, integrating faculty input into the process, and negotiating an exit from big deals."[33] In some cases, libraries have reversed course, having renegotiated better business terms with the publishers. Some statewide groups, like the University of California system, have canceled their statewide contracts with publishers like Taylor & Francis, but the individual libraries have in some cases individually pursued separate Big Deals.[34]

Likewise, many librarians have pronounced the Big Deal to be on its way out—its demise being only a matter of time. On the Scholarly Kitchen blog, Rick Anderson started a discussion about a growing number of libraries that are walking away from Big Deals. In it he predicts that as collection budgets continue to decline or remain flat, and as more libraries show that it is possible to walk away from Big Deals, there will be even more Big Deal cancellations in the coming years.[35]

CONCLUSION

The life cycle of serials is cyclical and ongoing. From the time a journal subscription begins, until the day it is canceled, regular evaluation will always have a role in this cycle. Annual renewals are a yearly reminder of the role assessment has in ensuring the vitality of the serials collection. It is imperative that technical services professionals create systems of review in order to make sure that the library's collections of journals and continuing resources are meeting patrons' collection needs, are sustainable within the library's budget, and are being effectively delivered to patrons. The pace of development in new fields of study will always outpace the available funding. So until there is a way for libraries and publishers to move away from the current subscription model, and its constant price increases, budgets will continue to be a driving force in serials reviews and cancellations.

Technical services must embrace a culture of assessment in order to keep pace with trends and stay in front of patrons' expectations for access to content. Acquisitions models are continually evolving, making content delivery less certain than when receiving issues through subscriptions was the only pathway for patrons to access the content. Staffing models need to become equally flexible and include positions that reflect the skill sets necessary to adequately manage access to this content. Unlike books, print simply has no place in the future of serials. These print collections linger for now, but they will become increasingly marginalized over the next decade. Concerns over space and accessibility will continue to drive questions over the value of these print materials and their place in the modern library.

NOTES

1. Susanne Clement, Gaele Gillespie, Sarah Tusa, and Julie Blake, "Collaboration and Organization for Successful Serials Cancellation," *The Serials Librarian* 54, no. 3-4 (2008): 230.

2. Recent studies include Jane Skoric and Carol Seiler, "Taming the Information Frontier," *The Serials Librarian* 68 (2015), who undertook a comprehensive review and created a framework for smaller ongoing reviews; Jacob L. Nash and Karen R. McElfresh, "A Journal Cancellation Survey and Resulting Impact on Interlibrary Loan," *Journal of the Medical Library Association* 104, no. 4 (2016), who monitored interlibrary loan demand after a cancellation project; Todd Enoch and Karen R. Harker, "Planning for the Budget-ocalypse: The Evolution of a Serials/ER Cancellation Methodology," *The Serials Librarian* 68 (2015), who underwent a multiyear, multimillion-dollar reduction to electronic resources and serials; and finally John S. Spencer and Christopher Millson-Martula, "Serials Cancellations in College and Small University Libraries: The National Scene," *The Serials Librarian* 49, no. 4 (2006), who conducted a multi-study review of the decision-making factors used for cancellation in college and small university libraries.

3. There are two studies worth noting here. Trey Lemley and Jie Li, "'Big Deal' Journal Subscription Packages: Are They Worth the Cost?" *Journal of Electronic Resources in Medical Libraries* 12, no. 1 (2015): 1–10, found that, in terms of cost-per-article, Big Deal packages were more cost-efficient than relying on pay-per-view or interlibrary loan. However, Jonathan Nabe and David C. Fowler, "Leaving the 'Big Deal' . . . Five Years Later," *The Serials Librarian* 69, no. 1 (2015): 20–28, argue that download statistics are not the best measurement for value or need and have found that "it is only possible [to determine the value/need of a journal package] when titles have been cancelled or otherwise lost." After canceling Big Deal packages, they found that while ILL requests increased, the demand for non-subscribed titles was not at a "high enough level" to change their decision. For Nabe and Fowler, cost savings and greater budget flexibility outweigh the downsides to losing these packages.

4. Mike Olson, David Killian, Debbie Bezanson, and Robin Kinder, "A Tale of Two Serials Cancellations," in *Proceedings of the 2016 Charleston Library Conference* (West Lafayette, IN: Purdue University Press, 2016), 187.

5. Bart Harloe, Pat Hults, and Adam Traub, "What's the Use of Use? Return on Investment Strategies for Consortial DDA Programs," *Journal of Library Administration* 55 (2015): 254–55.

6. Jill Grogg, "Using a Subscription Agent for E-Journal Management," *Journal of Electronic Resources Librarianship* 22, no. 1–2 (2010): 8, doi: 10.1080/1941126X.2010.492649.

7. Mark Ware, *ALPSP Survey of Librarians on Factors in Journal Cancellation* (Worthing, UK: Association of Learned and Professional Society Publishers, 2006), 1–19.

8. Thomas E. Nisonger, and Gloria Guzi, "Approaches, Techniques, and Criteria for Serials Evaluation in the Electronic Environment," *The Serials Librarian* 40, no. 3-4 (2001): 394, doi: 10.1300/J123v40n03_28.

9. Stephen Bosch and Kittie Henderson, "New World, Same Model: Periodicals Price Survey 2017," *Library Journal*, April 28, 2017, http://lj.libraryjournal.com/2017/04/publishing/new-world-same-model-periodicals-price-survey-2017/.

10. Clement, Gillespie, Tusa, and Blake, "Collaboration and Organization," 232.

11. Diane Carroll and Joel Cummings, "Data-Driven Collection Assessment Using a Serial Decision Database," *Serials Review* 36, no. 4 (2010): 227–28, doi: 10.1016/j.serrev.2010.09.001.

12. There is a two-hour webinar on prepping spreadsheets and using VLOOKUP referenced by Melissa Belvadi on SERIALST@listserv.nasig.org, December 12, 2017, Serials in Libraries Discussion Forum, www.nasig.org/site_page.cfm?pk_association_webpage_menu=308&pk_association_webpage =4955.

13. Diane Carroll, "Procedures for Using a Serials Decision Database," Washington State University Research Exchange, http://hdl.handle.net/2376/2277.

14. "Using Content for Inter Library Loan," Copyright Clearance Center, wwwdem1.copyright.com/Services/copyrightoncampus/content/ill_contu.html.

15. Paula Sullenger, "The Promise of the Future: A Review of the Serials Literature 2012–13," *Library Resources and Technical Services* 60, no. 1 (2016): 13, doi: http://dx.doi.org/10.5860/lrts.60n1.12.

16. Ingrid Moisil, "Renew or Cancel? Applying a Model for Objective Journal Evaluation," *Serials Review* 41, no. 3 (2015): 161. Moisil considers an embargo greater than twelve months the equivalent of having no aggregator access. Eighteen months may be acceptable for some disciplines or journals.

17. Cindy Sjoberg, "E-Journals and the Big Deal: A Review of the Literature," *SLIS Student Research Journal* 6, no. 2 (2017): 4–5.

18. TERMS 2.0 provides scheduling suggestions based on the library's fiscal year. See "5. Annual Review," TERMS: Techniques for Electronic Resource Management, https://library.hud.ac.uk/blogs/terms/terms/annual-review.

19. Clement, Gillespie, Tusa, and Blake, "Collaboration and Organization," 234; Beatriz B. Hardy, Martha C. Zimmerman, and Laura A. Hanscom, "Cutting without Cursing: A

Successful Cancellation Project," *The Serials Librarian* 71, no. 2 (2016): 16, http://hdl
.handle.net/11603/3061 (author final version).

20. Google Forms make for an easy way to set up feedback mechanisms. See "Google
    Forms in the Library," *The Tech Lady from Texas Blog*, May 30, 2014, https://techladytx
    .wordpress.com/2014/05/30/google-forms-in-the-library for a library perspective.

21. Olson, Killian, Bezanson, and Kinder, "A Tale of Two Serials Cancellations," 188.

22. Nash and McElfresh, "A Journal Cancellation Survey," 297–99; Kristin R. Calvert,
    William Gee, Janet Malliet, and Rachel M. Fleming, "Is ILL Enough? Examining
    ILL Demand after Journal Cancellations at Three North Carolina Universities," in
    Proceedings of the 2013 Charleston Conference (West Lafayette, IN: Purdue University
    Press 2013), 299.

23. Rajia C. Tobia and Susan C. Hunnicutt, "Print Journals in the Electronic Library:
    What Is Happening to Them?" *Journal of Electronic Resources in Medical Libraries* 5,
    no. 2 (2008): 166.

24. Lisa Spagnolo, Buddy Pennington, and Kathy Carter, "Serials Management in
    Turbulent Times," *Serials Review* 36, no. 3 (2010): 163.

25. "Cooperative Journal Retention," Association of Southeastern Research Libraries,
    www.aserl.org/programs/j-retain.

26. José Luis Andrade, Heather D'Amour, Gloria Dingwall, and Julie Tao Su, "'Shelf-
    Ready' Print Serials Acquisitions," *Serials Review* 37, no. 1 (2011): 29–30.

27. Sarah Glasser, "Disappearing Jobs: Staffing Implications for Print Serials Management,"
    Serials Review 36, no. 3 (2010): 142.

28. Patrick L Carr, "The Claim," *The Serials Librarian* 51, no. 1 (2006): 79.

29. Rebecca Schroeder and Jared L. Howland, "Shelf-Ready: A Cost-Benefit Analysis,"
    Library Collections, Acquisitions, & Technical Services 35, no. 4 (2011): 131.

30. Lila A. Ohler, "The Keys to Successful Change Management for Serials," *The Serials
    Librarian* 51, no. 1 (2006): 51.

31. Björn Brembs, "So Your Institute Went Cold Turkey on Publisher X. What Now?"
    björn.brembs.blog, December 20, 2016, http://bjoern.brembs.net/2016/12/so-your
    -institute-went-cold-turkey-on-publisher-x-what-now.

32. Diane Kwon, "A Growing Open Access Toolbox," *The Scientist*, November 28, 2017,
    https://www.the-scientist.com/?articles.view/articleNo/51048/title/A-Growing-Open
    -Access-Toolbox.

33. Greg Tananbaum to SPARC mailing list, November 29, 2017, https://groups.google
    .com/a/sparcopen.org/forum/#!forum/liboer.

34. "Big Deal Cancellation Tracking," SPARC*, https://sparcopen.org/our-work/big-deal
    -cancellation-tracking/; Chan Li, "UC Libraries' Taylor & Francis Systemwide Journals
    License," CDL: California Digital Library, April 5, 2017, www.cdlib.org/services/
    collections/current/TF/index.html.

35. Rick Anderson, "When the Wolf Finally Arrives: Big Deal Cancellations in North American Libraries," *The Scholarly Kitchen* (blog), May 1, 2017, https://scholarlykitchen .sspnet.org/2017/05/01/wolf-finally-arrives-big-deal-cancelations-north-american -libraries.

RESOURCES
Serials Review Fundamentals

Clement, Susanne, Gaele Gillespie, Sarah Tusa, and Julie Blake. "Collaboration and Organization for Successful Serials Cancellation." *The Serials Librarian* 54, no. 3–4 (June 2008): 229–34. doi: 10.1080/ 03615260801 974172.

"Introduction to Techniques for Electronic Resources Management (TERMS)." https:// library hud.ac.uk/blogs/terms/announcing-terms-ver2–0.

Spencer, John S., and Christopher Millson-Martula. "Serials Cancellations in College and Small University Libraries: The National Scene." *The Serials Librarian* 49, no. 4 (February 2006): 135–55. doi: 10.1300/J123v 49n04_10.+

Serials Review Examples

Website examples of ways to present collection review projects:

New Mexico State University's LibGuide presents cancellations over multiple years and includes articles for further information about trends with publishers and libraries. http://nmsu.libguides.com/c.php?g=206139&p=1360279.

North Carolina State University's website has a cancellation FAQ and timelines for projects. www.lib.ncsu.edu/collections/collections review2014.

The University of Wisconsin-Milwaukee's website offers an example of how to communicate final cancellation decisions. http://uwm.edu/libraries/crm/cancellations/ final-cancellations.

The University of Oklahoma's LibGuide about serials cancellations, specifically Big Deals, communicates what they are, the trends, and information about the decision to cancel. http://guides.ou.edu/c.php ?g=113949&p=739282.

Mississippi State University's library newsletter discusses cancellations and alternative options for accessing content. http://lib.msstate.edu/news/2017/database_cancella tions.php.

Western Washington University's website offers information about the culture of assessment at the library and how it is undertaken. Strategic goals are clearly placed. https://library .wwu.edu/about/budget_planning_assessment.

Western Carolina University's LibGuide provides information about reasons for the review and displays changes to resources in multiple ways. http://researchguides.wcu.edu/ collection-news.

Data and Project Management Tools

- Open Refine is an open source program for manipulating and editing data. http://open refine.org.
- Gantt charts are project management visualization tools that are used for tracking tasks and events against a timeline. www.gantt.com.
- Arizona State University offers an introduction to process mapping. https://service.asu .edu/blog/an-introduction-to-process-mapping.

Request for Proposals

Westfall, Micheline B. "Using a Request for Proposal (RFP) to Select a Serials Vendor: The University of Tennessee Experience." *Serials Review* 37, no. 2 (2011): 87–92.

Westfall, Micheline B., Justin Clarke, and Jeanne M. Langendorfer. "Selecting a Vendor: The Request for Proposal (RFP) from Library and Vendor Perspectives." *The Serials Librarian* 64 (2013): 188–95.

Wilkinson, Frances C., and Linda K. Lewis. *Writing RFPs for Acquisitions: A Guide to the Request for Proposal.* Chicago: American Library Association, 2008.

Legal and Licensing

General license information checklists:

- University of North Carolina at Charlotte, https://legal.uncc.edu/legal-topics/contracts #advisory.
- University of Texas, https://www.utsystem.edu/offices/general-counsel/contract-checklists.

Model licensing agreements that offer help with language and terms that are desirable for libraries:

- Liblicense model license, http://liblicense.crl.edu/licensing-information/model -license.
- Association of Research Libraries (ARL) license models and clauses, www.arl.org/ focus-areas/scholarly-communication/marketplace -licensing.

Tokens and On-Demand Article Providers

- "Get It Now," Copyright Clearance Center, www.copyright.com/rightsholders/get-it-now.
- "Article Galaxy's Academic A-Z DocDel Collection," Reprints Desk, http://info.reprints desk.com/your-business/academia.

Hosburgh, Nathan. "Getting the Most Out of Pay-per-View: A Feasibility Study and Discussion of Mediated and Unmediated Options." *Journal of Electronic Resources Librarianship* 24, no. 3 (2012): 204–11. https://doi.org/10.1080/194116X.2012 .706112.

Big Deal Resources

Glasser, Sarah. "Judging Big Deals: Challenges, Outcomes, and Advice." *Journal of Electronic Resources Librarianship* 25, no. 4 (November 2013): 263–76. doi: 10.1080/1941126X.2013.847672.

Schöpfel, Joachim, and Claire Leduc. "Big Deal and Long Tail: E-Journal Usage and Subscriptions." *Library Review* 61, no. 7 (2012): 497–510. https://doi.org/10.1108/00242531211288245

SPARC* offers a way to track Big Deal cancellations: https://sparcopen.org/our-work/big-deal-cancellation-tracking.

Vogel, Gretchen, and Kai Kupferschmidt. "A Bold Open-Access Push in Germany Could Change the Future of Academic Publishing." *Science,* August 23, 2017. www.science mag.org/news/2017/08/bold-open-access-push-germany-could-change-future -academic-publishing.

REFERENCES

Anderson, Rick. "When the Wolf Finally Arrives: Big Deal Cancellations in North American Libraries." *The Scholarly Kitchen* (blog). May 1, 2017. https://scholarlykitchen.sspnet.org/2017/05/01/wolf-finally-arrives-big-deal-cancelations-north-american-libraries.

Andrade, José Luis, Heather D'Amour, Gloria Dingwall, and Julie Tao Su. "'Shelf-Ready' Print Serials Acquisitions." *Serials Review* 37, no. 1 (2011): 29–34. doi: 10.1016/j.serrev.2010.12.008.

"Big Deal Cancellation Tracking," SPARC*. https://sparcopen.org/our-work/big-deal -cancellation-tracking.

Bosch, Stephen, and Kittie Henderson. "New World, Same Model: Periodicals Price Survey 2017." *Library Journal*, April 28, 2017. http://lj.libraryjournal.com/2017/04/publishing/new-world-same-model-periodicals-price-survey-2017/.

Brembs, Björn. "So Your Institute Went Cold Turkey on Publisher X. What Now?" *björn .brembs.blog*, December 20, 2016. http://bjoern.brembs.net/2016/12/so-your-institute -went-cold-turkey-on-publisher-x-what-now.

Calvert, Kristin R., William Gee, Janet Malliet, and Rachel M. Fleming. "Is ILL Enough? Examining ILL Demand after Journal Cancellations at Three North Carolina Universities." In *Proceedings of the 2013 Charleston Conference.* West Lafayette, IN: Purdue University Press, 2013.

Carr, Patrick L. "The Claim." *The Serials Librarian* 51, no. 1 (2006): 73–81. doi: http://dx.doi.org/10.1300/J123v51n01_04.

Carroll, Diane, and Joel Cummings. "Data-Driven Collection Assessment Using a Serial Decision Database." *Serials Review* 36, no. 4 (2010): 227–39. doi: 10.1016/j.serrev.2010.09.001.

Clement, Susanne, Gaele Gillespie, Sarah Tusa, and Julie Blake. "Collaboration and Organization for Successful Serials Cancellation." *The Serials Librarian* 54, no. 3–4 (June 2008): 229–34. doi: 10.1080/03615260801974172.

"Cooperative Journal Retention." Association of Southeastern Research Libraries. www.aserl .org/programs/j-retain.

Enoch, Todd, and Karen R. Harker. "Planning for the Budget-ocalypse: The Evolution of a Serials/ER Cancellation Methodology." *The Serials Librarian* 68, no. 1–4 (2015): 282–89. doi: 10.1080/0361526X.2015.1025657.

Glasser, Sarah. "Disappearing Jobs: Staffing Implications for Print Serials Management." *Serials Review* 36, no. 3 (2010): 138–46. doi: 10.1016/j.serrev.2010.06.002.

Grogg, Jill. "Using a Subscription Agent for E-Journal Management." *Journal of Electronic Resources Librarianship* 22, no. 1–2 (2010): 7–10. doi: 10.1080/1941126X.2010.492649.

Hardy, Beatriz B., Martha C. Zimmerman, and Laura A. Hanscom. "Cutting without Cursing: A Successful Cancellation Project." *The Serials Librarian* 71, no. 2 (2016): 1–19. Author final version. http://hdl.handle.net/11603/3061.

Harloe, Bart, Pat Hults, and Adam Traub. "What's the Use of Use? Return on Investment Strategies for Consortial DDA Programs." *Journal of Library Administration* 55 (2015): 249–59. doi:10.1080/01930826.2015.1034055.

Kwon, Dian. "A Growing Open Access Toolbox." *The Scientist,* November 28, 2017. https:// www.the-scientist.com/?articles.view/articleNo/51048/title/A-Growing-Open-Access -Toolbox

Lemley, Trey, and Jie Li. "'Big Deal' Journal Subscription Packages: Are They Worth the Cost?" *Journal of Electronic Resources in Medical Libraries* 12, no. 1 (2015): 1–10. doi: 10.1080/15424065.2015.1001959.

Moisil, Ingrid. "Renew or Cancel? Applying a Model for Objective Journal Evaluation." *Serials Review* 41, no. 3 (2015): 160–64. doi: 10.1080/00987913.2015.1065466.

Nabe, Jonathan, and David C. Fowler. "Leaving the 'Big Deal' . . . Five Years Later." *Serials Librarian* 69, no. 1 (2015): 20–28.

Nash, Jacob L., and Karen R. McElfresh. "A Journal Cancellation Survey and Resulting Impact on Interlibrary Loan." *Journal of the Medical Library Association* 104, no. 4 (2016): 296–301. doi: http://dx.doi.org/10.3163/1536–5050.104.4.008.

Nisonger, Thomas E., and Gloria Guzi. "Approaches, Techniques, and Criteria for Serials Evaluation in the Electronic Environment." *The Serials Librarian* 40, no. 3–4 (2001): 393–407. doi: 10.1300/J123v40n03_28.

Ohler, Lila A. "The Keys to Successful Change Management for Serials." *The Serials Librarian* 51, no. 1 (2006): 37–72. doi: http://dx.doi.org/10.1300/J123v51n01_03.

Olson, Mike, David Killian, Debbie Bezanson, and Robin Kinder. "A Tale of Two Serials Cancellations." In *Proceedings of the 2016 Charleston Library Conference.* West Lafayette, IN: Purdue University Press, 2016. doi: 10.5703/1288284316441.

Schroeder, Rebecca, and Jared L. Howland. "Shelf-Ready: A Cost-Benefit Analysis." *Library Collections, Acquisitions, & Technical Services* 35, no. 4 (2011): 129–34. doi: 10.1016/j.lcats.2011.04.002.

Sjoberg, Cindy. "E-Journals and the Big Deal: A Review of the Literature." *SLIS Student Research Journal* 6, no. 2 (2017): 1–11. http://scholarworks.sjsu.edu/slissrj/v016/iss2/3.

Skoric, Jane, and Carol Seiler. "Taming the Information Frontier." *The Serials Librarian* 68, no. 1–4 (2015): 370–77. doi: 10.1080/0361526X.2015.1021218.

Spagnolo, Lisa, Buddy Pennington, and Kathy Carter. "Serials Management Transitions in Turbulent Times." *Serials Review* 36, no. 3 (2010): 161–66. doi: 10.1016/j.serrev.2010.05.011.

Spencer, John S., and Christopher Millson-Martula. "Serials Cancellations in College and Small University Libraries: The National Scene." *The Serials Librarian* 49, no. 4 (2006): 135–55. doi: 10.1300/J123v49n04_10.

Sullenger, Paula. "A Serials Format Inventory Project: How Far Can Academic Libraries Go with 'Electronic Only'?" *Serials Review* 37, no. 3 (2011): 174–80. doi: 10.1016/j.serrev.2011.06.001.

Tobia, Rajia C., and Susan C. Hunnicutt. "Print Journals in the Electronic Library: What Is Happening to Them?" *Journal of Electronic Resources in Medical Libraries* 5, no. 2 (2008): 161–70. doi: 10.1080/15424060802064360.

"Using Content for Inter Library Loan." Copyright Clearance Center. wwwdem1.copyright.com/Services/copyrightoncampus/content/ill_contu.html.

Ware, Mark. 2006. *ALPSP Survey of Librarians on Factors in Journal Cancellation.* Worthing, UK: Association of Learned and Professional Society Publishers, 2006.

CATALOGING AND METADATA ASSESSMENT
An Overview

Karl Pettitt

The time when catalogers and metadata specialists could take for granted the need of their services within libraries has long passed. The work that cataloging and metadata personnel do is often hidden and misunderstood even by those trained as professional librarians. While cataloging and metadata departments have long performed certain types of assessment, such as statistics-keeping, these have often been for internal use only or shared via general institutional annual reports. A broader understanding of what assessment is and how it can be applied to cataloging and metadata work is needed. This chapter will outline some of the various types and applications of assessment that have been used within cataloging and metadata environments. The advantages and challenges for each type of assessment will be explored, along with specific examples of application. However, it is first necessary to outline the need or purpose for assessment within cataloging and metadata departments.

THE NEED OR PURPOSE OF ASSESSMENT
IN CATALOGING AND METADATA SERVICES

The purpose of the assessment will, in many ways, dictate the type of assessment necessary to achieve the desired goals set forth in the beginning. An example would be if a cataloging department wished to convey the amount of work being done by its personnel. In this case, a simple statistical breakdown of the number of items handled by the department, along with the various types of work and the hours dedicated to those types of work, would probably suffice. However, what if the department needs to justify a position or show how the department is contributing to the library's wider strategic plan and goals? In such a case, merely showing the administration a spreadsheet of statistics detailing the amount and types of work performed by the department will not be likely to achieve the desired results. Therefore, the purpose matters, and it must be clearly understood before moving on to any planning stages for the assessment.

The purpose of an assessment can vary widely and can range from productivity to marketing. Examples of purposes for carrying out an assessment in cataloging and metadata services include:

focus is internal, not users

- Marketing cataloging and metadata services to others (including administrators both within and outside the library)
- Streamlining procedures and improving workflow efficiencies
- Making the case for current or additional resources (money, personnel, etc.)
- Setting performance standards for individuals and the department
- Setting departmental priorities, including strategic goals
- Evaluating metadata quality

This list is by no means exhaustive. It simply contains some of the more prevalent reasons why cataloging and metadata departments would perform an assessment. A more in-depth look at these purposes will provide a greater understanding of the need for assessment in cataloging and metadata services.

Marketing and outreach are perhaps the least likely candidates that come to mind when thinking of the reasons to perform assessment in cataloging and metadata services. However, they should probably be one of the first reasons, given the need to project the value and need of cataloging to both library and university administrators. Mugridge and Poehlmann (2015) point out that an internal public service survey performed by a cataloging department is a useful tool in and of itself, but a side benefit is that the "follow-up actions taken based on the results of a customer service survey can serve as a public relations or marketing tool for a division or unit."[1] This is primarily accomplished through the sharing of results from cataloging and metadata services assessments with those outside the department. In so doing, the often hidden activities of those in cataloging and metadata services are brought to light, and the relevance and usefulness of those activities are highlighted. If consistent updates are also advertised to outside stakeholders, then the work done by cataloging and metadata services can be tied into their everyday work and shown to be relevant to what those outside of those departments do.

Streamlining workflows and procedures is probably the most common reason for cataloging and metadata services to perform some kind of assessment.[2] Cataloging and metadata creation are time-intensive activities. As such, it is often imperative to ensure that materials, whether they be physical or digital, move through the department as efficiently as possible so that users can access the information as soon as possible after it is acquired by the library. Any change in systems, personnel, or vendors can require a review of existing workflows and procedures to create better efficiencies within the department.

As more and more institutions move toward reliance on data-driven decision-making, it has become imperative that individuals and departments within those institutions have data to back up both the need for their services and the means by which those services are provided. As noted above, cataloging and metadata creation are time-intensive activities that still require a human's touch. In times when a library is asked to do more with less, it may become necessary to show how the work of cataloging and metadata services supports core services and fulfills vital aspects of the library's mission. Furthermore, it may become necessary to show that the work being done in cataloging and metadata services could not be done more effectively by any other means. As an example, a cataloging department may need to show that the library's mission and services could not be supported at an acceptable level by outsourcing some or many of the activities which that department performs.

Setting performance standards and departmental priorities and goals are also important reasons for conducting an assessment. However, the performance standards for cataloging and metadata personnel are replete with issues. Foremost, perhaps, is the difficulty in comparing productivity measurements between individuals or departments at different institutions that have varying policies and workflows.[3] Examples of other difficulties to overcome include personnel buy-in, quality vs. quantity, and determining peer institutions.[4] Nonetheless, there are advantages to setting and measuring performance standards. Some of these advantages include "the ability to improve performance, assess staff knowledge and skills, assess quality, assess processes, and manage expectations."[5] Setting department priorities and goals is less controversial. In a survey given to Pennsylvania academic libraries, Mugridge found that 55.5 percent of the respondents reported that the reason for assessing technical services was "to inform strategic planning activities."[6]

Last but not least, the assessment of cataloging and metadata services can be performed to determine metadata quality. Though there is little agreement found among the definitions of quality cataloging in the literature, Snow has found that descriptions generally "[fall] largely into four major categories: the technical details of the bibliographic record, adherence to standards, the cataloging process, and the impact of cataloging on users."[7] Since the quality of cataloging and metadata creation is tied directly to the user experience with the database, it is imperative that cataloging and metadata services maintain a consistent program of metadata maintenance. For example, Miksa argues for greater work to be done in authority control because "any bibliographic database worth using must have a corresponding authority database to ensure successful searching by subject or name headings."[8] Furthermore, whether records are created in-house or supplied by an external resource, such as WorldCat or a vendor, the record was still created by a human and, therefore, is prone to include errors.[9]

There are other reasons for conducting assessments in cataloging and metadata services. Sassen, Welch, and Loafman discuss some of these, such as learning more about the external and internal users, determining if record enhancement leads to greater use of materials, and evaluating the online tools used by catalogers, such as departmental websites.[10] As stated previously, this is by no means an exhaustive list. However, it does provide a starting point from which to begin to think about ways in which assessment can be applied to the work of cataloging and metadata services.

Assessment can be a useful tool when applied correctly and for the right purpose. The remainder of this chapter will focus on three specific assessment techniques that can be used in cataloging and metadata services: benchmarking, user surveys, and the Balanced Scorecard (BSC). Each of these will be explored through specific implementations, which highlight both the advantages and challenges to using them. These assessment techniques are well-established in business settings, both for profit-making and nonprofit organizations, and have been adapted to work within the library environment. There are a number of good resources for understanding these techniques, both in general and within the library. For a list of these titles, see the additional recommended reading list at the end of this chapter.

Good for further reading

TYPES OF ASSESSMENT IN CATALOGING AND METADATA SERVICES

Benchmarking

→ only useful for certain types of libraries

Benchmarking is a process in which a comparison is made between the unit being assessed and a similar unit in another organization or department that is considered a model in some way. Benchmarking is an assessment tool that is often used to measure performance, such as measuring the quantity of cataloging production.[11] However, Mugridge and Poehlmann consider benchmarking useful for assessing "not only production quantity but also quality, efficiency, and effectiveness."[12] In addition, Haswell argues that benchmarking in libraries can be used reactively, proactively, and strategically. It is used reactively when a librarian needs to justify something such as spending or personnel. It is used proactively when a librarian evaluates the efficiency of something compared to another library. Finally, it is used strategically when a librarian uses the data to convince administrators of continued support.[13] It is clear that benchmarking can be a useful tool for cataloging and metadata services in a number of different scenarios. Some may involve setting internal benchmarks based on samples taken internally. Others may involve using another institution as a means of measurement and comparison.

Although there are two types of benchmarking, internal and external, most cataloging and metadata benchmark assessments fall under the external category. Internal benchmarking can include comparison between departments within the same organization, or the comparison of processes within a single department. External benchmarking compares one organization to another similar organization. The process of benchmarking often follows a five-step process known as the *benchmarking wheel* (see figure 5.1). The steps are *plan, find, collect, analyze,* and *improve.*[14] While the process of benchmarking is an iterative one, it starts with a good *plan.* Here the planning may be conducted

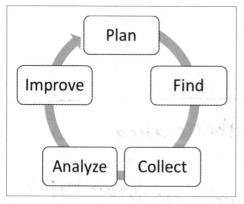

FIGURE 5.1 • Benchmark wheel

by an individual or by a team, depending on the size and needs of the institution performing the assessment. If a team or committee is being used, a chair or facilitator should be chosen to coordinate the work of the group. The first stage, or planning stage, clearly defines what needs to be compared, or assessed. Once this has been decided, the means of collecting data can be determined. This could include using available statistical information or collecting the data directly from the peer group used for benchmarking. The next task is to *find* suitable external institutions or, if internal, another department or process to benchmark against. In external benchmarking this is often one of the most difficult tasks to complete. Variations in library structure, procedures, personnel, and other differences can make it difficult to find another institution with which to compare. Policies and procedures must be clearly defined so that they can be compared to other institutions. Once other institutions have been chosen to serve as benchmarks, it is time to *collect* the data. Data collection methods can vary depending upon the type of data that needs to be collected. If, for example, a cataloging department wished to benchmark its cataloging quality with other institutions, it would first need to define what constitutes quality. If error rates within a record were considered part of what affects the quality of a record, then the department could then define what an error in a record is and begin collecting data on it. Likewise, the department serving as the benchmark would need to collect and supply this data for comparison. Next, the data must be *analyzed*. Questions should be asked about the meaning of the data and what impact it should have on the operations of the department. This is the point where the raw data is turned into practical and useful information for the final step. Finally, the analyzed data can be used to *improve* the processes or other aspects of the department. These improvements should also be monitored and tracked so that the changes can be evaluated for their effectiveness at achieving the desired outcomes.[15] The purpose of benchmarking is to achieve continual improvement through comparison with another department which is considered a model in some way. An example of an implementation of this assessment tool will provide some useful insights into how a department could

Rider U - Case study

go about using benchmarking in cataloging and metadata services. Although the following example uses an internal benchmark, the same basic principles and practices apply to external benchmarking.

Rider University, a private institution located in New Jersey, went through a significant budget reallocation process which resulted in a large increase in the print monograph budget. The sudden increase in print materials being added to the collection led the library to investigate a productivity benchmark in order to determine the "*rate* at which copy catalogers can be *anticipated* to do copy cataloging."[16] Finding no standard benchmark that could be applied to their library, Buschman and Chickering went about the process of establishing their own benchmark at Rider. To accomplish this, they decided to look at the number of records that a copy cataloger touched in aggregate, where "touch" is defined as modifying, adding, or deleting a record. They came up with the aggregate number by looking at the statistics over a longer period of time. This was done so that other factors such as sickness, absence, or the difficulty of cataloging the item would not affect the overall aggregate either positively or negatively. Lastly, Buschman and Chickering calculated the copy cataloger's time at work for the period in which the aggregate number of records touched was calculated. With this information, it was now possible to calculate productivity in terms of records touched per hour by dividing the number of records touched by the number of hours worked.[17]

Although this is an example of an internal benchmark and was exploring productivity in terms of quantity, it still provides useful insights into conducting any benchmark assessment. First, it is important to measure over time. The collection of data over short time spans will not yield the most accurate results, which could in turn affect the outcome of the assessment and set unrealistic benchmarks. Second, the data collected should be representative of the average of whatever is being measured. Anyone familiar with cataloging will understand that there are times when cataloging, either copy or original, can go quickly, with many items being cataloged, while there are other times when very few things are cataloged due to the difficulty and complexity of the issues involved in cataloging those items. For this reason, the length of time that data is collected for any benchmarking assessment should err on the longer side.

Another lesson to learn from the previous example is that benchmarking should be locally defined. What is meant by this is that local personnel, procedures, systems, and other circumstances should be taken into consideration when forming benchmarks. As Buschman and Chickering found out, there are no nationally accepted standards by which cataloging and metadata services

temper does an academic librarian by stressing internal focus benchmarks can be measured. This is important if the benchmark is to be compared to another institution. Care should be taken to consider the differences in size, workflow, and systems when looking for comparable departments outside of your own institution.

A point not easily seen in the example given above is that the staff for whom the standard will apply should be involved in the planning process from the beginning. Charbonneau argues that this is imperative for successful staff buy-in and implementation.[18] Similarly, Goodson contends that "employees are happier when they feel that they have some input into the standards by which they will be evaluated."[19]

An advantage to using benchmarking as an assessment method in cataloging and metadata services is that processes can be improved through the study of what are considered to be exemplary institutions. In studying other institutions, a gap analysis can be performed that shows where there may be deficiencies or overcomplicated processes.[20] A survey conducted by Mugridge and Poehlmann found that other advantages to benchmarking included assessing the knowledge and skills of staff and the quality of work being done.[21] Perhaps the biggest advantage to benchmarking is providing qualitative data for staff performance appraisals. As noted above, staff to whom the benchmarked standards will apply should be involved in the process from the very beginning. Goodson notes that having specific performance standards by which all staff in a particular department will be evaluated relieves the supervisor from having to evaluate the staff on "attitudes" and "vague qualities," which are always subjective.[22] Having these standards set allows staff to work towards concrete and specific goals. Benchmarking can play a significant role in setting these standards, so long as they are set and agreed upon by all involved in the process.

A disadvantage that comes up time and again in the literature on benchmarking is the difficulty in finding peer institutions to compare to. The variables involved in cataloging are many, and these complicate the task of trying to find other institutions by which fair and accurate measurements can be compared. Perhaps the biggest hurdle that must be overcome when looking for peer institutions is the issue of definitions. There are no standard definitions for cataloging activities. Dougherty gives the example of copy cataloging. For one institution, copy cataloging excludes professional librarians, while another includes them in the process.[23] Without common standards that everyone follows, it can be impossible to establish useful benchmarks. Another disadvantage to benchmarking is the misinterpretation of the data resulting from these activities. Depending on who is viewing the data, more context may be necessary. One institution of similar size to another may be getting by with fewer staff by creating metadata with more errors or lower quality. Although administrators inside or outside the library may see the overall output as a sign of efficiency, it may in fact show a lack of institutional investment in the support of quality metadata for the library's collections. In this example, it would be important to show the difference between quantity and quality and what effect that difference has on the user experience.

User Survey *focus on users here*

User surveys are one of the most recognized forms of assessment in libraries. Though often used in public-facing departments, they are also helpful in departments such as cataloging and metadata services. These assessments are often performed to determine whether the organization is meeting the needs of its users, and are otherwise known as "needs assessments." The users of the work that cataloging and metadata services perform can be both internal and external to the library. Internal users are those who work in the library and rely on the metadata produced by cataloging and metadata departments to perform their jobs in service to external users. External users are those who come to the library, either physically or digitally, and who use the metadata to find resources the library has access to that will satisfy their information needs. Other cataloging and metadata assessment activities that use surveys include interdepartmental interaction assessment,[24] customer satisfaction,[25] and a form of needs assessment called Customer Value Discovery,[26] to name but a few.

Since surveys are one of the most prevalent types of assessment used in libraries, the process for creating, disseminating, and analyzing the data of a survey is well represented in the library literature. The following will provide a brief overview of the steps involved in creating and disseminating a survey, but will leave the data analysis to other publications. The reason for this is that data analysis is very dependent on the type of data collected, and given the plethora of types of data that can be collected through a survey, the discussion of data analysis goes beyond the scope of this chapter.[27]

The three-step process that Applegate outlines for surveys is:

1. Designing the survey
2. Administering the survey
3. Analyzing the results[28]

The first step, designing the survey, begins with a clear understanding of the purpose which the survey is meant to serve. A clear research problem must be identified before beginning to craft the questions that will make up the survey. An example of a clear research problem related to cataloging and metadata services would be, "How well does cataloging serve the needs of its internal users?" It is also imperative that the potential respondents have insight into the research problem that is to be the focus of the survey. In either case, if the questions are unclear or the respondents don't have useful knowledge, the survey will not be successful. The next issue to be considered in designing a survey is the length of the survey or the amount of time it should take to complete it. Applegate recommends no more than two pages/sheets or ten minutes as the maximum length.[29] It must be remembered that surveys are very prevalent in all parts of society. This is especially true in certain pockets of society like schools and colleges. The ease with which a survey can be created and aimed at constituents from these institutions makes them frequent targets and can result in what Applegate terms "survey burnout."[30] Care should be taken to ensure that the information sought in the survey cannot be collected by any other means. Once the general research problem and the appropriate user group have been identified and it is determined that a survey is the best instrument for collecting the necessary data to solve this problem, then it is time to move on to creating the individual questions that will make up the survey.

Applegate outlines some basic considerations when creating specific questions for the survey. First, the survey should be created with the appropriate reading level in mind. Although a senior in college will have a higher level of reading comprehension than a senior in high school, the survey questions should still be worded as simply as possible in order to get their point across. Second, library jargon should be excluded from the survey. Even if the survey is to be administered to internal users, the use of jargon can be confusing and may lead to conflicting results when it comes time to analyze the data. If administered to external users, common verbiage should be used that reflects signage or other common naming conventions that are well known to the users. Third, the survey questions should be concrete and not vague. For example, when asking how often someone uses a service, don't include answers such as "frequently" or "infrequently," but instead use concrete language such as "once a week" or "more than five times a week." Fourth, use complete sentences with correct grammar. Complete sentences leave the least room for interpretation and have the best chance of producing consistent and useful information. Fifth, see if there have been previous surveys that covered some of the same content as the survey being created. There is no need to reinvent the wheel. If a question was well-worded and it collected useful responses on a past survey, then it should be reused. Last, it is important that each question deal with one point. There should never be two questions hidden in a single survey question. To do so makes it difficult for the respondent to determine which question they are answering and will, inevitably, lead to confusing results.[31] Keep in mind that at any point during the survey, if the respondent has difficulty deciphering the question or coming up with an answer, they are likely to skip the question or not finish the survey.

Furthermore, there are six different types of questions that can be asked on a survey. These are:

1. **Dichotomous:** this question asks the respondent to choose between two answers.
2. **Multiple-choice:** it asks the respondent to select one or more answers from a set.
3. **Multiple-choice choose one:** it asks the respondent to choose only one answer from a set.
4. **Likert-scale:** it asks the respondent to choose on a scale which consists of one to five, with an equal number of negative and positive responses and one neutral response.
5. **Ask-exact:** it asks the respondent to write their own response based on a specific question.
6. **Open-ended:** it asks the respondent to write their own response to a general question.[32]

Although open-ended questions seem like a good way to garner specific feedback from the respondent, they are also more labor-intensive to produce from the respondent's perspective, and thus are less likely to be completed by the respondent. They also require greater analysis in the end and don't provide generalizable results. Therefore, these questions should be used sparingly and only when no other question type will suffice. Once the questions that will be included in the survey have been identified, then it is time to construct the survey.

A survey in many ways follows the basic pattern of writing a research paper (see figure 5.2). An introduction is used to supply basic information, including

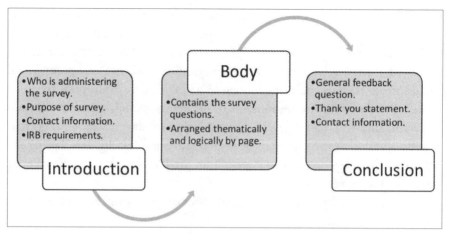

FIGURE 5.2 • Basic layout of a survey

who is administering the survey and for what purpose, what the information will be used for, the confidentiality of the data in the survey, and the contact information of the person/s administering the survey. There may be other information that needs to be covered in the introduction, especially as it relates to institutional review boards and meeting certain disclosure requirements for research involving human subjects. Next is the body of the survey. It should be arranged thematically and follow a predictable or logical sequence. The questions regarding specific subjects or areas should be kept together. At the end of a survey should be a conclusion. The conclusion will include a general feedback question that is open-ended, as well as a thank-you for completing the survey, and possibly the contact information for the person/s administering the survey again. If feedback about the survey is desired, then questions specific to the survey itself and the respondent's experience participating in it can be included in the conclusion as well.

Once the survey has been constructed, it is wise to perform a test run of it on some colleagues. They can provide valuable feedback about whether the questions are specific and understandable, as well as the overall experience of taking the survey. If need be, tweaks to the survey can be made at this time, before it is administered to the specific population for which it was created.

At this point a sample population, sample size, and sampling technique need to be chosen. A sample population refers to a group that shares some specific characteristics. An example would be the students at a university, all of whom share the common trait of being a student at a particular university.

Sample size refers to the number of members from a sample population that will represent the sample population in a survey or study. Calculating sample size can be rather complicated and confusing. However, there are tools available that can ease some of the pain in choosing a sample size.[33] The sampling technique refers to the method that is used to draw a sample from the broader sample population. An example of a sampling technique would be random sampling where members are chosen at random from the sample population. The sampling technique will determine how generalizable the results of the survey can be. Usually, the more generalizable sampling techniques require more work and can have lower participation rates, whereas the less generalizable techniques are easier to accomplish and can create higher response rates. Whichever route is taken, make sure that the consequences of the sampling technique are fully understood, because this will greatly impact the final results and how they are reported.

Another consideration is whether this survey will be distributed to respondents via electronic means, paper, or both. The population to be surveyed should influence this decision. If it is a population that may not have easy access to the Internet or computers, then a paper survey is probably best. However, if the population does have easy computer and Internet access, then an electronic survey is best, since it doesn't require manually inputting data into a computer for data analysis at the conclusion of the survey.

These are the basic steps involved in creating a survey, whether it be electronic or paper. There are many resources that cover this topic in more depth, and the reader is encouraged to consult these resources prior to creating a survey.[34] These resources will also cover the data analysis performed at the end of the survey, which has not been covered here. Keep in mind that the questions asked on the survey will in large part determine the type of data that is available at the end of the survey. Certain questions can only be analyzed in certain ways and may not produce the type of data sought by the creators. However, when done correctly and with forethought, a survey is a simple type of assessment that can yield useful data. real world example

An example of an internal customer service survey comes from the University at Albany, State University of New York's Technical Services and Library Systems Division. The survey was prompted by a desire to determine internal customers' satisfaction with technical services and systems services and ascertain whether there were areas for improvement.[35] Although the survey covered other departments within the library, cataloging was one of these and so will serve as an example that could be implemented by any cataloging and metadata service department. In designing and conducting the survey, the division hoped to accomplish six outcomes: (1) gather new information on customer perceptions and opinions about the division's services, (2) corroborate perceived customer satisfaction or dissatisfaction with current division services, (3) identify service gaps, (4) support change and funding, and provide direction to division managers, (5) convey to others the importance of their opinion of the division, and (6) serve as a public relations or marketing tool for the division.[36] A survey was decided upon as the most appropriate means of assessment to meet these outcomes.

In designing and implementing the survey, a number of issues had to be taken into consideration. First and foremost was the issue of privacy. Honest responses were desired from those taking the survey, so it had to be shown that respondents who gave negative responses would not be subject to repercussions. Likewise, it had to be shown that favor would not be shown to individuals who gave positive responses. To help alleviate these fears, the IP addresses of respondents were not collected. To further ensure anonymity, it was determined that department heads would see all of the responses prior to anyone else seeing them, and any responses that singled out individuals would be evaluated on an individual basis for whether they would be shared or not. Furthermore, any future publishing of the survey would be focused on the process of conducting the survey, while leaving out individual responses which could be "embarrassing" or "reflect unfavorably" on the library.[37] As is best practice, and is often required, institutional review board approval was sought and obtained, since this research involved humans as subjects.

The online tool SurveyMonkey was used to create and distribute the actual survey to employees of the library. After the first page providing the usual details about the survey and the users' rights pertaining to participation and completion of the survey, there were four pages for each of the departments within the division. For each page pertaining to a department, a description of the department's responsibilities was included at the beginning. This was done to ensure that each participant was clear as to what processes belonged to what department. After this, a Likert scale was used to evaluate the department on twelve characteristics. Other general questions pertaining to all four departments were then asked, followed by specific questions developed by each department that pertained particularly to their area of service. Finally, the survey ended with a section that asked questions pertaining to the entire division.[38]

Once the survey was created, it was distributed to the division department heads and staff for approval. Prior to distributing the survey to the entire library, a test was conducted with a select few librarians. Their input was taken into consideration in the final draft of the survey that was distributed to the library personnel. In retrospect, the division would have included more granular questions in the individual department sections to better assess specific functions of the department.[39] However, overall the division felt that the survey went well and provided the useful kind of insight that they had hoped to gather from the survey. ADVANTAGES

There are a number of advantages to the survey form of assessment. Surveys can be an inexpensive and quick form of assessment to carry out. They are especially useful in answering numerically oriented questions.[40] However, qualitative data can be gathered from surveys as well. Constructing, distributing, collecting, and analyzing surveys are made much easier with the widespread availability of software designed for this specific purpose. The questions in the surveys can be tailored to the individual situations that are under study, making them ideal for gathering data on specific issues. Disadvantages

There are, however, a number challenges to conducting successful surveys. One of these challenges is in the design of the questions to be used in the survey. The responses and answers gained from a survey are only as good as the questions being asked. If questions are not worded carefully, the responses may not speak to the areas which the department hopes to gain insight about. Another challenge with surveys is that they are self-reporting. The answers that are received through a survey are the opinions and views of those filling it out. The answers are not necessarily objective or scientifically verifiable. A further challenge with surveys is the response rate. A good response rate is usually seen as 30 percent for most surveys.[41] However, this low response rate is not considered by most authorities to accurately represent the entire population under study, and so it affects the generalizability of the survey results. Closely tied with response rate is the issue of sampling. Sampling is the process by which a representative group is drawn out of the total population. The composition of the sample population as it relates to the characteristics of the total population under study will also significantly impact the generalizability of the survey results.[42] However, if these challenges are considered in the beginning phases of creating a survey, many of them can be compensated for through other measures.

Balanced Scorecard

The Balanced Scorecard (BSC) method of assessment is still finding its way into libraries, let alone cataloging and metadata services. It comes by way of the business world, in which it has been used to assess the alignment of certain measurements with the mission and strategy of the organization.[43] This is accomplished by focusing on four unique perspectives: the user, finance, internal processes, and learning and growth. Part of the popularity of this assessment technique lies in the fact that it does not simply focus on financial issues, but rather focuses on a wider range of factors that affect success. Within each of these perspectives, three to five measures are chosen that in turn reflect the strategic goals of the organization.[44] Measures can be further defined as either outputs or outcomes, otherwise known as lag and lead measures respectively. A frequently used lag measure is customer satisfaction, while a typical lead measure is the number of outreach activities performed by a department.[45] The user perspective, and consequently the measurements chosen for this perspective, focus on how the organization is serving its users' needs. The finance perspective measures the efficiency with which services are rendered to the user. The internal processes perspective attempts to evaluate the activities that enable the organization to meet its users' needs, and often includes measures of quality. Finally, the learning and growth perspective measures how well an organization can meet changes, including whether the employees of the organization are trained and developed in such a way as to adapt to changes.[46]

Developing a BSC assessment requires six steps according to Matthews, a slightly modified version of which will be outlined below.[47] The process begins with the library's strategic plan or its mission and vision statement. One of the greatest strengths, and a major advantage, of the BSC is that it ties assessment activities into the larger organization's strategic goals and mission. This is especially useful to cataloging and metadata services departments, which often have a hard time seeing their work represented in library-wide strategic plans.

The next step involves developing a strategy map. The strategy map "provides a visual framework for a library's strategy—how it intends to create value for its customers."[48] This step is especially important and will require a little more explanation before moving on. For the purposes of implementing a BSC in a cataloging and metadata services department, the strategy map is a tool that visually illustrates how the strategic objectives of that department support the overall goals and strategy of the library as a whole. To build such a mapping you begin with the four perspectives. Each of the four perspectives will serve as a container, stacked in a hierarchical structure, in which each of the strategic objectives in the library's strategic plan that pertain to the cataloging and metadata services department will be placed, as seen in figure 5.3. Ideally, these strategic objectives would be taken directly from the library's strategic plan, but if this is not possible, then they should align as closely as possible with the existing goals of the library. The strategy map is often organized so that the most important perspective sits atop the other three. As an example, for a nonprofit organization, the financial perspective would be at the bottom of the hierarchy, with the learning and growth perspective above that. Next would be the internal process, with the user perspective sitting at the top of the hierarchy.[49]

Beginning at the top with the user perspective, strategic objectives should be created for each user group the library serves.[50] These can include external users such as students, faculty, and the public, as well as internal users such as other departments within the library. Keep in mind, however, that Matthews recommends no more than three or four strategic objectives, since any more than that can dilute the overall quality of the final results.[51] With these objectives in mind, strategic objectives for each of the other three perspectives can be created that support the strategic objectives related to the users. A good strategy map will link these objectives from the various perspectives together in cause-and-effect relationships (represented by the arrows in figure 5.3). The internal process perspective will show the necessary productivity goals to achieve the user perspective objectives. The learning and growth perspective will include the training and professional development necessary to meet the productivity goals. Finally, the financial perspective will include the necessary financial resources needed to achieve all of the department's strategic objectives. The graphical representation of this strategy map will play an important role in the creation of the BSC going forward.

The third step is to select the performance measurements that will be collected within each strategic objective. Although the suggested number of performance measures to collect varies depending on the author, Matthews suggests three to five, at the most.[52] There are a number of types of performance measures that can be used, including input, process, output, and outcome measures. A good BSC will use some of each of these as they work best within the strategic objectives outlined in the strategy map. Examples of possible performance measures for a cataloging and metadata services department include a survey of users, the number of training sessions, the time from receiving to shelf, collection use percentage, and many others. These measures provide an

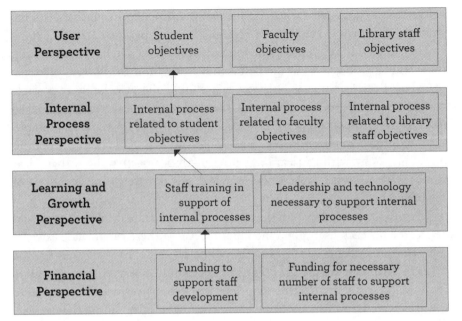

FIGURE 5.3 • Strategy map example

ongoing picture of how the department is, or is not, achieving success in the strategic objectives laid out previously. A good rule of thumb is to choose performance measures using the <u>SMART (Specific, Measurable, Action-oriented, Relevant, Timely) method.[53]</u>

The fourth step involves establishing targets for each performance measure that will determine levels of success in achieving the performance measure. The target should be attainable but still require the department to stretch to achieve it.

The fifth step is to "integrate" the library scorecard.[54] What this means is that the BSC becomes a regular part of the department's meetings and focus. As the performance measures are being monitored, issues that arise can be solved and adjustments can be made to departmental processes or procedures in order to meet the targets that were set.

The sixth and final step is to communicate the results of the BSC. In this way the BSC can serve as a marketing device, showing in measurable ways how the cataloging or metadata services department is contributing in real time to the strategic objectives of the library.

An example of how this can be applied within a library setting will be of assistance. Although the following example did not follow the exact process outlined above, it does show that there are multiple ways to go about conducting a BSC assessment. another real-world example

The Hanyang University Library (in South Korea) decided to outsource its entire cataloging operation with the exception of one cataloging supervisor, who would remain on staff with the library. A contractor was hired to supply employees who would perform the cataloging for the library. The employees of the contractor worked on-site in the library and were hired and managed by the contractor. The contractor was paid based on the amount of data created by the catalogers. The cataloging supervisor did not evaluate the contract workers, but rather "reviewed and revised the input data and calculated the costs."[55] In order to provide a fair and common ground for measuring the performance of the contract catalogers, as well as to help solve one of the greatest issues with outsourcing—namely, the disparity of institutional buy-in from outside contractors and library employees—a BSC was conducted.

Before the BSC was begun, a SWOT (Strengths, Weaknesses, Opportunities, and Threats) analysis was conducted to aid in the process of creating metrics in the BSC. A matrix, similar to a strategy map, was drawn up, with the correlation between the four elements serving as the basis for the strategies that the cataloging department would use to establish the key areas to focus on during the BSC. The strengths and weaknesses of the current setup with outsourced cataloging were then further evaluated based upon opportunities and threats. As an example, a weakness in the current setup was the difficulty of quality control. An opportunity was the greater number of universities in South Korea that were turning to outsourced cataloging, thereby creating a greater supply of individuals with cataloging experience. A strategy developed from the intersection of these two elements was to only hire contract workers who had a minimum of three years of experience in university library cataloging.[56] With this and other strategies in hand, the library was able to begin working on those areas within the four perspectives of the BSC.

Eight goals were established within each of the four perspectives. For the user perspective two goals were set, which focused on improving the quality and detail of the catalog. The metrics established to measure success in achieving these goals included conducting a user satisfaction survey, reducing errors in records, and greater use of authority controls. For the internal processes perspective three goals were established, focusing on the utilization of existing resources, expediting cataloging processes, and increasing the rate of collection-building. Some of the metrics chosen for this perspective included utilizing CIP data in cataloging, reducing backlogs, and focusing on rare editions and donated materials. For the learning and growth perspective, two goals were set that focused on developing the cataloging staff and sharing the department's vision with other departments in the library. The metrics used to measure success in this area include participation in professional training and departmental workshops. Finally, the financial perspective included one goal, which was to reduce costs. The metrics used to measure this included a quantitative evaluation of the contract cataloging service, as well as differentiating the cost based upon the level of difficulty in the cataloging.[57] All of these metrics were concrete performance measures that could be quantified or easily tracked and reported upon. With these metrics, the cataloging department was able to measure its progress towards meeting the goals established in the four perspectives. Using these results, the department could set new goals and metrics for the next year that continued to align it with the library's strategic goals.

There are obvious differences between the method outlined at the beginning of this section and the one used by the Hanyang University Library. However, the basic principles still remain in that multiple perspectives are used to determine the areas in which metrics will be collected. The metrics were established to measure progress towards achieving certain goals or strategies of the cataloging department that aligned with the overall strategic goals of the library. Although the Hanyang University Library did not use a strategy map, their matrix served a similar purpose. The situation at that library may be atypical in that most cataloging and metadata departments will not be looking to completely outsource their work. However, the example serves as a good illustration of how the BSC can be implemented specifically in a cataloging and metadata department and what kinds of metrics could be collected.

There are many advantages to the BSC method of assessment, including being able to demonstrate in measurable ways how the particular department contributes to the library's larger strategies and goals. This is especially important for nonpublic-facing departments such as cataloging and metadata services. Because so much of the library focuses on the user, it is important for those departments that do not directly interact with users to show their impact on the users' experiences. Another advantage to the BSC is that it helps focus the assessment process on a few select measurables. As James Self put it with regard to the University of Virginia Library's implementation of a BSC, it "made us figure out what areas are important, and what constitutes success in those areas."[58] Last but not least, the balanced aspect of the BSC also helps ensure that assessment activities are not just focused on specific areas, but are spread across a number of what the BSC calls "perspectives." Although the BSC was originally intended to help for-profit businesses focus on areas outside of financial measures to assess their success or failure, the BSC can help broaden a library's perspective of assessment beyond what it traditionally focuses on, namely customer service. This is good news for departments like cataloging and metadata services, since it allows the work done there to be included and valued in assessment practices.[59]

Challenges in using the BSC method of assessment include the possibility of including too many metrics, thereby making the assessment more difficult and time-consuming without adding any overall benefit. It is generally recommended to include three to five metrics per perspective so as not to become overloaded with information.[60] This creates another challenge, namely, choosing what to measure. Although this can certainly be more difficult when working with the entire library, there are still challenges to be faced by those looking to use the BSC in a cataloging or metadata services department. It can be a challenge not only to decide what metrics to focus on, but also in deciding how to measure those metrics. Furthermore, Self has rightly pointed out that the old adage "what gets measured, gets managed" can apply in this circumstance, with negative results for those areas not being measured.[61] Another challenge that a department is likely to face is generating staff buy-in. Numerous libraries that have implemented a BSC have noted that it can be difficult to achieve buy-in from staff who often view assessment in general, and especially assessments from the business world, as suspicious busywork.[62] The changes that result from any assessment are also viewed suspiciously if the proper context and need for the assessment are not discussed from the beginning.

Other examples of BSC use in libraries exist, but few focus on cataloging departments specifically. The University of Virginia Library has been an example to many wishing to implement a BSC. The work that the University of Virginia Library has done with BSC goes back to 2001 and is well documented by James Self, who was then director of management information services.[63] The Association of Research Libraries has also focused on BSC use and its implementation within academic libraries in particular.[64] The BSC method of assessment holds a great deal of promise in helping cataloging departments show how their work aligns with the library's strategic plan and goals in specific measurable ways, which can go a long way toward fulfilling some of the reasons discussed earlier for carrying out assessment activities in cataloging.

CONCLUSION

Assessment is a well-established practice in most libraries. However, the specific application of various assessment techniques in cataloging and metadata services departments is just recently being explored. Recent publications that have focused on assessment in cataloging and metadata services include a special issue of the *Cataloging & Classification Quarterly* edited by Rebecca Mugridge which includes a number of papers on various topics related to assessment in cataloging and metadata services environments.[65] In her introduction to this special issue Mugridge says: "I have long felt that cataloging and metadata departments regularly conduct a variety of forms of assessment, but that we are not good at sharing those assessment activities or communicating the results of our efforts."[66] This is true, but we have also not always chosen the correct assessment technique for the specific circumstance that requires assessment. As noted in the introduction to this chapter, the purpose of the assessment should drive the type of assessment. If an administrator asks why the library should replace an open cataloging or metadata position, the response should not be how many items were cataloged last month or year. A better response would be to show how the department, and the empty position, have contributed to the goals and work of other departments, as well as the overall mission of the library. Assessment should become an everyday activity that guides and forms the work done in cataloging and metadata services departments. In many ways, the shift of libraries to a greater awareness and use of assessment is a great benefit to those working in nonpublic-facing departments. After all, assessments are all about data and that, at the end of the day, is exactly what cataloging and metadata specialists are all about.

NOTES

1. Rebecca Mugridge and Nancy M. Poehlmann, "Internal Customer Service Assessment of Cataloging, Acquisitions, and Library Systems," *OCLC Systems & Services: International Digital Library Perspectives* 31, no. 4 (2015): 222.

2. A list of studies performed for this purpose can be found in Catherine Sassen, Rebecca Welch, and Kathryn Loafman, "Assessment of Cataloging Services in an Academic Library," *Technical Services Quarterly* 33, no. 1 (2016): 25.

3. John Buschman and F. William Chickering, "A Rough Measure of Copy Cataloging Productivity in the Academic Library," *Library Philosophy and Practice,* July (2007): 1, https://digitalcommons.unl.edu/libphilprac/139/.

4. Claire-Lisa Bénaud, Sever Bordeianu, and Mary Ellen Hanson, "Cataloging Production Standards in Academic Libraries," *Technical Services Quarterly* 16, no. 3 (1999): 46–48.

5. Rebecca L. Mugridge and Nancy M. Poehlmann, "Benchmarking as an Assessment Tool for Cataloging," *Technical Services Quarterly* 32, no. 2 (2015): 153.

6. Rebecca L. Mugridge, "Technical Services Assessment: A Survey of Pennsylvania Academic Libraries," *Library Resources and Technical Services* 58, no. 2 (2014): 104.

7. Karen Snow, "Defining, Assessing, and Rethinking Quality Cataloging," *Cataloging and Classification Quarterly* 55, no. 7–8 (2017): 445.

8. Shawne D. Miksa, "You Need My Metadata: Demonstrating the Value of Library Cataloging," *Journal of Library Metadata* 8, no. 1 (2008): 26.

9. Ibid., 27.

10. Sassen, Welch and Loafman, "Assessment of Cataloging Services," 25–26.

11. See, for example, Buschman and Chickering, "A Rough Measure of Copy Cataloging."

12. Mugridge and Poehlmann, "Benchmarking as an Assessment," 142.

13. Martha Haswell, "Benchmarking: A Powerful Management Tool," *Information Outlook* 16, no. 5 (2012): 15.

14. Peter Brophy, *Measuring Library Performance: Principles and Techniques* (London: Facet, 2006), 150.

15. Ibid., 151.

16. Buschman and Chickering, "A Rough Measure of Copy Cataloging," 3.

17. Ibid., 4.

18. Mechael D. Charbonneau, "Production Benchmarks for Catalogers in Academic Libraries: Are We There Yet?" *Library Resources and Technical Services* 49, no. 1 (2005): 42.

19. Carol F. Goodson, *The Complete Guide to Performance Standards for Library Personnel* (New York: Neal-Schuman, 1997), 14.

20. Haswell, "Benchmarking," 14.

21. Mugridge and Poehlmann, "Benchmarking as an Assessment," 153.

22. Goodson, *Complete Guide to Performance Standards,* 14.

23. Richard M. Dougherty, *Streamlining Library Services: What We Do, How Much Time It Takes, What It Costs, and How We Can Do It Better* (Lanham, MD: Scarecrow, 2008), 182.

24. See, for example, Andrea Payant, Becky Skeen, and Liz Woolcott, "Initiating Cultural Shifts in Perception of Cataloging Units through Interaction Assessment," *Cataloging & Classification Quarterly* 55, no. 7–8 (2017): 467–92.

25. See, for example, Sassen, Welch, and Loafman, "Assessment of Cataloging Services," 23–41.

26. See, for example, Sue McKnight, "Acquisition and Cataloging Processes: Changes as a Result of Customer Value Discovery Research," *Evidence-Based Library and Information Practice* 2, no. 4 (2007): 22–36.

27. See the recommended reading list at the end of this chapter for suggested resources on data analysis.

28. Rachel Applegate, *Practical Evaluation Techniques for Librarians* (Santa Barbara, CA: Libraries Unlimited, 2013), 3–4.

29. Ibid., 4.

30. Ibid., 5.

31. Ibid., 5–6.

32. Ibid., 6–8.

33. See, for example, Peter Hernon, "Determination of Sample Size and Selection of the Sample: Concepts, General Sources, and Software," *College and Research Libraries* 55, no. 2 (1994): 171–79. Although dated, this article offers an easy-to-understand explanation of sampling and sample size calculation.

34. See the recommended reading list at the end of this chapter for suggested resources on data analysis.

35. Mugridge and Poehlmann, "Internal Customer Service Assessment," 220.

36. Ibid., 221–22.

37. Ibid., 224–25.

38. Ibid., 226.

39. Ibid., 227.

40. Rosalind Farnam Dudden, *Using Benchmarking, Needs Assessment, Quality Improvement, Outcome Measurement, and Library Standards,* How-to-Do-It Manuals for Librarians 159 (New York: Neal-Schuman, 2007), 82.

41. Applegate, *Practical Evaluation Techniques for Librarians,* 3.

42. Barbara M. Wildemuth and Leo L. Cao, "Sampling for Intensive Studies," in *Applications of Social Research Methods to Questions in Information and Library Science,* ed. Barbara M. Wildemuth (Westport, CT: Libraries Unlimited, 2009), 133.

43. James Self, "Metrics and Management: Applying the Results of the Balanced Scorecard," *Performance Measurement and Metrics* 5, no. 3 (2004): 101.

44. Joseph R. Matthews, *Scorecards for Results: A Guide for Developing a Library Balanced Scorecard* (Westport, CT: Libraries Unlimited, 2008), 1.

45. Despina Dapias Wilson, Theresa del Tufo, and Anne E. C. Norman, *The Measure of Library Excellence: Linking the Malcolm Baldridge Criteria and Balanced Scorecard Methods to Assess Service Quality* (Jefferson, NC: McFarland, 2008), 139.

46. Matthews, *Scorecards for Results,* 3–7.

47. Ibid., 27.

48. Ibid., 58.

49. See, for example, Robert S. Kaplan and David P. Norton, *Strategy Maps: Converting Intangible Assets into Tangible Outcomes* (Boston: Harvard Business School Press, 2004), 432.

50. This is a slightly modified version of the strategy map used by the Boston Lyric Opera example in Kaplan and Norton, *Strategy Maps,* 430–33.

51. Matthews, *Scorecard for Results,* 58.

52. Ibid., 28. Wilson, del Tufo, and Norman recommend a slightly different approach where each perspective has two to three objectives and each objective has two to three

performance measures; see Wilson, del Tufo, and Norman, *The Measure of Library Excellence,* 183.

53. Matthews, *Scorecards for Results,* 71.
54. Ibid., 29.
55. Dong Suk Kim, "Using the Balanced Scorecard for Strategic Operation of the Cataloging Department," *Cataloging & Classification Quarterly* 48, no. 6–7 (2010): 576.
56. Ibid., 581.
57. Ibid., 582.
58. Self, "Metrics and Management," 104.
59. Ibid.
60. Matthews, *Scorecards for Results,* 87.
61. James Self, "From Value to Metrics: Implementation of the Balanced Scorecard at a University Library," *Performance Measurement and Metrics* 4, no. 2 (2003): 59.
62. Vivian Lewis, Steve Hiller, Elizabeth Mengel, and Donna Tolson, "Building Scorecards in Academic Research Libraries: Performance Measurement and Organizational Issues," *Evidence Based Library and Information Practice* 8, no. 2 (2013): 196, https://doi.org/10 .18438/B8T02Z.
63. See Self, "From Values to Metrics," 57–63; and Self, "Metrics and Management," 101–5.
64. See Lewis, Hiller, Mengel, and Tolson, "Building Scorecards in Academic Research Libraries," 183–99, https://doi.org/10.18438/B8T02Z.
65. For an introduction to the contents of this issue, see Rebecca L. Mugridge, "Assessment of Cataloging and Metadata Services: Introduction," *Cataloging & Classification Quarterly* 55, no. 7–8 (2017): 435–37, https://doi.org/10.1080/01639374.2017.1362913.
66. Ibid., 435.

REFERENCES

Applegate, Rachel. *Practical Evaluation Techniques for Librarians.* Santa Barbara, CA: Libraries Unlimited, 2013.

Bénaud, Claire-Lisa, Sever Bordeianu, and Mary Ellen Hanson. "Cataloging Production Standards in Academic Libraries." *Technical Services Quarterly* 16, no. 3 (1999): 43–67. https://doi.org/10.1300/J124v16n03_04.

Brophy, Peter. *Measuring Library Performance: Principles and Techniques.* London: Facet Publishing, 2006.

Buschman, John, and F. William Chickering. "A Rough Measure of Copy Cataloging Productivity in the Academic Library." *Library Philosophy and Practice* (July 2007): 1–9. http://digitalcommons.unl.edu/libphilprac/139.

Charbonneau, Mechael D. "Production Benchmarks for Catalogers in Academic Libraries: Are We There Yet?" *Library Resources and Technical Services* 49, no. 1 (2005): 40–48.

Dougherty, Richard M. *Streamlining Library Services: What We Do, How Much Time it Takes,*

What it Costs, and How We Can Do it Better. Lanham, MD: Scarecrow Press, 2008.

Dudden, Rosalind Farnam. *Using Benchmarking, Needs Assessment, Quality Improvement, Outcome Measurement, and Library Standards*, How-To-Do-It Manuals for Librarians 158. New York: Neal-Schuman Publishers, 2007.

Goodson, Carol F. *The Complete Guide to Performance Standards for Library Personnel*. New York: Neal-Schuman Publishers, 1997.

Haswell, Martha. "Benchmarking: A Powerful Management Tool." *Information Outlook* 16, no. 5 (2012): 13–15.

Hernon, Peter. "Determination of Sample Size and Selection of the Sample: Concepts, General Sources, and Software." *College and Research Libraries* 55, no. 2 (1994): 171–79.

Kaplan, Robert S. and David P. Norton. *Strategy Maps: Converting Intangible Assets into Tangible Outcomes*. Boston: Harvard Business School Press, 2004.

Kim, Dong Suk. "Using the Balanced Scorecard for Strategic Operation of the Cataloging Department." *Cataloging & Classification Quarterly* 48, no. 6-7 (2010): 572–84. https://doi.org/10.1080/01639374.2010.496305.

Lewis, Vivian, Steve Hiller, Elizabeth Mengel and Donna Tolson. "Building Scorecards in Academic Research Libraries: Performance Measurement and Organizational Issues." *Evidence Based Library and Information Practice* 8, no. 2 (2013): 183–99. https://doi.org/10.18438/B8T02Z.

Matthews, Joseph R. *Scorecards for Results: A Guide for Developing a Library Balanced Scorecard*. Westport, CT: Libraries Unlimited, 2008.

McKnight, Sue. "Acquisition and Cataloging Processes: Changes as a Result of Customer Value Discovery Research." *Evidence Based Library and Information Practice* 2, no. 4 (2007): 22–36. https://doi.org/10.18438/B8D61X.

Miksa, Shawne D. "You Need My Metadata: Demonstrating the Value of Library Cataloging." *Journal of Library Metadata* 8, no. 1 (2008): 23–36. https://doi.org/10.1300/J517v08n01_03.

Mugridge, Rebecca L. "Assessment of Cataloging and Metadata Services: Introduction." *Cataloging & Classification Quarterly* 55, no. 7-8 (2017): 435–37. https://doi.org/10.1080/01639374.2017.1362913.

———. "Technical Services Assessment: A survey of Pennsylvania Academic Libraries." *Library Resources and Technical Services* 58, no. 2 (2014): 100–10. http://dx.doi.org/10.5860/lrts.58n2.100.

Mugridge, Rebecca, and Nancy M. Poehlmann. "Benchmarking as an Assessment Tool for Cataloging." *Technical Services Quarterly* 32, no. 2 (2015): 141–59. https://doi.org/10.1080/07317131.2015.998465.

———. "Internal Customer Service Assessment of Cataloging, Acquisitions, and Library Systems." *OCLC Systems & Services: International Digital Library Perspective* 31, no. 4 (2015): 219–48. https://doi.org/10.1108/OCLC-12-2014-0037.

Payant, Andrea, Becky Skeen and Liz Woolcott. "Initiating Cultural Shifts in Perceptions of Cataloging Units Through Interaction Assessment." *Catalog & Classification Quarterly* 55, no. 7-8 (2017): 467–92. https://doi.org/10.1080/01639374.2017.1350775.

Sassen, Catherine, Rebecca Welch, and Kathryn Loafman. "Assessment of Cataloging Services in an Academic Library." *Technical Services Quarterly* 33, no. 1 (2016): 23–41. https://doi.org/10.1080/07317131.2015.1093820.

Self, James. "From Values to Metrics: Implementation of the Balanced Scorecard at a University Library." *Performance Measurement and Metrics* 4, no. 2 (2003): 57–63. https://doi.org/10.1108/14678040310486891.

———. "Metrics and Management: Applying the Results of the Balanced Scorecard." *Performance Measurement and Metrics* 5, no. 3 (2004): 101–5. https://doi.org/10.1108/14678040410570111.

Snow, Karen. "Defining, Assessing, and Rethinking Quality Cataloging." *Cataloging and Classification Quarterly* 55, no. 7-8 (2017): 438–55. https://doi.org/10.1080/01639374.2017.1350774.

Wildemuth, Barbara M., and Leo L. Cao. "Sampling for Intensive Studies." In *Applications of Social Research Methods to Questions in Information and Library Science*, ed. Barbara M. Wildemuth, 116–28. Westport, CT: Libraries Unlimited, 2009.

Wilson, Despina Dapia, Theresa del Tufo and Anne E. C. Norman. *The Measure of Library Excellence: Linking Malcolm Baldrige Criteria and Balanced Scorecard Methods to Assess Service Quality*. Jefferson, NC: McFarland and Company, 2008.

ADDITIONAL RECOMMENDED READING

Andersen, Bjørn, and Per-Gaute Pettersen. *The Benchmarking Handbook: Step-by-Step Instructions*. London: Chapman & Hall, 1996.

Babbie, Earl. *Survey Research Methods*. 2nd ed. Belmont, CA: Wadsworth, 1990.

Connaway, Lynn Silipigni, and Ronald R. Powell. *Basic Research Methods for Librarians*. 5th ed. Library and Information Science Text Series. Santa Barbara, CA: Libraries Unlimited, 2010.

Dillman, Don A., Jolene D. Smyth and Leah Melani Christian. *Internet, Phone, Mail, and Mixed-Mode Surveys: The Tailored Design Method*. 4th ed. Hoboken, N.J.: John Wiley & Sons, 2014.

Fink, Arlene. *How to Conduct Surveys: A Step-by-Step Guide*. 4th ed. Los Angeles: Sage, 2009.

Kaplan, Robert S., and David P. Norton. *The Balanced Scorecard: Translating Strategy into Action*. Boston: Harvard Business School Press, 1996.

Niven, Paul R. *Balanced Scorecard: Step-by-Step for Government and Nonprofit Agencies*. 2nd ed. Hoboken, N.J.: John Wiley & Sons, 2008.

Peterson, Robert A. *Constructing Effective Questionnaires*. Thousand Oaks, CA: Sage Publications, 2000.

Pickard, Alison Jane. *Research Methods in Information*. London: Facet Publishing, 2007.

Punch, Keith F. *Survey Research: The Basics*. Thousand Oaks, CA: Sage Publications, 2003.

Sapsford, Roger. *Survey Research*. 2nd ed. Thousand Oaks, CA: Sage Publications, 2007.

Spendolini, Michael. *The Benchmarking Book*. New York: AMACOM, 1992.

Stapenhurst, Tim. *The Benchmarking Book: A How-to-Guide to Best Practices for Managers and Practitioners*. Boston: Elsevier, 2009.

Stephen, Peter, and Susan Horby. *Simple Statistics for Library and Information Professionals*. 2nd ed. Thousand Oaks, CA: Sage Publications, 1999.

Vaughan, Liwen. *Statistical Methods for the Information Professional: A Practical, Painless Approach to Understanding, Using, and Interpreting Statistics*. ASIST Monograph Series. Medford, N.J.: Information Today, 2001.

PRESERVATION ASSESSMENTS

Fletcher Durant

I n the forty years since Stanford and Yale undertook the first large-scale preservation assessments of library collections, American libraries and the understanding of their responsibilities to patrons and collections have grown, even as funding has failed to keep pace with that growth. Evaluating the condition and preservation needs of collections is essential for preserving their materials for current and future users, and it enables librarians to direct their limited time and resources to more impactful actions. This chapter will examine the four primary types of preservation assessments undertaken in libraries and archives: preservation needs assessments, collection condition surveys, collection assessments, and item-level condition reports. Each of these assessment formats offers different insights into the condition of library collections and serves distinct purposes in developing preservation priorities.

A *preservation needs assessment* is a broad, holistic evaluation of how an organization cares for and preserves its collections. Any institution can benefit from a needs assessment, since it examines both the strategic and practical aspects of caring for collections in a preventive fashion. A *collection condition survey* can be undertaken by any organization with consistent collections (such as books) in order to provide data on the risks and damage to collection materials. Basic statistical sampling allows organizations to extrapolate trends in their collections to allow for strategic planning and resource allocation in order to better meet collection needs and reduce risks. *Collection assessments* are an intensive method of assessment that is more suited to diverse or unique collections such as special collections or archival holdings. This structured evaluation of individual collections allows for improved project planning for housing and reformatting interventions. *Item–level condition reports* are vital for documenting the condition of high-value or high-risk items, such as items on exhibition loan. However, the time-intensive nature of the condition reports should limit their use across collections.

Preservation assessments are tools to assist libraries in better understanding and caring for their collections. While existing preservation knowledge and experience can facilitate speedier or more in-depth data collection, at least some specialized knowledge is required to conduct basic assessments and surveys to strengthen collections. Outside funding and specialists are also available to conduct assessments of collections and institutions that may need the additional support.

PRESERVATION NEEDS ASSESSMENTS

A preservation needs assessment (also known as a general preservation planning survey) is a comprehensive evaluation of an organization's ability to care for and preserve its collection materials. The goal of the preservation needs assessment is to describe the impact of the existing conditions and policies on the collections, and provide corresponding short-, medium-, and long-term steps that an organization can take to benefit the materials under its care. The scope and recommendations of this kind of assessment should be tailored to fit the realities of a given institution, its staffing levels, and budget constraints. Aspirational goals can be included, but the report should be clear that perfect is the enemy of good.

The needs assessment is a truly holistic look at an organization in order to understand how everything from the building structure to staff food policies can impact the condition of materials over the life span of the collections. The categories of assessment used are descriptive and qualitative, and a given assessor or institution may categorize specific aspects differently without impacting the overall value of the report. It is also important to consider that, due to the interrelated nature of the risks to collections, the different categories assessed interact with each other. For example, temperature and relative humidity (RH) are the primary factors in the aging of collections, but high temperatures and high RH increase the risk of mold growth and pest infestations, while low temperatures and low RH can temporarily increase the brittleness of some materials, leading to handling issues and impact accessibility. These interactions need to be understood in the context of a given institution and its mission in order to provide meaningful guidance that can be implemented successfully.

The starting point for any organization considering a preservation needs assessment is to determine whether internal staff or an outside consultant should conduct the assessment. While staff members should be expected to have insights into the recurring and long-term preservation issues of their collections, outside consultants bring fresh eyes, a neutral perspective, and a significant amount of preservation experience.[1] In reality, few organizations have staff members with the time or background to conduct the assessment internally. For these organizations, state libraries or the American Institute for Conservation's "Find a Conservator" tool are key starting places for locating a preservation specialist to conduct an assessment.[2]

Expected Areas of Assessment

In her analysis of thirty years of needs assessments, Karen E. K. Brown identifies six primary areas for assessment. Regardless of who is conducting the assessment, an organization should expect that the following areas and topics will be reviewed:

- Administration (mission, collecting policies, intellectual control, staffing/training needs, budgets)
- Building and facilities.
- Environmental factors (monitoring and control of temperature, relative humidity, light, pollutants)
- Protection against loss (pest management, emergency preparedness and prevention, security)
- Condition, storage, and handling of collections in various formats (including exhibition)
- Remedial treatment (reformatting, repair and conservation, library binding)[3]

Conducting the Needs Assessment

Since the needs assessment is a qualitative assessment, there is no formal instrument to design, although assessors may have prepared checklists or interview forms. Rather, the needs assessment takes place in three distinct phases: (1) pre-site background information collection, (2) stakeholder interviews, and (3) site inspection. Needs assessments do require a commitment of staff time, whether conducted by the staff or by consultants. Brown's 2005 analysis of needs assessments shows that 73 percent of assessments required less than 40 hours of staff time, and 86 percent of consultant site visits took fewer than two days to complete.[4]

Pre-Site Background Information

The pre-site background information collection is intended to provide the assessor with all of the relevant documents to understand the organization, its mission and structure, the scale and scope of the collections, previous grant applications, environmental data, blueprints or design drawings, processing manuals, and other formal or informal documents that an organization may have for the collections. These documents help the assessor understand the organization and prepare the assessor to formulate the scope of their interviews and on-site inspection. The absence of documentation may indicate that informal policies could benefit from formalization or initial development. Formal documentation is especially important for organizations that rely on volunteer labor or have high turnover, since informal best practices may not survive staffing transitions.

Stakeholder Interviews — *typically done by a manager*

Following the collection of written documents, the stakeholder interviews provide the assessor with firsthand input and institutional knowledge from the staff. The assessor should interview staff or volunteers with executive, curatorial, preservation, and patron responsibilities. In a smaller institution, these responsibilities may all reside in a single person. The staff can provide a wealth of information and insight that would otherwise be difficult to glean from limited site visits. It is important for the assessor to try to establish trust at the beginning of the interview process, since the unvarnished truth from the staff will provide the greatest opportunity for understanding the needs of the organization. The assessor is not there to pass moral judgment on the functioning of the staff or the organization, only to assist in addressing needs and evaluating areas for improvement.

In particular, long-term staff are a valuable source of information about the functions and problems within a collection. They may recall collection disasters that have impacted materials, or explain procedures or unusual storage choices that the assessor may encounter. Long-term staff are likely to have opinions about the functioning of certain aspects of the organization, such as the service desk operations, stacks security, or space rentals, that are not reflected elsewhere. Newer staff may offer a different type of perspective, highlighting operations and functions that "have just always been done this way." New staff also tend to notice minor issues, such as water stains or seasonal pest sightings, that longer-tenured staff have come to accept.

The assessor should focus the staff interviews on risks and issues that are either historic or procedural in nature. Examples of historic risks could be events that happened in the past that may not be immediately apparent to the assessor when they are on-site, whether it is a disaster from which an organization has already recovered or the acquisition of a collection that caused difficulties and forced workflow adjustments. Procedural issues are the recurring problems that might arise when helping patrons, such as lack of coverage in the reading room exposing a security risk, or event rentals leaving food behind after parties. The interviews should help establish what the staff understand to be their immediate needs and should convey priorities and risks that could otherwise be missed. Additionally, the interviews should begin to frame the types of risks that a collection faces and its preservation priorities.

Site Inspection

The site inspection is the final step of data collection. The inspection primarily focuses on the areas of collection storage, display, and use, but it needs to consider all areas of the facilities. Preservation issues frequently arise when the staff store collections at their desks or convert closets into unlabeled storage areas. Security and environmental issues can also arise when collections are stored in areas that are not intended for collections use.

The site inspection collects as much qualitative data as possible about the current state of the collections and about potential risks. The information collected from background documents and stakeholder interviews guides the assessor, but the assessor must also use their experience to identify risks and issues that staff may overlook or be unaware of. The assessor should document the range of risks or damage that they observes, whether those risks are vulnerable formats, poor storage conditions, or structural risks. Frequently staff no longer "see" those boxes in the corner or the rolled posters that are stored atop shelving units. Because of the broad scope of the needs assessment, the assessor typically does not focus on item-level issues in a collection ("Book X has detached boards"), but should identify repetitive risks that are apparent across the collection ("Significant numbers of volumes in Special Collections have detached boards, which threaten the usability of the collection for researchers").

After the site inspection, follow-up interviews with select stakeholders may be needed to provide added information or clarification of the assessor's findings.

Analysis and Reporting

Once the data collection is completed, it is the role of the assessor to analyze the findings and compile them into a concise and understandable report. The report should describe the organization's mission, structure, and collections, as well as identifying both the strengths and the areas of improvement for caring for the collections. Differing institutions and assessors may structure reports differently, but the heart of the report should be a list of the major issues identified during the assessment, including an accessible explanation of the risks that each issue poses to the collections. The assessment report should provide a list of actions and/or potential solutions to the identified risks, as well as a sense of the relative importance of each action to the well-being of the collection.

Many organizations that receive preservation needs assessments may not have any staff members with backgrounds in preservation. The report must be written clearly and concisely to provide these organizations with the information they need to care for their collections. Suggestions for improved housings should include contact information for reputable vendors; updating or creating a disaster plan should include links to online and print resources; and conservation treatment needs should include listings of local conservators or point to the American Institution for Conservation's "Find a Conservator" tool. A successful report should lead to both immediate and long-term actions by the organization. The nature of those actions will vary greatly based upon local needs, but an organization should expect that guidance on improving housing and storage conditions, the care and handling of materials by staff and users, facility recommendations, disaster planning and response, and security issues may be addressed.

COLLECTION CONDITION SURVEYS

A collection condition survey, or condition survey, is a survey of a statistically significant, representative, random sample of collections that is undertaken to provide data on the physical condition and needs of the collection. The collection condition survey is a particularly effective tool for analyzing library collections that typically hold large numbers of similar materials (books) in similar conditions, with similar patterns of use and similar rates of damage. The data should provide insights into the issues facing the collections that may provide strategic direction for the library's preservation and conservation programs. The survey may also identify types of damage that are better mediated by user education and outreach, such as damage from handling, misshelving, or poorly designed book drops.

Condition surveys can be a valuable tool for both general, circulating collections and special collections. The collection of data from a random sample of holdings, if done on a scale large enough to be considered statistically significant, can accurately depict the issues in a collection to within +/–5 percent. Considering the scale of many library holdings, evaluating every volume is impractical, and condition surveys are an effective way to gather a snapshot of vital data.

The condition survey should reflect the local needs, issues, and capabilities of the library. While we might expect the rate of damage found in research libraries and public libraries to vary, the survey tool to collect the data may look very similar for all of them, since the primary preservation problems that are found in books are fairly universal across collections. The survey tool may also reflect the level of institutional commitment to preservation: the greater the expected investment in preservation, the greater the level of detail of the data collected in the survey. While more data to track preservation issues is always a welcome thing, the cost-benefit ratio for the institution needs to be clear, and collecting more data points will require both a better-trained staff to identify specific damage and more time to record that additional information.

Designing and Implementing the Survey

A wide variety of data may be collected during a condition survey. Organizations with greater capacity can include more data points, but any organization should benefit from collecting the following key points:

- Volume size
- Format
- Date of imprint
- Location (or region) of imprint
- Binding style
- Condition of the binding
- Leaf attachment method
- Condition of the text block
- Paper type
- Types of damage

A more detailed list of survey questions can be found in Brian J. Baird's *Library Collection Assessment through Statistical Sampling*[5] or from other published condition surveys such as the Yale[6] and Stanford[7] surveys. However, the basic data points listed above should enable an institution to understand the rates and types of damage to its collection, as well as some of the underlying conditions that may contribute to that damage. Data entry must be structured to facilitate analysis. Drop-down menus and checkboxes should be used as much as possible. If paper survey forms or free-text fields are being used for data collection, instruction sheets with standardized language or abbreviations should be provided to every survey team.

Sample Size

Once the survey tool is developed, the next step is to determine the number of volumes to survey for the sample set. There are helpful in-depth resources[8] to explain statistical significance and confidence levels, but a good rule of thumb is that to have a 95 percent confidence level at a +/–5 percent confidence interval, the sample size must be at least 384 items. To have 99 percent confidence at a +/–5 percent confidence interval, the sample size must be at least 600 items. To achieve a smaller confidence interval, the sample size needs to approximately double for every percentage point. But 384 volumes is a suitable number to start with, which can be rounded off upward to 500 volumes to account for variation or errors in the sample selection process.

When designing the survey, the surveyors must note that the data can only represent the body of the collection that the sample is drawn from. If a research library includes multiple library facilities, the sample population must draw its sample from across all libraries, collections, or locations in order for the survey to accurately represent all holdings. If the expectation is to describe the conditions of both individual collections (Campus Library A and Campus Library B) and the broader library collections, then statistically significant samples must be surveyed from each individual library collection or location (384 from Library A and 384 from Library B). As long as the same survey tool is used, the survey data from multiple libraries or collections can be combined to describe the condition of the entire library system.

Random Sample Formulation

For the sample to be statistically significant, it must also be random. Simply walking down the stacks and selecting books to survey until the sample size is met will not achieve this requirement. There are a variety of ways to ensure a random sample. It may be possible to run a query in an ILS to produce a random selection of volumes. This method could also be used to automatically input some catalog data into survey forms, thus reducing the time required to fill out the survey tool for each sample item.

Less technologically inclined methods involve calculating the number of shelves in a collection and dividing that by the sample size to identify which shelf a sample would be pulled from, and then selecting a set, arbitrary book to survey (e.g., always the third book from the left side). For example, if a library has 1,900 shelves and the predetermined sample size was 500 volumes, $1900/500 = 3.8$. Rounding down from 3.8 to ensure that the sample size met the minimum requirement of 500, the surveyor would look on every third shelf and inspect the third book from the left. Rounding down also provides flexibility in case there are empty shelves or shelves with fewer than three books on them.

A related method would be to assign consecutive numbers to each shelving bay, and then use a random number generator to randomly select a bay number, a shelf number on that bay (always counted from top to bottom or vice versa), and a volume number on that shelf (always counted from the same side). For example, in a library with 1,900 bays and 7 shelves per bay, we could use a spreadsheet or other program to fill out 3 columns, where the first column contains random numbers from 1 to 1,900 for the bays, the second column contains random numbers from 1 to 7 for the shelves, and 1 to 30 for the volume on the shelf. An output might read 917, 3, 24, which would lead the surveyor to the 917th bay, the 3rd shelf from the top, and the 24th book from the left side. If there were only eighteen books on the shelf, the survey instructions would have to provide a standard guidance that the surveyor could either use a random number generator to create a new number for the volume, or skip that entry completely and move to the next randomly generated line in the spreadsheet. This method needs to account for differing shelf counts and can result in the creation of nonexistent sample locations, but more random locations can easily be created to ensure a large enough sample size.

Conducting the Survey

With the tool designed and the random sample selected, the process of surveying is fairly straightforward. The surveyor should have a book cart and a laptop or tablet. Paper printouts of the sample locations may be helpful in facilitating the process. The surveyor will locate the item to be surveyed, pull it from the shelf, inspect it, complete the survey form, and return the book before moving on to the next item. Baird estimates that an experienced surveyor can complete the inspection in one to two minutes per book, although in large libraries additional time should be allotted to move between survey locations.[9] Teams of surveyors can be used to speed up the data entry, with one person inspecting the item and another recording the information. Multiple surveyors or survey teams can also be used with cloud-based platforms, such as Google Forms or Qualtrics, which allow multiple surveyors to simultaneously input data.

Surveyors must be given some basic training to correctly identify issues, with the level of training correlated with the level of detail being collected by the survey tool. The focus of the training should be on correctly identifying formats, materials, and types of damage. Physical examples of damage are particularly helpful for students who may not have much exposure to typical preservation issues. Developing consistency across surveyors is important for producing meaningful data. With appropriate training and a clearly designed survey instrument, student workers or volunteers can successfully conduct the data collection portion of the preservation survey.

Analyzing the Data

With the raw data in hand, the important work of analysis can begin. Depending on the formulation of the survey instrument, different sets of information may be gleaned from the data. Most organizations without an active preservation program will find simple calculations, such as the percentage of the collection with damage or the percentage with brittle paper, the most helpful in being able to allocate resources to support conservation, binding, and boxing budgets. More detailed correlations may emerge between the volume size, date of publication, or region of publication and the damage noted; these correlations may guide acquisitions or shelf-prep activities that can reduce wear and damage. High rates of graffiti or marking in the volumes may provide the impetus for a public outreach campaign, or to provide mechanical erasers to student workers at the reference desk to erase graffiti when they are not assisting patrons.

As with all assessments, the results of the analysis should be readily calculated and highlighted so as to be easily understood by administrators and funders. The findings from preservation surveys are particularly well-suited to graphics and visualizations that convey both basic information about the collection as well as more detailed points, such as the relative rates of formats and damage types across a collection. *real world example*

The University of Florida's Baldwin Library Physical Condition Survey (1992) provides an excellent example of some of the basic visualizations that can better inform collection managers.[10] The Baldwin Library of Historical Children's Literature had long been known to have condition issues, but its needs had not previously been quantified. A sample of 540 volumes was drawn from the collection of 85,000 titles. From the data collected, the institution could better understand the relative age of the collections (see figure 6.1), as well as the extent of brittleness as measured by the double-fold test (figure 6.2).

From these charts, it is apparent that this collection comprises volumes primarily from the mid- to late nineteenth century, and there are serious and widespread issues with brittle paper. Additional analysis (figure 6.3) shows that the brittleness is not distributed equally, but rather reflects historic transitions to lower-quality wood pulp paper in the middle of the nineteenth century.

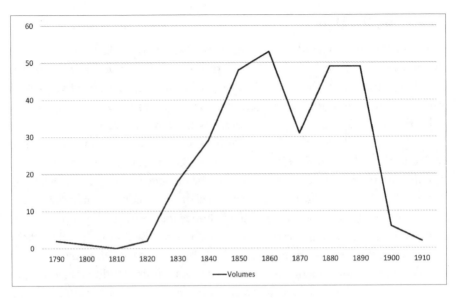

FIGURE 6.1 • Volumes in the Baldwin Library by publication date

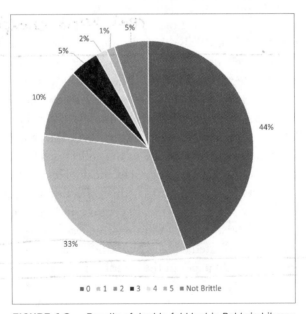

FIGURE 6.2 • Results of double-fold test in Baldwin Library

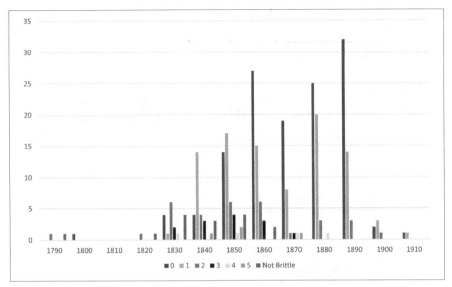

FIGURE 6.3 • Distribution of double-fold test results in Baldwin Library by decade

By changing the volume count to a percentage (figure 6.4), the rates of embrittlement per decade can be better understood, allowing curators to plan for additional preservation support when they acquire new collections in the future.

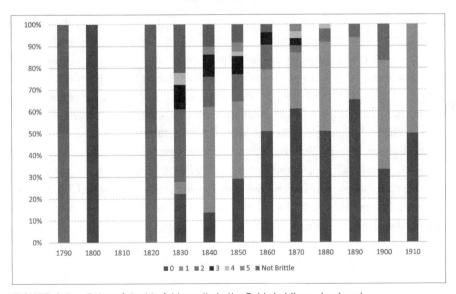

FIGURE 6.4 • Rates of double-fold results in the Baldwin Library by decade

A more contemporary survey of active, unbound serials in the University of Florida's Marston Science Library shows the presence of damage in serials titles by the cover materials (figure 6.5).[11]

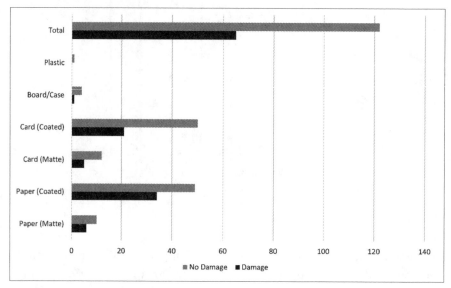

FIGURE 6.5 • Count of damage in serial titles by cover material

It is clear from this figure that there are meaningful amounts of damage to serials with both card and paper covers, with the majority of damaged titles having either coated card or coated paper covers. By shifting the X-axis to a percentage rather than a simple numerical count (figure 6.6), it becomes more apparent that the rates of damage are correlated to the paper/card stock covers rather than the coated or matte surface, with the paper covers seeing damage rates around 40 percent, card covers with damage around 30 percent, and serials bound in boards at 20 percent.

For a library with a limited budget to spend on serials binding, these rates provide valuable insight into where to focus the binding budget. Other institutions will have their own local concerns that condition surveys can address to improve the long-term access to the collections.

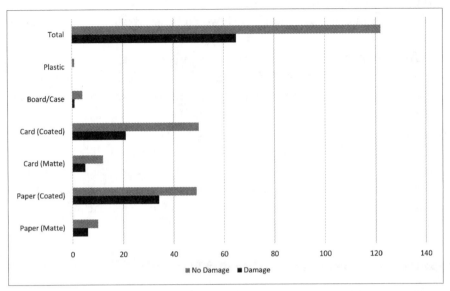

FIGURE 6.6 • Rates of damage in serial titles by cover material

COLLECTION ASSESSMENT

A collection assessment is a long-term data collection program to evaluate archival collections based on housing conditions, material conditions, and/ or formats in order to better understand the composition of large, complex collections and their short- and long-term preservation needs. The collection assessment typically involves the inspection of archival collections undertaken at the box, folder, and/or item level to record basic condition information. A well-designed and executed assessment should allow for organizations to plan for both box-level interventions, such as rehousing unique artifacts, and for collection-wide projects, such as replacing all acidic folders. Due to the unique nature of archival collections, collection assessments may not always be used to guide long-term programmatic changes to preservation workflows, although the data may be able to identify improvements in existing processing workflows in order to reduce retrospective interventions.

Collection assessment is a tool that enables special collections and archives to better understand their collections. Because of the commitment of time and resources to the development of a tool and the box- or item-level assessment, these projects are not an efficient use of resources for large library collections, although a library may possess a smaller subset of materials, such as a map collection or fine art collection, which would be appropriate for a collection assessment.

As with other preservation surveys and assessments, a collection assessment should be designed to meet the specific needs and existing resources of a given institution. The amount of data collected should reasonably reflect the organization's commitment to and understanding of preservation. There is little reason to spend significant amounts of time and labor collecting detailed data points if there is little expectation that the results can and will be acted upon. Institutions with more developed preservation programs may benefit from more intensive data collection, such as identifying specific audiovisual or digital formats in order to provide support for grant-funded reformatting projects.

Collection Assessment Design and Planning

At its essential formulation, the collection assessment is designed to collect basic archival holdings information, such as collection title, box count, and box sizes or linear feet of collections, tied to the assessment of the collection's storage environment, housing condition and quality, the physical condition of the collection items, and the risk of damage or loss posed by the item format (with risk being a judgment call based on the format stability as it is understood by the preservation and archival communities). The title, box count, and box sizes or linear feet are entered as free text and numbers, while the assessment data (environment, housing, condition, and risk) should be entered on a numerical scale. Different organizations have used different scales, primarily a 3- or 5-point scale (figure 6.7). A simplified scale minimizes the decision-making for novice assessors and allows for easier clustering of issues for analysis and project planning. Whichever scale is decided upon for a given assessment must be followed consistently.[12]

The assessment should also include checkboxes to clearly identify the presence of vulnerable or problematic formats. In a fashion similar to the assessment ratings, minimizing the detail of the categories reduces the amount of knowledge and time required for the assessors to complete each collection assessment. Basic categories such as film/photographs, audiovisual, digital media, oversize, and bound can convey essential format information and guide staff to the collections for additional follow-up without forcing the initial

Sample 3-Point Scale	Sample 5-Point Scale
1 = **Good.** No need for attention.	**1** = **Perfect condition.**
2 = **Fair.** Stable, but will likely need attention in the future.	**2** = **Good.** Minor signs of wear.
3 = **Poor.** At risk for loss or causing damage. Needs attention immediately/short-term.	**3** = **Fair.** Some damage to materials/ housings, but stable and fully functional.
	4 = **Poor.** Widespread damage. Some pieces heavily damaged or inaccessible to researchers. Housing needs attention.
	5 = **At risk.** Ongoing loss or damage from format issues or inappropriate housings. Potential mold or pests. Needs attention immediately.

FIGURE 6.7 • Point scales for two samples

assessor to collect data that may not be usable by an organization. Larger organizations may benefit from additional details in the assessment process, including format specifics, item counts (or linear inches/feet of a given format), and more detailed material types. The assessment can also include a free text field, but free text entries should only be made in addition to the formal assessment areas, since free text is difficult to quantitatively analyze.

Any assessment platform should be designed to link to or fit within existing institutional databases and collection management systems if possible, to ensure that collection- or item-specific data is not siloed from existing records. Linking the collection assessment tool with collection management systems can also expedite the assessment process because basic information, such as the collection title, accession number, and box listing, can be drawn from the central database and be pre-filled in the collection assessment forms.

If there is no existing collections platform, the assessor should consider developing a database to input and maintain the data collected during the assessment. A database will provide a more functional interface than a spreadsheet for the recurring updates and entries. If an organization does not possess the technical ability to develop, support, or maintain an internal database, a spreadsheet may be used to arrange basic data, although the analysis and interpretation will be more time-intensive. Paper forms can be used for data collection prior to data entry.

An example of a complex, freestanding collection assessment database is the Columbia University Libraries' Special Collection Materials Survey Instrument.[13] This Microsoft Access 2003 database collects dozens of data points to provide an in-depth understanding of the complex holdings of the libraries' Special Collections and provide the robust Preservation Department with the opportunity to target individual items or collections for specialized attention and treatment. In comparison to the Columbia instrument, the Smithsonian Institution Archives' Preservation Assessment is a basic assessment form that is designed to integrate into an existing collections management system.[14] The form only collects seven data points, as well as a "flag" checkbox to request immediate attention for mold, pests, or conservation treatment. However, both assessments provide levels of data that are appropriate to meeting the needs of the institutions and collections.

Conducting the Assessment

Unlike the preservation survey, a collection assessment does not require a random sample to provide effective data. The ultimate goal of a collection assessment is to collect data on every box or item in every collection at an institution so that appropriate preservation interventions can be made. After improvements to the collection have been made, the assessment database can be updated to reflect new scores, thus providing a quantifiable measurement of the improvement of the collections, at least on a scale relative to their previous condition.

The best place to start with a collection assessment is with an organization's most heavily used or most valued collections. These collections can provide a benchmark for the assessment, but are also the most likely ones to spur institutional action if clear needs can be identified and articulated. In smaller institutions, the assessment could also start in one area of storage and proceed linearly until all collections have been inspected and assessed.

The assessment itself is a straightforward process once the database and entry method have been formalized. The assessor should have a cart or table to work on, a list of collections and their locations (including any secondary locations for collections that are not stored contiguously), and a data collection method (paper forms, tablet, or laptop). The assessor should locate the collection and then inspect each box individually, being sure to check folders for unusual formats or damaged items. The findings are recorded and entered into the database before moving on to the next collection on the list. While the box and archival collection data should be inspected together, the overall assessment process does not need to be undertaken at one time, and in fact should be set up to be supported over an extended period of time in order to measure changes in the collection and its needs.

Staffing
[handwritten: MAN HOURS + student workers]

The staffing of the assessment will vary from institution to institution. Because of the long-term nature of the assessment, the data collection portion is not a process that makes sense to outsource to contractors. Professional and para-professional collections staff should be able to make the necessary decision to provide numbered ratings. In smaller organizations or larger university settings, volunteers and student workers may be available, or may be the only labor available, to conduct assessments. Volunteers and students are capable of conducting collection assessments if they are provided with appropriate training to understand the expectations of housing quality and physical condition issues.[15] Volunteers and students frequently also struggle with format identification. A major point of emphasis for planning student and volunteer projects must be consistency. If different assessors have different understandings of what numerical ratings to assign to the same collection, then the results can end up less helpful than with consistent, if skewed, results.[16]

Analyzing the Data

The collection assessment does not need to be "completed" with every collection at a repository inspected before any analysis can be conducted. Basic benchmark numbers can be computed to help understand the collection. These benchmarks will vary depending on the design of the assessment database, but averaging the ratings for housing quality, physical condition, and risk can provide insights into overarching collection needs, such as rehousing projects or conservation treatments. These baseline numbers can also be compared year-over-year as additional collections are surveyed or interventions are made and initial assessment numbers are updated. Raw numbers can also be valuable for project planning, such as improving collections with low housing quality ratings or missing folders. The physical condition and risk numbers can be correlated with the data points collected on the basic formats of the collections to plan more intensive housing projects, such as rehousing glass-plate negatives, conservation treatments, or reformatting.

Proactive Collection Assessment

While collection assessments are primarily enacted as retrospective projects to understand what institutions already have on their shelves, the assessment can also be conducted before the collections reach the shelves during archival processing. Archives staff can be trained to conduct the collection assessment at the point of ingest or appraisal, allowing for the assessment data to grow along with an institution's collections.

ITEM-LEVEL CONDITION REPORTS

Item-level condition reports are the simplest form of preservation assessment in regard to technical needs. The goal of the condition report is to qualitatively describe a single object independent of any other object or collection function. Precision and accuracy are key for this type of assessment, and the report should take care to record essential characteristics such as the size, format, material characteristics, media type(s), visible damage, and distinguishing marks of the object. Like other types of assessments discussed, the level of description should be suitable to meet the needs of the project.

Different goals for item-level reports require differing levels of recorded detail and staff time. An object going out for an exhibition loan should be assessed to ensure that the object is returned in the same physical condition that it was in prior to the loan. An exhibit loan may also focus more on the description of content to ensure that the correct object is returned to the loaning institution. A condition report for a conservation treatment proposal would focus less on the content description and more on describing existing damage and potential risks inherent in the structure or materials. These details would be highlighted to convey specific needs to curators to better understand the reasons for suggested interventions. For some complex, but high-value items, staff may write a condition report to allow future staff to track, measure, or at least acknowledge changes that happened during display or storage. Such reports would duly focus on areas of risk or concern, such as the precise area covered by silver mirroring in a silver gelatin photograph, or the extent of fading of sensitive media such as watercolors or felt-tipped markers. Assessments can also go beyond the visual, describing the surface textures of paper, the odors of deteriorating film, or even the "rattle" of a plastic sheet.

Conducting the Item-Level Assessment

The assessment should begin with recording the available descriptive metadata, such as title, author/creator, call number, date of publication, and other existing bibliographic information. Next, take precise measurements of the item, either in two or three dimensions as appropriate, including a page count if applicable. If the item is a print or photograph, be sure to measure both the size of the paper and the size of the image area. Then provide a concise description of the physical item, including materials, binding style, format, and media.[17] If it is a photograph or work of art on paper, describe the imagery in broad detail. When describing the item, try to identify physical characteristics that may be unique to this copy of the item, such as inscriptions, damage, staining, ownership markings, or irregularities. These distinguishing features should also be measured and located on the item, for example, "there is a ¾-inch-long tear that extends from the bottom edge into the image area," or "the upper board shows abrasions 1 inch above the titling."

Item-level condition reports to document at-risk collection formats should include much of the same descriptive metadata, but should focus the documentation much more finely on the at-risk aspects of the item's composition. However, this type of documentation is time-intensive and may be of little value to many collections, since the documentation can only track changes to individual items that may happen over decades, not prevent or reverse such changes. In addition to creating the documentation, the institution also has to maintain that documentation indefinitely into the future so that comparisons can be made. Photographs can also be used to establish visual baselines or supplement written reports.

Maintaining Item-Level Condition Reports

Item-level condition reports can only serve their long-term purpose if they remain accessible over time. Paper reports should be kept in collection files for future reference. Digital files should be saved in stable file formats, in a permanent location with other collection records. Saving the report to an individual hard drive, a staff member's shared drive, or to cloud-storage may not ensure its continued existence as institutional hardware and systems are upgraded over time.

MUCH SMALLER SECTION

Digital Preservation Assessment

Digital preservation remains an evolving field, but over the past decade a number of methods for the programmatic assessment of digital materials have been developed. These assessment methods are measures of organizational commitment and capabilities with a focus on measurements of institutional governance, technical infrastructure, and digital object management. Each assessment requires different (but frequently overlapping) types of documentation based on the ISO 14721 Open Archival Information System (OAIS) reference model.[18] The expected time commitment to complete the assessments or audits also varies, but is frequently described as demanding 3–12 months, depending on the assessment process selected.[19]

The primary assessment and/or audit methods are:

Trusted Digital Repository ISO 16363: This evolved from the Trusted Repository: Audit and Checklist (TRAC) into a formal audit process. This ISO standard requires the completion of 109 criteria as measured by certified external auditors.[20]

Trusted Repository: Audit and Checklist (2007): This was developed as a self-assessment checklist for institutions and utilizes eighty-four criteria. It was used by the Center for Research Libraries to certify repositories prior to the publication of ISO 16363.[21]

Data Seal of Approval (DSA): This is a self-assessment of sixteen guidelines that is then peer-reviewed by a DSA board member. DSA was begun by the Data Archiving and Network Services (DANS), a research institute of the Dutch Academy.[22]

NESTOR Seal for Trustworthy Digital Archives: This is a self-assessment of thirty-four guidelines based on DIN 31644,[23] followed by a review of the assessment by two external reviewers. NESTOR is aimed primarily at German institutions, but the self-assessment can be conducted by anyone.[24]

Digital Repository Audit Method Based On Risk Assessment (DRAMBORA): This is a self-audit process developed by the Digital

Curation Centre (DCC) and Digital Preservation Europe (DPE) to evaluate institutional risk.[25]

Assessment as a Discovery Process

While preservation assessments are undertaken to better understand the risks and needs of a collection in order to provide a basis for thoughtful planning and resource allocation, the assessment process also forces staff to interact directly with collections and facilities. Walking through the storage areas and looking at volumes and into boxes, the surveyor may encounter situations or formats that require more in-depth consideration or immediate actions.

The most worrisome discoveries in the stacks are likely to be moldy or pest-infested collections. Unless a collection is wet from an ongoing leak (which should cause all other work to stop until resolved), mold that is encountered in collections usually will be inactive, appearing dry and powdery. There may be visible damage from where the mold has consumed the substrate that it grew on, including losses, staining, or changes to the surface texture. In this state, the mold is not an immediate threat to collections, although it could cause allergic reactions among staff and researchers. The affected materials should be separated and cleaned to reduce the risk of the mold reactivating and spreading.

Similarly, evidence of pests or pest infestations needs to be dealt with immediately in order to reduce the risk of damage to collections and to staff or researcher health. Common pests in North America include mice, silverfish, cockroaches, and webbing clothes moths, but other pests may be more of a threat depending on the location of the institution and collection formats. The damage is typically consumed paper or cardboard, with visible frass or scat. Infested collections should be inspected, rehoused, and frozen to eliminate the pests, if appropriate.

Some formats, particularly in archival collections, should also receive additional attention based on their physical or material vulnerabilities. While most paper-based collections will remain stable if provided with minimal standards of storage and housing, many other formats are at much greater risk of damage from poor storage, handling, or chemical deterioration:

> *Cellulose nitrate film:* This substance, the earliest plastic, was used as the base for motion-picture film and photographic negatives until the 1950s. Cellulose nitrate rapidly deteriorates in standard storage environments. The deteriorating film will off-gas acidic vapors and is an extreme fire hazard. The storage and handling

(including shipping) of nitrate film is regulated by the National Fire Protection Association standard NFPA 40, and all nitrate film should be separated from other collections and addressed immediately.[26]

Cellulose acetate film: Also known as safety film, cellulose acetate was introduced to replace the highly flammable nitrate film and can be found as the base for motion-picture film, photographic negatives, and microfilm produced from the 1950s through the 1980s. Acetate film deteriorates in an autocatalytic process known as Vinegar Syndrome, named because of the distinctive odor of vinegar from the deterioration of the film to acetic acid. Once the deterioration has begun, it cannot be stopped or reversed, but only slowed by storage at cold temperatures. Deteriorating acetate film should be separated from other collections and have its storage, replacement, and/or disposal addressed in the short term.[27]

Glass plate negatives: These negatives and lantern slides are particularly vulnerable to damage from poor handling. These fragile items should be noted in order to receive appropriate housing and storage on fixed shelving.[28]

Audiovisual formats: Audiovisual materials are at risk from a range of environmental and storage conditions, as well as accessibility issues from a lack of reliable playback equipment. Audiovisual formats should be noted for potential reformatting.

Preservation Assessments in Practice

The best assessment tool is the one that works for the specific needs of a project and an institution. Different institutions will have varying amounts of experience, resources, and existing systems and infrastructure to guide and support an assessment or a survey. There are few wrong ways to collect data, as long as it is done in a structured and standardized fashion.

The earliest preservation surveys in the 1970s and 1980s were collected on paper forms. That data was also collated and tabulated by hand, with later surveys using paper forms to collect data that was entered into a spreadsheet or database. Institutions with little technical support or funding for hardware and software may still find that paper forms provide the simplest means for data collection. Paper forms require no learning curve for volunteers, no power source to recharge batteries, and no Internet access to connect to cloud-based platforms; for these reasons, paper may also be the best choice for collecting data at off-site facilities or in disaster zones.

Spreadsheets, such as Microsoft Excel and Google Sheets, are excellent tools for organizing and tabulating data. However, for data collection purposes, they can be awkward when trying to collect more than a handful of data points, since the need to scroll through cells and rows of entries can result in errors during field surveys. Programs such as Google Forms or Qualtrics allow for structured survey forms that can output into spreadsheet or CSV formats. These programs allow the survey to be designed with standardized drop-downs, free text answers, and relevant follow-up questions. Google Forms and Qualtrics both offer some basic data analytics as well. Both programs are web-based platforms that require Internet access during data collection and analysis.

Databases, built in Microsoft Access, MySQL, or other formats, offer the greatest functionality and depth for data collection and analysis. They can be custom-designed to meet local needs, and they can connect with existing databases to provide for greater depth of analysis. Databases can also be structured to allow entries to be updated so that collection improvements can be measured and tracked. However, databases require more up-front design work and a commitment to maintain the software elements. Databases typically require a computer for data entry, but they are increasingly compatible with tablets and mobile devices for networked data collection.

A number of tools have been developed and are freely available to use for assessments of different types: *specific tools for recording assessment data*

"*Assessing Preservation Needs: A Self-Survey Guide*" is a manual published by the Northeast Document Conservation Center to assist institutions in conducting their own preservation needs assessments. It includes worksheets and questionnaires to collect information, and sample recommendations to provide examples of the types of recommendations that may be drawn from the assessment data.[29]

CALIPR is a web-based library preservation needs assessment survey tool that was designed for the California Preservation Program to provide a prioritized list of broad preservation actions. The tool walks the user through the steps to develop a random survey sample, provides the surveyor with two standard survey forms (one for print materials and one for audiovisual materials) that are easily filled out, and then conducts an automated preservation risk assessment based on the collected data. CALIPR is a basic tool that requires little specialized knowledge to utilize effectively in order to produce easily communicated priorities. However, the tool provides no customization and collects few specific data points to allow for deeper understanding for organizations with existing preservation support.[30]

The Preservation Self-Assessment Program (PSAP) is a web-based open-source tool to conduct basic needs assessments, condition surveys, and condition assessments on a wide variety of collection materials. PSAP was developed by the University of Illinois Urbana-Champaign (UIUC) with support from an Institute of Museum and Library Services National Leadership grant. The tool includes a thorough manual to walk novice surveyors through the process. There is also a Collection ID Guide to assist surveyors in identifying a range of common and less-common collection formats, including film, audio recordings, architectural drawings, and photographic images. PSAP was developed to collect data and analyze preservation needs at both an institutional level and an item or collection level. Number scores are given based on the interpreted risk, and updated data (such as improved collection housings or HVAC controls) can be added to receive an improved score. PSAP developed out of UIUC's earlier Audiovisual Self-Assessment Program, but was greatly expanded in scope.[31]

The Field Audio Collection Evaluation Tool (FACET) is a downloadable (Windows XP or Vista) tool developed by Indiana University to evaluate and prioritize audio collections for further preservation interventions. The prioritization is based on a number of risk factors, including format, storage environment, and known preservation problems. FACET assesses issues at the collection, not item level, although an assessment score is given for each format type within a collection. There is some local interpretation that is required for surveyors. Once data is entered, FACET outputs a comparative score based on a combined preservation score and curatorial value score, as well as a summary of known risks. This information can then be used by curatorial staff to determine priorities for action.[32]

The Columbia Mellon Survey Database is a downloadable collections assessment Microsoft Access 2003 database developed by Columbia University to survey archival and special collections materials. The database collects data on archival collections based on the PACSCL Consortial Survey Initiative model,[33] which includes curatorial value, housing information, and folder- and item-level formats and conditions. The database then produces a variety of ranked reports to prioritize preservation interventions. However, the Access 2003 format is no longer supported by current versions of Microsoft Access. The database remains available for download from Columbia University Libraries, but would require updating or emulation for use.[34]

Funding for Preservation Assessments

Funding to develop or conduct preservation assessments may be available from a variety of private, local, or state organizations. Currently there are two federal granting agencies that provide funding for preservation assessments: the Institute of Museum and Library Services (IMLS) and the National Endowment for the Humanities. The IMLS provides funding through its Museums for America Grants, Museum Assessment Program, and Conservation Assessment Program.[35] The National Endowment for the Humanities provides funding through its Preservation Assistance Grants for Smaller Institutions and through Humanities Collections and Reference Resource Grants.[36] Additional library funding and grants may be available through state-level organizations such as state libraries, archives, or historical commissions.

Communicating Findings to Institutional Stakeholders

Data collection is the goal of assessment, but to make an impact that data must be interpreted and communicated to stakeholders. Interpretation is a complex and multifaceted process that is likely unique to a given survey and a given organization, but a successful assessment will provide a list of potential actions that an organization can take to improve the preservation of its collections. Ideally, such a list would include a range of short-, medium-, and long-term steps that can be implemented. Large capital improvements, such as upgraded HVAC systems or fire suppression systems, can have the largest and broadest positive impact on reducing risks and preserving collections, but it is unlikely that most organizations will be able to immediately afford such improvements. However, if a series of low- or no-cost projects can be implemented from the assessment data, visible improvements may build trust and positive buy-in from management or donors in order to focus institutional efforts on larger investments.

CONCLUSION

Preservation assessments serve as the foundation for enacting structured improvements in order to ensure enduring access to collections and materials. Assessments are part of a long-term process that can provide an understanding of the needs and risks of a given collection in order to implement meaningful progress towards preserving that collection for future generations of users. While preservation may be a specialized field about which many librarians, archivists, and curators do not feel knowledgeable, there are types of preservation assessments that can be undertaken with minimal exposure to the field. Additionally, preservation specialists and funding streams are available to support institutions conducting assessments.

The data and analysis from assessments can and should be used to guide policies and projects for the continued development of preservation efforts. The assessment itself is not a silver bullet for caring for collections, but it can provide a pathway toward tangible improvements, both big and small, that support the institutional missions of collecting organizations and their communities. The data can point to large-scale needs, such as facilities improvements or HVAC upgrades, or small improvements, such as adding bookends to library stacks or coat racks for researchers. Preservation is a process. Small changes over the long life spans of collection materials can have outsized impacts on the durability and usability of materials, and every step that can be taken to improve the collections helps to sustain those collections.

NOTES

1. Sherelyn Ogden, "The Needs Assessment Survey," NEDCC Preservation Leaflets, 1994, https://www.nedcc.org/free-resources/preservation-leaflets/1.-planning-and -prioritizing/ 1.3-the-needs-assessment-survey.

2. "Find a Conservator," American Institute for Conservation, www.conservation-us.org/membership/find-a-conservator.

3. Karen E. K. Brown, "Use of General Preservation Assessments: Process," *Library Resources & Technical Services* 49, no. 2 (2005): 91.

4. Ibid., 97.

5. Brian J. Baird, *Library Collection Assessment through Statistical Sampling* (Lanham, MD: Scarecrow, 2004), 20–64.

6. Gay Walker et al., "The Yale Survey—A Large-Scale Study of Book Deterioration in the Yale-University-Library," *College & Research Libraries* 46, no. 2 (1985): 111–32.

7. Sally Buchanan and S. Coleman, "Deterioration Survey of the Stanford University Libraries Green Library Stack Collection," in *Preservation Planning Program: Resource Notebook* (Washington, DC: Association of Research Libraries, Office of Management Studies, 1982), 159–91.

8. Douglas Shafer and Zhiyi Zhang, "Introductory Statistics," Saylor Academy, 2012, https://saylordotorg.github.io/text_introductory-statistics/.

9. Baird, *Library Collection Assessment*, 75.

10. Erich Kesse, "Baldwin Library Physical Condition Survey," University of Florida Institutional Repository, 1992, http://ufdc.ufl.edu/UF00076105.

11. Fletcher Durant, "Marston Serials Survey," unpublished report, University of Florida, 2017.

12. In the author's opinion, a three-point scale is the simpler, more readily standardized scale that can easily be interpreted by assessment staff and volunteers regardless of their experience level.

13. "Special Collections Materials Survey Instrument," Columbia University Libraries, http://library.columbia.edu/services/preservation/survey_tools.html.

14. "Preservation Assessment," Smithsonian Institution Archives, https://siarchives.si.edu/sites/default/files/pdfs/preservation%20assessment.pdf.

15. Jennifer Waxman, "A Survey in the Making: Archives and Preservation," The Backtable, https://wp.nyu.edu/specialcollections/2010/10/12/a-survey-in-the-making-archives-and-preservation/.

16. Joel Taylor and Siobhan Stevenson, "Investigation Subjectivity within Collection Condition Surveys," *Museum Management and Curatorship* 18, no. 1 (1999): 19–42.

17. Philip Gaskell, *A New Introduction to Bibliography* (Oxford: Oxford University Press, 1972). Corrections incorporated into subsequent reprintings. [1995 reprint: Winchester, UK: St. Paul's Bibliographies; New Castle, DE: Oak Knoll Press.]

18. "ISO 14721:2012 (CCSDSS 650.0-P-1.1) Preview Space Data and Information Transfer Systems—Open Archival Information System (OAIS)—Reference Model," International Organization for Standardization, https://www.iso.org/standard/57284.html.

19. Ana Krahmer and Mark Edward Phillips, "Communicating Organizational Commitment to Long-Term Sustainability through a Trusted Digital Repository Self-Audit," paper presented at the International Federation of Library Associations and Institutions' World Library and Information Conference, Columbus, OH, 2016.

20. "ISO 16363:2012 (CCSDS 652.0-R-1) Preview Space Data and Information Transfer Systems—Audit and Certification of Trustworthy Digital Repositories," International Organization for Standardization, https://www.iso.org/standard/56510.html.

21. "Trustworthy Repositories Audit & Certification: Criteria and Checklist (TRAC)," Center for Research Libraries, https://www.crl.edu/archiving-preservation/digital -archives/metrics-assessing-and-certifying/trac.

22. Data Seal of Approval, https://www.datasealofapproval.org/en/.

23. "DIN 31644 Information and Documentation—Criteria for Trustworthy Digital Archives," DIN, https://www.din.de/en/getting-involved/standards-committees/nid/ standards/wdc-beuth:din21:147058907.

24. "NESTOR Seal for Trustworthy Digital Archives," nestor, www.dnb.de/Subsites/ nestor/EN/Siegel/siegel.html.

25. "DRAMBORA," Digital Curation Centre, www.repositoryaudit.eu/.

26. "NFPA 40: Standard for the Storage and Handling of Cellulose Nitrate Film," National Fire Protection Association, http://catalog.nfpa.org/NFPA-40-Standard-for-the -Storage-and-Handling-of-Cellulose-Nitrate-Film-P1176.aspx.

27. "Vinegar Syndrome," National Film Preservation Foundation, https://www.filmpreserva tion.org/preservation-basics/vinegar-syndrome.

28. "How Do I House Glass Plate Negatives?" National Archives and Records Administration, https://www.archives.gov/preservation/storage/glass-plate-negatives.html.

29. Beth Patkus, "Assessing Preservation Needs: A Self-Survey Guide," Northeast Document Conservation Center, 2003, https://www.nedcc.org/assets/media/ documents/apnssg.pdf.

30. "CALIPR," California Preservation Program, www.lib.berkeley.edu/preservation/ CALIPR/.

31. "The Preservation Self-Assessment Program," University of Illinois Urbana-Champaign, https://psap.library.illinois.edu/.

32. "The Field Audio Collection Evaluation Tool," Indiana University Digital Library Program, www.dlib.indiana.edu/projects/sounddirections/facet/index.shtml.

33. "The PACSCL Consortial Survey," Philadelphia Area Consortium of Special Collections Libraries, http://pacscl.org/consortial_survey.

34. "Special Collections Materials Survey Instrument," Columbia University Libraries, http://library.columbia.edu/services/preservation/survey_tools.html.

35. "Grants," Institute of Museum and Library Services, https://www.imls.gov/grants.

36. "Grants," National Endowment for the Humanities, https://www.neh.gov/grants.

REFERENCES

Baird, Brian J. *Library Collection Assessment through Statistical Sampling*. Lanham, MD: Scarecrow, 2004.

Brown, Karen E. K. "Use of General Preservation Assessments: Process." *Library Resources & Technical Services* 49, no. 2 (2005): 90–106.

Buchanan, Sally, and S. Coleman. "Deterioration Survey of the Stanford University Libraries Green Library Stack Collection." In *Preservation Planning Program: Resource Notebook*, 159–91. Washington, DC: Association of Research Libraries, Office of Management Studies, 1982.

"CALIPR." California Preservation Program. www.lib.berkeley.edu/preservation/CALIPR/.

Dataseal of Approval. https://www.datasealofapproval.org/en/.

"DIN 31644 Information and Documentation—Criteria for Trustworthy Digital Archives." DIN. https://www.din.de/en/getting-involved/standards-committees/nid/standards/wdc-beuth:din21:147058907.

"DRAMBORA." Digital Curation Centre. www.repositoryaudit.eu/.

Durant, Fletcher. "Marston Serials Survey." Unpublished report, University of Florida, 2017.

"Field Audio Collection Evaluation Tool." Indiana University Digital Library Program. www.dlib.indiana.edu/projects/sounddirections/facet/index.shtml.

"Find a Conservator." American Institute for Conservation. www.conservation-us.org/membership/find-a-conservator.

Gaskell, Philip. *A New Introduction to Bibliography*. Oxford: Oxford University Press, 1972. Corrections incorporated into subsequent reprintings. [1995 reprint: Winchester, UK: St. Paul's Bibliographies; New Castle, DE: Oak Knoll Press.]

"Grants." Institute of Museum and Library Services. https://www.imls.gov/grants.

"Grants." National Endowment for the Humanities. https://www.neh.gov/grants.

"How Do I House Glass Plate Negatives?" National Archives and Records Administration. https://www.archives.gov/preservation/storage/glass-plate-negatives.html.

"ISO 14721:2012 (CCSDSS 650.0-P-1.1) Preview Space Data and Information Transfer Systems—Open Archival Information System (OAIS)—Reference Model." International Organization for Standardization. https://www.iso.org/standard/57284.html.

"ISO 16363:2012 (CCSDS 652.0-R-1) Preview Space Data and Information Transfer Systems—Audit and Certification of Trustworthy Digital Repositories." International Organization for Standardization. https://www.iso.org/standard/56510.html.

Kesse, Erich. "Baldwin Library Physical Condition Survey." University of Florida Institutional Repository, 1992. http://ufdc.ufl.edu/UF00076105.

Krahmer, Ana, and Mark Edward Phillips. "Communicating Organizational Commitment to Long-Term Sustainability through a Trusted Digital Repository Self-Audit." Paper presented at the International Federation of Library Associations and Institutions'

World Library and Information Conference, Columbus, OH, 2016. https://digital
.library.unt.edu/ark:/67531/metadc854117/.

"NESTOR Seal for Trustworthy Digital Archives." nestor. www.dnb.de/Subsites/nestor/EN/
Siegel/siegel.html.

"NFPA 40: Standard for the Storage and Handling of Cellulose Nitrate Film." National Fire
Protection Association. http://catalog.nfpa.org/NFPA-40-Standard-for-the-Storage
-and-Handling-of-Cellulose-Nitrate-Film-P1176.aspx.

Ogden, Sherelyn. "The Needs Assessment Survey." NEDCC Preservation Leaflets, 1994.
https://www.nedcc.org/free-resources/preservation-leaflets/1.-planning-and-prioritiz
ing/1.3-the-needs-assessment-survey.

"PACSCL Consortial Survey." Philadelphia Area Consortium of Special Collections
Libraries. http://pacscl.org/consortial_survey.

Patkus, Beth. "Assessing Preservation Needs: A Self-Assessment Guide." Northeast
Document Conservation Center, 2003. https://www.nedcc.org/assets/media/
documents/apnssg.pdf.

"Preservation Assessment." Smithsonian Institution Archives. https://siarchives.si.edu/sites/
default/files/pdfs/preservation%20assessment.pdf.

"Preservation Self-Assessment Program." University of Illinois Urbana-Champaign. https://
psap.library.illinois.edu/.

Shafer, Douglas, and Zhiyi Zhan. "Introductory Statistics." Saylor Academy, 2012. https://
saylordotorg.github.io/text_introductory-statistics/.

"Special Collections Materials Survey Instrument." Columbia University Libraries. http://
library.columbia.edu/services/preservation/survey_tools.html.

Taylor, Joel, and Siobhan Stevenson. "Investigation Subjectivity within Collection Condition
Surveys." *Museum Management and Curatorship* 18, no. 1 (1999): 19–42.

"Trustworthy Repositories Audit & Certification: Criteria and Checklist (TRAC)." Center
for Research Libraries. https://www.crl.edu/archiving-preservation/digital-archives/
metrics-assessing-and-certifying/trac.

"Vinegar Syndrome." National Film Preservation Foundation. https://www.filmpreservation
.org/preservation-basics/vinegar-syndrome.

Walker, Gay, Jane Greenfield, John Fox, and Jeffrey S. Simonoff. "The Yale Survey—A Large-
Scale Study of Book Deterioration in the Yale University Library." *College & Research
Libraries* 46, no. 2 (1985): 111–32.

Waxman, Jennifer. "A Survey in the Making: Archives and Preservation." The Backtable.
https://wp.nyu.edu/specialcollections/2010/10/12/a-survey-in-the-making-archives
-and-preservation/.

KEY RESOURCES

Baird, Brian J. *Library Collection Assessment through Statistical Sampling*. Lanham, MD: Scarecrow, 2004.

Baird, Brian J., Jana Krentz, and Brad Schaffner. "Findings from the Condition Surveys Conducted by the University of Kansas Libraries." *College & Research Libraries* 58, no. 2 (1997): 115–26.

Baird, Brian J., Milissa Boyer, Judith Emde, Nancy Jaeger, Jana Krentz, and Brad Schaffner. "Findings from the Collection Condition Surveys Conducted by the Preservation Task Force, 1995–1996." Technical report, University of Kansas, 1996.

Bell, Nancy. "The Oxford Preservation Survey 2: A Method for Surveying Archives." *The Paper Conservator* 17, no. 1 (1993): 53–55.

Bell, Nancy, and Helen Lindsay. *Benchmarks in Collection Care for UK Libraries*. London: Library and Information Commission, 2000.

Bond, Randall, Mary DeCarlo, Elizabeth Henes, and Eileen Snyder. "Preservation Study at the Syracuse-University-Libraries." *College & Research Libraries* 48, no. 2 (1987): 132–47.

Brown, Karen E. K. "Use of General Preservation Assessments: Outputs." *Library Resources & Technical Services* 50, no. 1 (2006): 58–68.

———. "Use of General Preservation Assessments: Process." *Library Resources & Technical Services* 49, no. 2 (2005): 90–106.

Buchanan, Sally, and S. Coleman. "Deterioration Survey of the Stanford University Libraries Green Library Stack Collection." In *Preservation Planning Program: Resource Notebook*, 159–91. Washington, DC: Association of Research Libraries, Office of Management Studies, 1982.

Child, Margaret. "1.2 Preservation Assessment and Planning." Northeast Document Conservation Center. 1994. https://www.nedcc.org/free-resources/preservation-leaflets/1.-planning-and-prioritizing/1.2-preservation-assessment-and-planning.

Dardes, Kathleen, Erica C. Avrami, Marta de la Torre, Samuel Y. Harris, Michael Henry, and Wendy Claire Jessup. *The Conservation Assessment: A Proposed Model for Evaluating Museum Environmental Management Needs*. Los Angeles: Getty Conservation Institute, 1999. http://hdl.handle.net/10020/gci_pubs/evaluating_museum_environmental_mngmnt_english.

Darling, Pamela. *Preservation Planning Program: An Assisted Self-Study Manual for Libraries*. Rev. 1993 edition, revised by Jan Merrill-Oldham and Jutta Reed-Scott. Washington, DC: Association of Research Libraries, 1993.

Decandido, R. "Condition Survey of the United States History, Local History and Genealogy Collection of the New York Public Library." *Library Resources & Technical Services* 33, no. 3 (1989): 274–81.

De Stefano, Paula, and Mona Jimenez. "Commercial Video Collections: A Preservation Survey of the Avery Fisher Center Collection at NYU." *The Moving Image: The Journal of the Association of Moving Image Archivists* 7, no. 2 (2007): 55–81.

Drott, M. Carl. "Random Sampling: A Tool for Library Research." *College & Research Libraries* 30, no. 2 (1969): 119–25.

Eden, Paul, Nancy Bell, Naomi Dungworth, and Graham Matthews. "Developing a Method for Assessing Preservation Needs in Libraries." *Library Management* 20, no. 1 (1999): 27–34.

———. "Preservation Needs Assessment in Libraries and Archives: Piecing Together the National Jigsaw." *Library Management* 19, no. 4 (1998): 228–37.

Gertz, Janet, and Susan Blaine. "Preservation of Printed Music: The Columbia University Libraries Scores Condition Survey." *Fontes Artis Musicae* 41, no. 3 (1994): 261–69.

Gertz, Janet, Charlotte B. Brown, Jane Beebe, Daria D'Arienzo, Floyd Merritt, and Lynn Robinson. "Preservation Analysis and the Brittle Book Problem in College Libraries: The Identification of Research-Level Collections and Their Implications." *College & Research Libraries* 54, no. 3 (1993).

Gunselman, Cheryl. "Assessing Preservation Needs of Manuscript Collections with a Comprehensive Survey." *The American Archivist* 70, no. 1 (2007): 151–69.

Krueger, Holly, Sarah Melching, and Kitty Nicholson. "Written Documentation." The Book and Paper Group Wiki. 2018. www.conservation-wiki.com/wiki/Written _Documentation_(PCC).

Matthews, Graham. "Surveying Collections: The Importance of Condition Assessment for Preservation Management." *Journal of Librarianship and Information Science* 27, no. 4 (1995): 227–36.

New York State Archives. "Archival Needs Assessment Guidelines and Template." New York State Archives Publication no. 59 (2001).

Ogden, Sherelyn. "1.3: The Needs Assessment Survey." Northeast Document Conservation Center. 1994. https://www.nedcc.org/free-resources/preservation-leaflets/1.-planning -and-prioritizing/1.3-the-needs-assessment-survey.

Oneill, Edward T., and Wesley L. Boomgaarden. "Book Deterioration and Loss—Magnitude and Characteristics in Ohio Libraries." *Library Resources & Technical Services* 39, no. 4 (1995): 394–408.

Patkus, Beth. "Assessing Preservation Needs: A Self-Assessment Guide." Northeast Document Conservation Center. 2003. https://www.nedcc.org/assets/media/ documents/apnssg.pdf.

"A Public Trust at Risk: The Heritage Health Index Report on the State of America's Collections." *Chronicle of Philanthropy* 18, no. 9 (2006): 59.

Reinke, Scott. "Condition Survey of the Circulating Collection: Joseph Anderson Cook Memorial Library, University of Southern Mississippi." *SLIS Connecting* 1, no. 2 (2012): 13.

Rinio, Tyson. "Collection Condition Assessment in a Midsized Academic Library." *Collection Management* 41, no. 4 (2016): 193–208.

Smith, Merrily A., and Karen Garlick. "Surveying Library Collections." *Technical Services Quarterly* 5, no. 2 (1988): 3–18.

Teper, J. H., and S. M. Erekson. "The Condition of our 'Hidden' Rare Book Collections—A Conservation Survey at the University of Illinois at Urbana-Champaign." *Library Resources & Technical Services* 50, no. 3 (2006): 200–213.

Walker, Gay. "Assessing Preservation Needs." *Library Resources & Technical Services* 33, no. 4 (1989): 414–19.

Walker, Gay, Jane Greenfield, John Fox, and Jeffrey S. Simonoff. "The Yale Survey—A Large-Scale Study of Book Deterioration in the Yale University Library." *College & Research Libraries* 46, no. 2 (1985): 111–32.

THE FUTURE
OF TECHNICAL SERVICES
Data Governance and Analytics

Nina Servizzi

eyes on the future

The history of technical services is one of continual adaptation to changing information needs. While current advances in technology continue to drive innovation development, the rise of digital scholarship and increasing expectations of user-centeredness have challenged academic libraries to redefine their traditional collection, research support, and curation models. The resulting changes to core library services will require technical services departments to prioritize data governance and analytics in support of library assessment. This chapter will discuss the development of a data warehouse to support technical service assessment, and it will present practical guidelines to consider when building a data warehouse. *data warehouse*

PREPARING FOR THE FUTURE: ASSESSMENT WITHIN TECHNICAL SERVICES

What is the future of technical services in libraries? This question has elicited debate within the library community since 1841, when Antonio Panizzi's standardized cataloging rules first challenged traditional library practice to better serve the user.[1] Yet, despite nearly 175 years of continual evolution, many authors paint a dire image of a field collapsing under the weight of constant change and unable to keep up with technological trends. Fortunately, others present a more positive picture. Based on the innate understanding that adaptation to evolving information needs is the very essence of technical services, progressive scenarios properly situate the current digital landscape and its demands along a continuum of paradigm shifts that will continue to shape technical services practices.

For academic libraries, interest in "big data" has accompanied the rise of digital scholarship and has fostered new forms of research that are deeply rooted in data-mining, predictive analytics, and machine learning. As digitally savvy users accustomed to client-customized services challenge libraries to redefine their traditional models of collection development, research support, and curation, technical services must adapt their processes and workflows in response to changes in core library services. These changes necessitate that acquisitions departments move away from traditional ordering and expand into resource licensing and access. They compel cataloging departments to replace old standards and formats with new ones—AACR2 with RDA, MARC with BIBFRAME. They demand discovery systems that seamlessly expose library collections to users regardless of where the research query is initiated. They oblige preservation departments to embrace the intricacies of born-digital conservation. In all of these cases, technical services librarians have responded to the challenges within the current environment with innovation and leadership.

So where does the apprehension come from? If advances in technology drive change and encourage innovation, this is often accompanied by the tacit expectation to "do more with less." In recent years, academic institutions, in the midst of growing concerns over the cost of higher education, have faced increasing pressure to demonstrate a better return on investment (ROI) and develop initiatives to maintain affordability. In order to remain effective in an increasingly complex research environment, academic libraries have turned to the evidence-based assessment of library services in order to mitigate the impact of fiscal restrictions. As Carol Tenopir, lead principal investigator of the LibValue project, observed, "When there are decreasing resources and increasing alternatives for information and attention, libraries of all types find that they need to measure and demonstrate the value of all of their collections and services. And, sometimes, measuring value means choosing to eliminate some traditional roles in order to take on or re-emphasize new ones."[2] A similar sentiment was expressed by members of the Technical Services Directors of Large Libraries Interest Group, who, when surveyed, identified the seemingly irreconcilable contradiction between technological development and fiscal restraints as a major change agent that is simultaneously threatening legacy processes while driving new iterative development cycles.[3] Although it is easy to see how this condition can provoke anxiety, the coupling of technological advancement with fiscal accountability is, in fact, not new to technical services. The traditional pillars of technical services, fiscal control and bibliographic control, bear a long history of technological advances in the discovery and access of library resources.

Moving beyond fiscal accountability, data-driven decision-making has allowed libraries to gain a more thorough understanding of their users' needs and to focus on the development of user-centered services. Given their long history of metadata creation and curation, technical services are uniquely positioned to provide the data governance and analytics that are necessary to support the assessment and strategic development of collection-related services. To be effective in this new role, technical services must first recognize that "collection metadata has evolved from basic catalogue descriptions to include content licensing, preservation, and access information. Its continuing development is driven by the challenges of: digital migration, rising audience expectations and diminishing resources," and the field must accept that "traditional metadata generation, management, and dissemination methods are not scalable or appropriate in this new environment."[4] The prioritization of data governance within the technical services portfolio challenges technical services to create new evidence-based processes and workflows that are truly sustainable within the current library environment and meet user expectations. However, to effectively support increasingly complex assessment and user needs, technical services must expand their capacity to meaningfully interact with the full array of library data assets, whether structured, semi-structured, or unstructured—and whether internally or externally sourced.

The remainder of this chapter will discuss the advantages of a data warehouse; explore its role in data governance, analytics, and assessment; and present practical guidelines for building a data warehouse. Key considerations discussed will include identifying stakeholders, articulating data needs, projecting development cycles, and guaranteeing data delivery. Afterwards, a case study of the New York University Libraries will illustrate how one library applied these guidelines to develop its data warehouse and will provide examples of how the data warehouse currently supports technical services assessment and informs the development of user-centered services.

User focus

BUILDING A DATA WAREHOUSE TO SUPPORT ASSESSMENT

Analytics and the Case for Data Integration

As libraries struggle to balance mounting user expectations with limited means, the importance of correctly identifying high-impact user-centered services has led to an increase in library assessment and a growing demand for readily accessible data. To meet this demand, libraries must be able to pull data from a complex array of sources and create coherent data sets that can facilitate in-depth analysis and visualization. In technical services assessment, access to comprehensive data sets is particularly challenging. First, the required data is rarely confined to transactional data, and it often requires delimiting transactions by the information held in master and reference data; for example, a report requesting all line items paid in the first quarter of the fiscal year (transactional data—invoice line item) for European imprints (master data—bibliographic record) with related expenditures expressed in USD (reference data—currency conversion table). Second, technical services assessment often demands data from succinct library systems to be integrated; for example, a comparison of local MARC records (first source system—integrated library system) for leased content (second source system—electronic resource management system) with holdings on the aggregator's platform (third source system—OpenURL knowledge base). Finally, assessment needs may require data from library systems to be combined with data from external systems; for example, a report identifying order records (integrated library system—library source system) that have full-level catalog records available for overlay (cooperative bibliographic catalog—external source system). As can be seen in these examples, the integration of data across types and sources is a critical factor in technical services assessment, and is often the main determinant of a data set's suitability. Poor integration can negatively impact the accuracy and comprehensiveness of the data and impede meaningful analysis.

The best approach to maximize the data integration required for a successful assessment program is to consolidate the data from multiple source systems in a data warehouse. Figure 7.1 shows a simple data warehouse with internal library data sources and external data sources. In this example, source systems such as an integrated library system (ILS) or electronic resource management system (ERMS) maintain the operational data (transactional, master, and reference) that are necessary to carry out library processes. In data management, transactional systems such as an ILS are referred to as online transaction processing (OLTP) systems. These systems provide the source data to the data warehouse via an extract, transform, and load (ETL) process. This process begins by extracting data from the OLTP. Once the data has been retrieved from the source system, ETL proceeds to read, transform, and integrate the extracted data. The data is then loaded into a dimensional data store (DDS). The combination of ETL and DDS forms the basic data warehouse system.[5] Since the DDS stores data using a fundamentally different model than the OLTP, querying a DDS has two distinct advantages over querying the source system directly: (1) the DDS arranges data in a dimensional format optimized for analysis, and (2) the DDS integrates data from multiple source systems.[6]

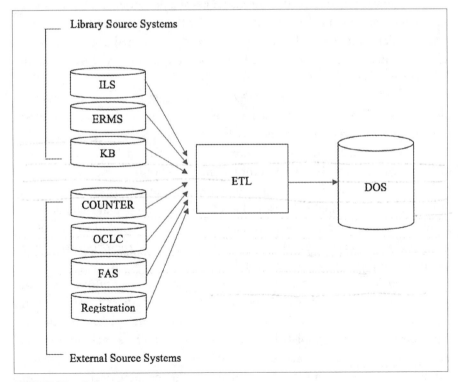

FIGURE 7.1 • Data warehouse system

explanation of benefits

From this brief introduction, the advantages of developing a data warehouse to support technical services assessment become obvious. A data warehouse allows different data types from multiple systems to be consolidated, integrated, and stored in a single system that has been optimized for complex querying. Access to rich data sets inherently facilitates greater analysis of workflows, and ultimately leads to the design and development of tools that enhance technical services' operations. As big data and data science become more and more pervasive, the potential library use cases are endless and extend well beyond the technical services department. However, to successfully build a data warehouse requires a deep understanding of operational needs and a carefully delimited scope.

checklist / guide

Key Considerations for Building a Data Warehouse

In order to build a successful data warehouse, it is important to take time to establish the organization's data needs and available resources. The following seven steps will provide key considerations for the planning and implementation of a data warehouse. There is also a checklist provided at the end of this chapter which can be used to identify key local requirements at each step, and help ensure maximum strategic alignment.

1. *Build consensus among key stakeholders.* In order to fully understand the depth of operational need and the types of assessment the data warehouse will support, it is important to first identify key stakeholders. Potential stakeholders should be the primary consumers of library systems data, including users outside of technical services. It is important to find stakeholders who can provide a comprehensive view of the library's operations in relation to its strategic priorities. Stakeholders should, therefore, be able to define immediate data demands as well as anticipate future needs. Once identified, the stakeholders should be included in the earliest stages of warehouse planning so their concerns can be addressed and the proper scope established.

2. *Identify cross-departmental teams.* Once there is a commitment to build the data warehouse, care should be taken to identify a core team. The team should have a deep knowledge of both the library's data context and the systems environment. A well-balanced team must therefore include members who understand data and its structure within a given source system (systems administrators) and members who understand the meaning of the data within the context of library operations (catalogers, acquisitions librarians, access

librarians, etc.). The team should also include programmers/developers and IT specialists.

3. *Analyze data needs.* It is essential to gain a comprehensive understanding of core library operations and related data needs early in the process of building a data warehouse. Knowing how users consume data within individual library departments will help determine data sources both within the library and without. Use cases should be collected from across a broad range of operational areas, including ones from external stakeholders such as auditors, consortial partners, and library associations. Documenting a comprehensive set of use cases will expose the most highly demanded data sets and inform functional requirements.[7] Once primary data requirements have been established and probable data sources identified, data samples will need to be evaluated to ascertain their integrity, time variance, and accessibility. A key to this evaluation will be determining an appropriate level of data granularity that will afford meaningful analysis without overwhelming the data warehouse.[8]

[handwritten margin note: user focus]

4. *Evaluate server options: dedicated vs. cloud.* The decision to maintain a local dedicated server or to use a cloud-based platform must take into consideration several factors: the content volume of data, frequency of ingest, scalability, security requirements, performance needs, and local IT capacity. When considering a locally hosted solution, server maintenance and failover system development must also be budgeted for. The increased stress on local IT resources that accompanies dedicated server environments should be carefully weighed. For many libraries, new technologies and rapid advances in cloud-based data warehousing environments, including the development of cloud ETL and increased self-service access, make cloud-based solutions viable options.

5. *Select an ETL software.* To effectively manage ETL processes, it is necessary to research and select the proper ETL software. Software packages must be compatible with local source systems and with the selected data warehouse platform. The ETL software should meet local functional requirements and be able to address the specific array of data integration issues present in the core library data set. The initial data needs analysis (see 3 above) should provide a solid understanding of the local data environment and define a clear set of functional requirements for the data warehouse, including ETL processes. There are many ETL vendors as well as open-source solutions that are available within all budgets. Whether commercial or open source, care should be taken to select a reputable provider in order to ensure ongoing product development.

6. *Employ iterative development cycles.* The preliminary data needs analysis will, if done properly, provide a thorough overview of operational needs and

[handwritten note at bottom: assessment as iterative/cyclical]

related data requirements. These needs/requirements should be considered the basis of an incremental development road map rather than fixed parameters for a comprehensive data model. Warehouse development should be iterative, prioritizing data needs shared across multiple use cases. As the warehouse is built out, high-use data sets will emerge and define a "portfolio of master conformed dimensions"[9] within the DDS data model. However, it is important that initial development be restricted to use cases requiring data from a single known internal source such as the ILS. This allows the initial DDS data model to be vetted and refined before addressing multi-source integration issues. Successive development should continue to be use case-driven, but should slowly introduce increasing levels of complexity. As more dimensions are added to the data model, the pace of development will naturally speed up. The linking of development cycles to the resolution of single-use cases keeps stakeholders vested in ongoing development by ensuring that the positive impact of the data warehouse on core library operations is visible from the beginning of the development process.

7. *Provide end user access.* Once data is available in the data warehouse, consideration needs to be given to user access. The most basic tool for user access is the creation and maintenance of a data dictionary that defines the relationship of data, as it is stored in the data warehouse, to its source system(s) and notes significant changes in context or meaning. Next, access rights and permissions need to be established for individual users. A subset of users across various areas of the library should be assigned direct access. These users are deeply involved with departmental assessment, have expert knowledge of operational context, and are regularly responsible for the analysis of assessment data. To facilitate the retrieval of large or complex data sets, these users must know how to query the data warehouse directly using regular expressions, structured query language (SQL), or other scripting languages as appropriate. A larger subset will need to access the data warehouse primarily for ad hoc analysis and reporting using visual analytics or business intelligence (BI) software. Like direct access users, they are routinely involved in analysis and assessment and often rely on data visualization to communicate data to external stakeholders. For users whose regular data interaction is limited to well-defined dynamic data sets, interactive dashboards, scorecards, and automated reports can be created.

New York University Libraries' Data Warehouse

Strategic Mandate for the Future

In response to the increased data dependence that is evident in the changing role of academic libraries, the New York University (NYU) Libraries ("the Libraries") formally recognized the need to incorporate regular assessment throughout the division's various departments. To foster data awareness throughout the organization, an emphasis on data-driven exploration and decision-making was highlighted in the Libraries' Strategic Plan 2013–2017. Goal 8 of the plan challenged the Libraries to "become a data-aware organization that promotes open exploration of data and grounds our decisions in evidence."[10] Although each department in the Libraries had its own history of data collection and *against* assessment, the information obtained was often siloed, and the data sets used *silos* were inconsistent across the departments. To effectively develop the data-rich environment needed to support creative inquiry, discovery, analysis, and decision-making as outlined in the strategic plan would require cross-departmental access to statistical sets and analyses. The need to consolidate library data became increasingly apparent. *strategic planning*

The strategic plan clearly defined several outcomes that would lay the *specific* groundwork for data access and use expectations across the Libraries. The *mention* outcomes included a program of well-specified data management and business intelligence supporting evidence-based resource allocation; a library-wide structure for data capture, warehousing, and reporting; an increase in staff skilled in the collection, analysis, and interpretation of data; and ready access to the data needed for decision-making, experimentation, and exploration.[11] The expressed desire for library-wide data capture and warehousing led to the creation of a dedicated strategic initiative. Strategic Initiative 8.3 mandated the implementation of "a robust and accessible data warehouse that extracts, integrates, and stores data from diverse sources and allows for the continual analysis and execution of complex queries."[12] The initiative further "ensure[d] that adequate, skilled staff is available for consultation when needed so that data requests are timely and efficiently handled."[13]

Due to the complexity of systems in use throughout the Libraries, the need to develop a centralized data repository was seen as critical to the division's

strategic plan

strategic plan. A successful data warehouse would have to provide locally defined, integrated data sets that could support the full range of assessment and analysis. Each department would identify relevant data sets that would be extracted from corresponding internal and external systems. The data would then need to be integrated into a repository that was nonvolatile and time-variant. The data warehouse would also need to be multifunctional—structured to meet not only immediate data needs but, more importantly, capable of accommodating unknown future requirements.[14]

Given the breadth of data required across the departments, the success of the data warehouse would rely on integrating data from multiple sources in a manner that is consistent and readily understood by staff throughout the Libraries. It would also require identifying a meaningful level of granularity that would serve the broad spectrum of queries and analyses without overwhelming data clients.[15] Once built, the data warehouse would allow departments to access integrated sets of data that would support their local assessments. More importantly, it was hoped that the greater consistency and integration of data sets would facilitate the much-needed interdepartmental assessment and information exchange that was already proving crucial in the creative development of new user services.

The importance of interdepartmental collaboration was clearly visible in the formation of the initiative team. The central team pulled together expertise from the library systems, technical services, and public services departments with sponsorship from the Libraries' budget and planning office. These departments were identified early on in the strategic planning process to be "data super-users" that were regularly involved in cross-departmental development projects. Individual team members were familiar with the newly launched NYU University Data Warehouse (UDW+), and many of the team were actively engaged in efforts to streamline library reporting needs using commercially available BI report-building applications. The team's deep knowledge of library data needs, potential for interoperability with UDW+, and experience employing BI applications provided a thorough understanding of library data management needs and their unique challenges. The team began working on the data warehouse in 2013 and had a working proof of concept developed the following year. Strategic Initiative 8.3 was completed in late 2016 when the Library Data Warehouse (LDW) was deemed fully operational.

The Library Data Warehouse Today

Currently, the LDW has over 200 jobs scheduled running back-office procedures and supporting assessment throughout the Libraries. The maintenance and development of the data warehouse resides in Knowledge Access and Resource Management Services (KARMS), the Libraries' technical services department, while the local Microsoft (MS) SQL server and failover are administered in collaboration with the Libraries' IT department.

ETL processes are designed and managed using SQL Server Integration Services (SSIS). Included as part of the Libraries' MS SQL Server license, SSIS provides an economic and robust integrated development environment. The software package includes a full suite of ETL tools that help automate efforts to pull data from diverse sources, standardize formats, and load the resulting data into the data warehouse. Data sources for the LDW include the integrated library system (Aleph—bibliographic, acquisitions, and circulation modules); the discovery system (PRIMO—PNX files); the university's financial system (FAME—General Ledger); the university registrar (student, faculty, and staff lists); interlibrary loan (ILLIAD); OCLC WorldShare; KBART files; COUNTER statistics, and so on. Data sources continue to be added as required by new use cases chosen for development.

LDW end users are able to access and manipulate the data independently using Tableau visualization software. As the primary front-end tool, Tableau supports a wide range of ad hoc analysis and reporting. The software also allows for the creation of interactive dashboards that provide staff access to regularly updated data sets when needed. Depending on the project, staff can also connect to the LDW using Excel. To allow for greater querying capacity, scripting, and data monitoring, advanced users can access the LDW using Open Data Base Connectivity (ODBC), SQL Server Management Studio (SSMS), and Toad.

Data Integration in Assessment

To better understand how the LDW supports technical service assessment for the Libraries, it is helpful to review several use cases. The first use case allows technical services staff to review cataloging output. The complete data for this report is contained in a single data set within the LDW. This data set is composed entirely of data extracted from the Libraries' integrated library system (ILS), and combines master data contained in the item records and related bibliographic records with transactional data capturing cataloger, cataloging data, and type of cataloging. Since the transactions are not permanently retained in the ILS, but are overwritten when the materials are shelved, it is impossible to run cataloging reports containing historic data directly from the ILS report services. Instead, cataloging data is extracted from the ILS and loaded into the LDW every evening. Ad hoc reports created using Tableau visualization software, such as the example in figure 7.2, allow technical services supervisors to access complete historical cataloging statistics with options to filter by cataloging date, fiscal year, cataloger ID, cataloging unit, material type, sub-library, cataloging type, original cataloging agency, and so on. As can be seen, the combination of the data warehouse with visualization software enables staff with minimal data skills to interact directly with a defined data set.

A second example, shown in figure 7.3, illustrates how data from multiple sources can be merged to form a single integrated data set within the LDW. The Libraries recently faced the migration of over 400,000 e-books from the Ebrary platform to Ebook Central. To ensure that (1) the holdings were complete on the new platform, (2) bibliographic records were properly uploaded in the local ILS, and (3) full-text resources were indexed for web-scale discovery, it was necessary to undertake a comprehensive audit of the e-books involved in this migration. The audit compared the Libraries' holdings in the local ILS

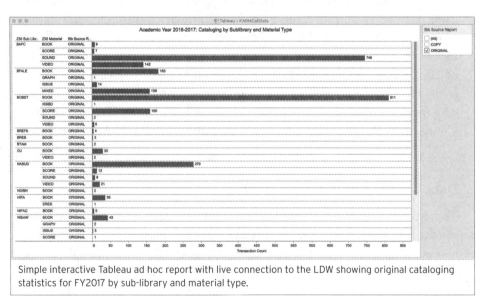

Simple interactive Tableau ad hoc report with live connection to the LDW showing original cataloging statistics for FY2017 by sub-library and material type.

FIGURE 7.2 • Original cataloging distribution by sub-library and material type

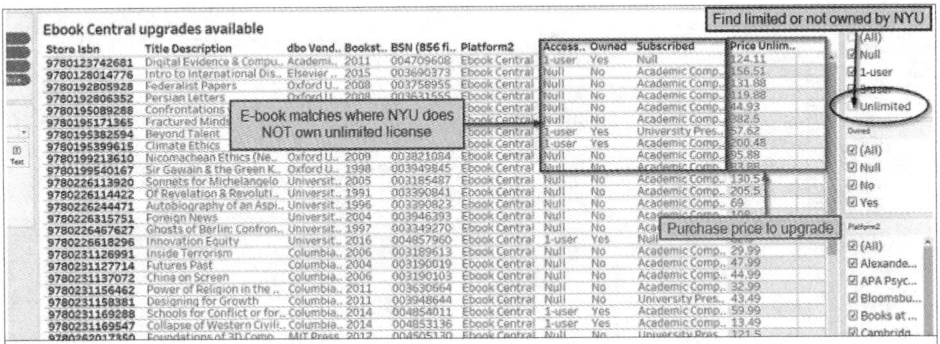

Comparison of integrated holdings from Ebook Central, NYU ILS, OCLC WS, and Summons within the LDW.

SOURCE: David Perry, Nancy Lin, and Camelia Anghel, "Let's Reconcile! How NYU Libraries Use SQL Server Integration Services and Tableau to Analyze E-Book Title and Usage Data," presentation at the IGeLU (International Group of Ex Libris Users) Annual Conference, St. Petersburg, Russia, September 9-14, 2017.

FIGURE 7.3 • E-Book audit reconciling holdings across multiple source systems

with holdings represented in various external systems—Ebook Central, the Libraries' main e-book platform; OCLC WorldShare knowledge base, the Libraries' source for MARC record sets; and Summon knowledge base, the Libraries' unified index for full-text searching. The goal was to reconcile the holdings in Ebook Central with the holdings information supplied by publishers to OCLC WorldShare in order to confirm that MARC record sets accurately reflected local e-book holdings. Bibliographic records and holdings were then updated in the Libraries' ILS. Finally, the fully reconciled e-book holdings were synchronized with the Summon knowledge base. The comparative analysis necessary for the audit was made possible by extracting master data from four distinct source systems—Ebook Central, OCLC WorldShare, Summon, and ILS—and integrating the data within the LDW. This required merging over one million lines of data into a single table within the data warehouse. Once the individual data sets representing the Libraries' holdings were loaded into the LDW, Tableau provided an ad hoc analytic layer that allowed staff to identify discrepancies and work with vendors and aggregators to reconcile the Libraries' holdings within their respective systems.

The final example (figure 7.4) demonstrates how data from multiple sources and types can be queried during the ETL process and loaded into the LDW parsed by query results. As an effort to support the NYU affordability initiative, the Libraries joined with the NYU Bookstore to identify titles on the faculty course reading list that are held by the Libraries. This required comparing

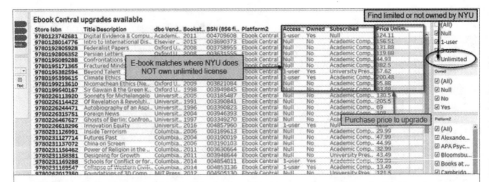

NOTE: Comparison course reading titles held by the Libraries in electronic format, with leased or single-user licenses. Bookstore data set initially parsed during ETL processing and then integrated with ILS and Ebook Central data in the LDW.

SOURCE: David Perry, Nancy Lin, and Camelia Anghel, "Let's Reconcile! How NYU Libraries Use SQL Server Integration Services and Tableau to Analyze E-Book Title and Usage Data," presentation at the IGeLU (International Group of Ex Libris Users) Annual Conference, St. Petersburg, Russia, September 9–14, 2017.

FIGURE 7.4 • Tableau view of title matches with leased or single-user access only

unique holdings identifiers in the Libraries' Discovery system (master data) with a list of books assigned by faculty for student purchase (transactional data) that was retrieved daily from the NYU Bookstore's inventory system. ISSNs contained in the NYU Bookstore's data feeds were matched against the ISSNs associated with the Discovery system's holding IDs during the ETL process. Matched titles were then integrated with holding and bibliographic data from the Libraries' ILS to form unique data sets for print and electronic holdings. Print holdings reports were sent to reserves for processing. Electronic holdings required further integration with data from Ebook Central titles lists (transactional data) to add access level, ownership, and, if available, the cost of multiuser upgrades to the LDW data set. If the Libraries held an unlimited license for a title, a link to the resource would be added to the NYU Bookstore's faculty-assigned course reading web page. Titles with leased or single-user access only were reviewed by the Libraries' collection development department for upgrade consideration. In the first semester of implementation, the Libraries supplied links to 855 full-text resources and purchased or upgraded an additional 180 titles. Based on the success of this pilot, the Libraries have decided to continue development of this service in direct response to student concerns with the rising cost of higher education.

Final Observations

good quote

The NYU case study demonstrates how a strategic commitment to data-driven exploration and decision-making has enabled the Libraries to develop increasingly user-centered services. The successful integration of data analytics into routine processing and workflows has fostered a culture of continual assessment and innovation. The LDW has supported these efforts by providing both centralized access to data resources and a shared space for analytic exploration. More importantly, the actual building of the LDW exemplifies the changing nature of technical services at the library and has led to the formation of a dedicated Data Analysis and Integration unit within KARMS that will provide systems administration and data management support for analytics work throughout the department. The need to develop an agile infrastructure that could support growing data demands challenged technical services librarians to acknowledge both the inherent constraints within traditional models of data stewardship and the need to occupy an expanding field of operations. For NYU, the data warehouse served as an effective vehicle for the concretization of new models for data governance within technical services.

By investigating how technical services departments can effectively employ a data warehouse to support growing assessment needs throughout the library, this chapter has demonstrated one approach for technical services to establish new forms of data governance. As current advances in technology continue to drive innovative development, the rise of digital scholarship and increasing expectations of user-centeredness challenge libraries to redefine traditional collection, research support, and curation models. To adapt to the rapidly changing data landscape, technical services will need to expand their capacity to retrieve, analyze, and assess data that can support the strategic development of collection-related services. The creation of new evidence-based processes and workflow in support of a growing suite of user-centered services will require technical services departments to fluently interact with the full spectrum of library data and to take a lead role in data governance and analytics. Building on their rich history of data curation, technical services departments are uniquely positioned to accept this challenge, effortlessly bridging the divide separating legacy traditions and future demands.

CHECKLIST

This checklist can be used to identify key local requirements at each step of building a data warehouse, and can help ensure maximum strategic alignment.

1. Build Consensus among Key Stakeholders

- Who are the greatest users of library data within Technical Services?
- Who are the greatest users of library data outside Technical Services but within the library? Public Services? Collection Development?
- Who are potential users of data outside the library? The university administration? Consortial partners?
- How will greater access to data support the library's core mission?

2. Identify Cross-Departmental Teams

- Who is directly involved in current assessment efforts? The assessment librarian?
- Who is in need of increased assessment capacity? Department heads? Supervisors?
- Who administers core library data repositories? The systems librarian? The database administrator?
- Who can identify the technical specifications for data needs?
- Who has basic programming skills?

3. Identify Data

- What do users want to do with library data?
- Do multiple use cases require access to similar data sets?
- Is the required data collected internally? Externally? Both?
- What is the quality of your data? Is the data consistent?
- Is the data dynamic? Time-variant? Current-value?
- What is the data's granularity?

4. Evaluate Server Options: Dedicated vs. Cloud

- What are the current/anticipated data demands? How much? How often?
- Can the platform scale effectively?
- What are the library's data security requirements?
- What are the local performance needs?

- What is the local IT capacity?
- What is the cost?

5. Select an ETL

- Is the ETL software compatible with existing data sources?
- Is the ETL software compatible with the data warehouse platform?
- Is the software source reliable?
- Does the ETL software meet local functional requirements?
- Does the ETL software match the staff's skill set?
- What is the cost?

6. Employ Iterative Development Cycles

- What library data is requested in multiple use cases? What data is "high priority"?
- Which use cases require "high priority" data from a single source? Multiple data sources?
- Is data needed from external sources? What permissions are needed to access external data?
- What are new data needs?

7. Provide End User Access

- How will the data dictionary be maintained? What information is needed?
- Who should receive direct access to the data warehouse?
- Who can link to the data warehouse for ad hoc analytics and reporting?
- How will routine data requests be handled? Scheduled reports? Interactive dashboards?
- What staff training is required?

NOTES

1. Antonio Panizzi, "Rules for the Compilation of the Catalogue," in *Catalogue of Printed Books in the British Museum* (London: Printed by order of the Trustees, 1941): [v]–ix, https://babel.hathitrust.org/cgi/pt?id=umn.31951001998306w;view=1up;seq=5.
2. Carol Tenopir, "Building Evidence of the Value and Impact of Library and Information Services: Methods, Metrics and ROI," *Evidence-Based Library and Information Practice* 8, no. 2 (2013): 270, doi: 10.18438/B8VP59.

3. Jeehyun Yun Davis, "Transforming Technical Services: Evolving Functions in Large Research University Libraries," *Library Resources & Technical Services* 60, no. 1 (2016): 63, doi: 10.5860/lrts.60n1.52.

4. British Library, "Unlocking the Value: The British Library's Collection Metadata Strategy 2015–2018" (internal publication, British Museum, 2015), 4, https://www .bl.uk/bibliographic/pdfs/british-library-collection-metadata-strategy-2015–2018.pdf.

5. Vincent Rainardi, *Building a Data Warehouse: With Examples on SQL Server* (Berkeley, CA: Apress L.P., 2018), https://ebookcentral.proquest.com/lib/nyulibrary-ebooks/ detail.action?docID=371486, p. 4.

6. Ibid., 3

7. Ibid., 65

8. W. H. Inmon, *Building the Data Warehouse, Fourth Edition* (Indianapolis, IN: Wiley, 2005), chap. 2, "Summary," http://common.books24x7.com/toc.aspx?bookid=12458.

9. Ralph Kimball and Margy Ross, *The Data Warehouse Toolkit: The Definitive Guide to Dimensional Modeling* (New York: John Wiley and Sons, 2013), 34, https://ebook central-proquest-com.proxy.library.nyu.edu/lib/nyulibrary-ebooks/ reader.action?doc ID=1313513.

10. NYU Libraries, "Strategic Plan 2013–2017" (internal publication, 2013), Goal 8, https://s3.amazonaws.com/nyulibraries-www-assets/nyu-libraries-strategic-plan.pdf.

11. Ibid.

12. NYU Libraries, "Strategic Planning Initiatives 2013–2017: Leads, Team Membership, and Status" (internal publication, 2016), 7, http://ezproxy.library.nyu.edu:2098/display/ DEAN/Home?preview=/11993321/376569899/Strat%20Plan%20teams%201eads%20 and%20status%20UPDATED%20April%202016.docx.

13. Ibid.

14. Inmon, *Building the Data Warehouse*, chap. 2, "Overview," http://common.books24x7 .com/toc.aspx?bookid=12458.

15. Ibid., chap. 2, "Summary."

REFERENCES

British Library. "Unlocking the Value: The British Library's Collection Metadata Strategy 2015–2018." Internal publication. British Museum, 2015. https://www.bl.uk/ bibliographic/pdfs/british-library-collection-metadata-strategy-2015–2018.pdf.

Davis, Jeehyun Yun. "Transforming Technical Services: Evolving Functions in Large Research University Libraries." *Library Resources & Technical Services* 60, no. 1 (2016): 52–65. doi: 10.5860/lrts.60n1.52.

Inmon, W. H. *Building the Data Warehouse, Fourth Edition.* Indianapolis, IN: Wiley, 2005. http://common.books24x7.com/toc.aspx?bookid=12458.

Kimball, Ralph, and Margy Ross. *The Data Warehouse Toolkit: The Definitive Guide to Dimensional Modeling.* New York: John Wiley and Sons, 2013. https://ebookcentral -proquest-com.proxy.library.nyu.edu/lib/nyulibrary-ebooks/reader.action?doc ID=1313513.

New York University Libraries. "Strategic Plan 2013–2017." Internal publication, NYU Libraries, 2013. https://s3.amazonaws.com/nyulibraries-www-assets/nyu-libraries -strategic-plan.pdf.

———. "Strategic Planning Initiatives 2013–2017: Leads, Team Membership, and Status." Internal publication, NYU Libraries, 2016. http://ezproxy.library.nyu.edu:2098/display/ DEAN/Home?preview=/11993321/376569899/Strat%20Plan%20teams%20leads%20 and%20status%20UPDATED%20April%202016.docx.

Panizzi, Antonio. "Rules for the Compilation of the Catalogue." In *Catalogue of Printed Books in the British Museum.* London: Printed by order of the Trustees, 1941. https://babel .hathitrust.org/cgi/pt?id=umn.31951001998306w;view=1up;seq=5.

Perry, David, Nancy Lin, and Camelia Anghel. "Let's Reconcile! How NYU Libraries Use SQL Server Integration Services and Tableau to Analyze E-Book Title and Usage Data." Presentation at the IGeLU (International Group of Ex Libris Users) Annual Conference, St. Petersburg, Russia, September 9–14, 2017.

Rainardi, Vincent. *Building a Data Warehouse: With Examples on SQL Server.* Berkeley, CA: Apress L.P., 2018. https://ebookcentral.proquest.com/lib/nyulibrary-ebooks/detail .action?docID=371486.

Tenopir, Carol. "Building Evidence of the Value and Impact of Library and Information Services: Methods, Metrics and ROI." *Evidence-Based Library and Information Practice* 8, no. 2 (2013): 270–74. doi: 10.18438/B8VP59.

ABOUT THE EDITORS AND CONTRIBUTORS

KIMBERLEY A. EDWARDS is the Information Analyst for Technical Services at George Mason University Libraries in Fairfax, Virginia. She received her MLIS degree from the University of Kentucky, and prior to her current role she worked in the circulation and technical services departments of several college and government libraries. Edwards has taught and presented on collection analysis and assessment tools and techniques at a range of national and international conferences.

MICHELLE LEONARD is a tenured librarian at the Marston Science Library, George A. Smathers Libraries, at the University of Florida. She is a collection manager for the natural resources and environmental sciences disciplines that span engineering, agriculture, and the geological sciences. She is a coauthor of *Implementing and Assessing Use-Driven Acquisitions* (2016). Leonard has conducted presentations on assessment and collection-building at a number of important library and science library conferences.

CECILIA BOTERO is the Dean of Libraries at the University of Mississippi and previously served as the Director of the Health Science Center Libraries at the University of Florida. She received her MLIS degree from the University of Texas at Austin, and early in her library career she worked as a serials cataloger and manager in technical services. Her many interests in the field of academic librarianship include conducting user studies and surveys; developing evidence-based collection and budget strategies; and performing library assessment and statistical analyses.

KRISTIN CALVERT is the Head of Content Organization and Management at Western Carolina University (Cullowhee, NC). Her research interests include the use patterns of serials and leadership development for librarians.

STEVEN CARRICO was employed as an acquisitions librarian at the University of Florida's Smathers Libraries for over twenty years, and retired as Chair of the Acquisitions Department and as Collections Coordinator in 2016. He has several conference presentations and library publications to his credit, with a research focus on use-driven acquisitions (e.g., DDA), collection-building, library budgets, and assessment studies in academic and special libraries.

FLETCHER DURANT is the Head of Conservation and Preservation at the University of Florida's George A. Smathers Libraries. Prior to joining the University of Florida, he was the Preservation Archivist for NYU Libraries and an Assistant Conservator for Special Collections at the New York Public Library. He received his MSIS degree and a CAS certificate in the Conservation of Library and Archival Materials from the University of Texas.

WHITNEY JORDAN is the Acquisitions Librarian at Western Carolina University in Cullowhee, North Carolina, where she is responsible for overseeing the collections budget and for licensing new and continuing resources. Her research interests include managing electronic resources and acquiring nontraditional materials.

MADELINE M. KELLY is the Director of Collections at Western Washington University (in Bellingham, Washington), where she oversees the full collection management life cycle for the Western Libraries. In her previous position as Head of Collection Development at George Mason University (in Fairfax, Virginia), she developed and implemented a holistic collection assessment program, undertook dozens of assessment projects on an as-needed basis, and served on a statewide consortial e-resource assessment task force. In addition to these roles, Kelly has authored articles and conference proceedings on collections assessment, and has presented and delivered workshops on the topic regionally and nationally.

KARL PETTITT is the Coordinator of Cataloging and Metadata Services at the University of Denver. He is also an adjunct instructor in the LIS program at the University of Denver's Morgridge College of Education, where he teaches cataloging and classification. His research interests have centered on the professional education of librarians and various subjects related to cataloging, including how assessment can be implemented within cataloging departments.

NINA SERVIZZI is Associate Dean for Knowledge Access and Resource Management Services at the Division of Libraries, New York University, where she is responsible for technical services, systems administration, and data integration and analysis. She has been deeply involved in defining functional specifications for the libraries' data warehouse since the project's inception, and she oversees the team responsible for its design and development.

TREY SHELTON is an Associate University Librarian and serves as the Chair of the Acquisitions and Collections Services Department of the George A. Smathers Libraries at the University of Florida. Previously, he served as the Electronic Resources Librarian for the Smathers Libraries. Shelton's scholarship focuses on the effectiveness of acquisition methods, collection assessment, and e-resource management. He frequently presents at national conferences, has coauthored multiple journal articles, and has authored or coauthored three book chapters.

STEPHANIE S. SMITH is a Collections Development Analyst at the Library of Congress in Washington, DC. Her work and research that contributed to this chapter were completed in her former position as a Collection Development Assessment Specialist at George Mason University in Fairfax, Virginia. At Mason she conducted holistic collection assessments by subject, co-built a database analyzing journal cost and use, and served on a DC-area consortial collections committee.

INDEX